The Rise and Fall of King Cotton

Picture Credits

The Rise & Fall of KING COTTON

Anthony Burton

André Deutsch
British Broadcasting Corporation

This book is published to accompany
a series of BBC Television Programmes
first broadcast in Autumn 1984

Series producer: Michael Garrod

Published to accompany a series of programmes in
consultation with the BBC Continuing Education Advisory Council

First published 1984
Published by the British Broadcasting Corporation
35 Marylebone High Street, London W1M 4AA
and André Deutsch Limited
105 Great Russell Street, London WC1B 3LJ

Printed in England by Jolly & Barber Limited, Rugby, England
This book is typeset in Apollo, 11pt leaded 2pts

ISBN 0 233 97148 3 (André Deutsch)
ISBN 0 563 21023 0 (BBC)

Contents

It may assist us to form a conception of the immense extent of the British cotton manufacture when it is stated, that the yarn spun in this country would, in a single thread, pass round the globe's circumference 203,775 times; it would reach 51 times from the earth to the sun, and it would encircle the earth's orbit eight and a half times. To complete the wonder – the manufacture is the creation of the genius of a few humble mechanics; it has sprung up from insignificance to its present magnitude within little more than half a century.

Edward Baines, *History of the Cotton Manufacture in Great Britain*, 1835.

Let any great social or physical convulsion visit the United States, and England would feel the shock from Land's End to John O'Groats. The lives of nearly two million of our countrymen are dependent upon the cotton crop of America. Should any dire calamity befall the land of cotton, a thousand of our merchant ships would rot idly in dock; ten thousand mills must stop their busy looms; two thousand mouths would starve, for lack of food to feed them.

E. N. Elliott, *Cotton is King and Pro-Slavery Arguments*, 1860

Preface

The process of industrialisation is central to our whole modern civilisation. In this book, I have looked at the growth of one industry, cotton textiles, in terms of three societies. The first is India, where the use of cotton can be traced back for millennia – a society where the intervention of European traders seemed at one time likely to destroy the industry for ever. That destruction would have been the consequence of a unique partnership between the other two societies: the American South, which developed as the most important producer of the raw material and Britain, which became the principal manufacturing area. For almost a century, these two depended on each other for their wealth; each developing its own social structure during the period of violent change which we call the industrial revolution. I have tried to explore the processes by which that industrial world was made, and the consequences that flowed from its making. Cotton seems to me to be a microcosm in which one can see, in its simplest yet most dramatic form, all those forces at work which have combined to make the world we live in today.

The pattern of development of the cotton industry was complex, involving many countries and many societies: India was not the only country with an ancient tradition of using cotton, Britain was not alone in turning to factories and America never developed a monopoly in growing. It is in these countries, however, that the issues can be most clearly seen, and it is on these that I have concentrated. This is not, then, a complete history. It is rather a study of change viewed through those societies most affected by it. Change has become the norm for the modern world. The appearance of computers, the silicon chip, microprocessors and the like in recent years suggests that change is likely to be with us for a long time. A study of the first, and still the greatest, upheaval of the modern world is not without relevance today.

Invariably in writing a book of this sort one accumulates many debts: in this case so many as to defy cataloguing. I should, however, like to record my special gratitude to the staff of the Southern Historical Collection of the University of North Carolina, the Textile Commissioners of Ahmedabad, Bombay and Delhi, the Manchester City Library and, as always, the Bodleian Library, Oxford. And once again I have to thank the BBC and, in particular, my producer Michael Garrod, for taking up this project for television and encouraging me to extend the scope of the work and Keith Wilton, editor of the series, who for the third time running has managed to make sense of my nonsense. Production of the book was immeasurably helped by the two editors, first Faith Evans and later Sara Mongue, and the book's designer Huw Davies: my thanks to all three.

The Cotton Plant: open seed bowls display the white lint. The dead leaves are not a natural phenomenon but are caused by defoliants used to help modern machine picking.

Towards a New World

A new world was made in the eighteenth century: it was neither a Utopia born in a philosopher's brain, nor a land opened up by exploration. It was our own world, the world of machine and factory. In that period, one country, Great Britain, went through a change so fundamental and traumatic that we can find nothing comparable in the whole of written history. We call the change the industrial revolution, and it is so central to our whole concept of society that now, two centuries later, we divide the world into two: the developed areas which have followed Britain through the transformation, and the undeveloped which have not.

The old world was one that was primarily concerned with keeping itself alive. It was an agricultural society, forever balanced on that edge of subsistence which marks off comfort from starvation. The new world is dynamic, geared to the notion of continuous economic growth. Very few would argue that starvation is preferable to comfort, nor could they argue that the change from the one condition to the other would have been possible without industrialisation. So it should logically follow that industrialisation is an essential stage through which man must pass if he is to enjoy a decent life. It does not, however, imply that the process of industrialisation will seem pleasant to those who have to live through the transition. If I have toothache I feel far better after the tooth is removed. I do not necessarily enjoy the process of removal. One could say that the industrial revolution was, for many people, very like having a tooth out, without the benefits of anaesthetic. Nowhere can both the benefits and the pain be seen more clearly than in the textile industry, and, in particular, in cotton. Starting with a few simple technical innovations, a transformation was begun that was permanently to change the lives of the people of three continents.

Textile making is one of the oldest of man's industries. It is also basically very simple. Take a natural fibre, stretch it and twist it to make a thread. Inter-twine the thread and you have cloth. In Britain, the textile industry was founded on wool. It was ideal in an age when transport was both expensive and difficult. The raw material was the fleece of locally-reared sheep, and all the processes could be carried out in the same area. Yet even in the days when wool reigned supreme, other textiles were made. Fibres from the flax plant were used to make linen. And for those who had a taste for something richer, and the means to gratify that taste, silk was imported to be woven into fine cloth. In seventeenth-century Lancashire, there was also a small trade in cotton, using raw material imported from the Middle East. The cloth was not considered very grand, and was chiefly used as a lining for other, better garments.

Anyone viewing the British textile scene at the beginning of the eighteenth century would have had an impression of great stability. He might have expected a steady improvement in manufacturing methods, but nothing very dramatic. He would certainly not have looked for any fundamental change. Why should he? The British woollen trade was the pride of the nation. Travellers noted with delight the wealth that it produced. 'It turns', said Celia Fiennes, viewing the trade in the West Country, at the end of the seventeenth century, 'the most money in a week of anything in England.'[1] While the poet John Dyer went even further, in verses extolling the happiness and prosperity that filled the manufacturing districts.

> Wide around
> Hillock and valley, farm and village, smile,
> And ruddy roofs, and chimney-pots appear
> Of busy Leeds, up-wafting to the clouds
> The incense of thanksgiving: all is joy.[2]

Why should any of this change? No one could prophesy a revolution that would transform the whole basis of the textile industry.

Domestic textile workers in eighteenth-century Yorkshire in a painting by Julius Caesar Ibbetson. Activities shown include washing, winding and spinning yarn.

One of the most astute and careful observers of the British scene was the novelist, essayist and pamphleteer, Daniel Defoe. Between 1724 and 1726, he published his account of a tour through Britain in which he gave very full details of the state of the country and especially of its thriving manufacturing districts.[3] Pride of place went to the wool districts of the West Country and, more importantly, to Yorkshire. Travelling from Blackstone Edge to Halifax, he was astonished to find the wild, hilly country thickly populated. Wherever he looked, he saw cloth hung out to dry beside the homes. There was not much sign of life, but when he knocked at the door of one of the master clothiers, 'we presently saw a house full of lusty fellows, some at the dye-fat, some dressing the cloths, some in the loom, some one thing, some another, all hard at work, and full employed upon the manufacture.' Everywhere there was ample evidence that the great woollen industry was thriving.

It is tempting to look back upon such a time as an idyll, a golden Arcadian interlude. And certainly there are aspects of the time whose passing we can mourn. The spinner at the wheel and the weaver at the loom could both work within their own homes and enjoyed a certain independence. They were paid for work done, not by the hour, which meant that provided the work was completed, they could choose when to do it. In practice this meant that many preferred to work extremely long hours in order to enjoy the luxury of time off later. But the picture is, in fact, more complex than that. To talk of spinner and weaver is to tell only part of the story.

Wool was bought by merchants who handed it out to the cottage workers. When it came from the fleece it was dirty and greasy, so the first job was to clean it, by soaking it in a mixture of urine and water. After drying, the fibre was loosened by beating. Spinning consists of stretching and twisting the fibres, but first the fibres have to be aligned by a process known as 'carding'. The wool was dragged through cards studded with metal wire. It was then ready for spinning on the wheel. It was a slow process, and at least five spinners were needed to keep one weaver busy.

After the wheel, came the loom: the thread was wound onto a frame known as a warping frame, from which it was fed to the loom as the warp. The mechanism of the loom allows alternate warp thread to be raised and lowered, leaving a gap through which the weft thread can pass. Warp and weft combine to form the cloth. It is again a simple process, but one that requires enough skill of the weaver to give a man pride in his craft; and, as payment was by the piece, the good weaver could expect more solid reward as well. In boom times, the best of them would display their earnings to the world, stuffing their money into the bands of their hats. At such times, the textile district did present something of the cheery appearance noted by Defoe. The women could take their wheels out of doors and gossip as they worked. Earnings were high enough for weavers to pay homage to their

The Jersey wheel. The spinner is drawing out the thread which is twisted as it flicks off the end of the spindle. A pair of cards can be seen on the floor.

patron saint, Saint Monday, drinking his health right through his name day. In such circumstances, independence was much prized.

That independence was, however, at best only partial. The weavers carried no stock of their own. The merchants supplied the wool and sold the cloth. They rarely had any money tied up in equipment, so they could ride out any trade storms by simply sitting tight, neither buying nor selling and living on their spare capital. No wool from the merchant, however, meant no work for weaver and spinner, and they had no spare capital. Such bad times came at least as often as the good.

In view of later developments it is as well to be aware of the role of the children in the textile working families. From an early age, they were put to such simple tasks as carding for the spinners, and soon the boys were expected to take their places at the loom. The latter role was very important for, up to the middle of the eighteenth century, the broad loom needed two pairs of hands. It was too wide for one man to cope with the job of throwing the shuttle, with its thread of weft, from side to side. The master weaver took charge of one side of the loom, throwing and catching the shuttle. He also had the job of controlling the movement of the warp through foot treadles. The second worker had to do no more than throw and catch at his side. It was boring, repetitive work and commanded little pay. It usually fell to one of the boys of the house or a young apprentice. So, the children too played their part in the household economy. The work was hard, but at least it could usually be carried out within their own homes and among their own families. That was some compensation.

Trade fluctuated over the years, but the overall pattern was stable. Had Britain been an isolated, inward-looking nation, then there would have been little reason why that system should not have remained stable. But she was not. She was a major figure in world trade, exporting her own surpluses and importing exotic goods from other countries. Not only was she not isolated but, by the beginning of the eighteenth century, she was already well on her way along the road of colonialism. British colonies had been established in North America and British traders, in the form of the East India Company, had founded small enclaves in India. They were rather late arrivals on the Oriental scene. By the time the East India Company had been founded in 1599, the Dutch had already established a near monopoly in the main attraction of the region, the spices of the East Indies. The islands were theirs, and the British had to accept second best on the mainland: and not even that second best could be monopolised, for the French and Portuguese were there as well. The British trade began as a mere fraction of the overall traffic between Europe and the Far East.

The British came to an India that was largely under the control of the Moghul empire. Although the Moghuls never controlled the entire subcontinent, they were by far the most powerful force in the land – and by far the wealthiest. The capital at Agra showed a degree of opulence scarcely to be matched in any city in Europe. It was here that the British were forced to wait, cap in hand, to solicit for trading rights. The ambassadors, men of rank and substance like Sir Thomas Roe, had to follow the Moghul court in its tours around the country and had to cope with the capricious nature of the Emperor's decrees. Jahangir, for example, seemed less impressed by the

13

The British in India: Mr William Fullerton receiving a visitor.

evidence of British might displayed when a handful of British merchantmen fought off the entire Portuguese fleet to establish a trading route to India, than he was by the fact that an English mastiff brought over as a present fought and killed a leopard. The truth was that neither Jahangir, nor his successor Shah Jahan, were particularly well disposed towards the British or indeed any other European traders. But their power was on the wane and they eventually gave way to pressure, permitting trading settlements to be established. Then the hunt for trade goods began.

Just as the British had developed excellent textiles from the best available local material, wool, so too the Indians had made the most of their

14

native raw material, cotton. Europeans had known about the Indian cotton plant since at least the fifth century BC, when Herodotus had described trees which 'bear fleeces on their fruit, surpassing those of sheep in beauty and excellence'. Now, two thousand years later, the British began to take an interest. They found many highly-sophisticated techniques in use, most of which had been perfected centuries before. The Elder Pliny, writing around AD 70, had described one particular method used by the Indians to decorate cloth. A mordant which would hold a dye was applied to the cloth, so that sections so treated would emerge as coloured from the dye vat. In the very best work, the designs were drawn separately and then transferred by laying the pattern on the cloth, pricking it out with fine needles and then rubbing charcoal through the pinholes to create the pattern. Then the mordant and dye were added. Using such methods, patterns of great intricacy and beauty could be obtained, and similar effects were later produced by using delicately carved wooden blocks to print on the design. These materials were known as 'chint', later to be Anglicised to the more familiar 'chintz'. Spinning and weaving of the very highest quality were combined to produce muslin of quite exceptional fineness and delicacy. This represented the affluent end of the trade. Spinning and weaving were universal activities,

The choukha, *the traditional spinning wheel of India.*   15

every village being able to supply the cloth to meet its own needs. The craftsmen who produced the best – and most expensive – cloth followed the court in its migrations or set up business near the palace of some great noble. The British in their long sojourns at the Moghul court had ample time to inspect such goods, which were so very different from anything they had known in Europe. Where the woollens tended to be heavy and dull, the cottons were light, colourful and attractive. There was trading potential here, but at first all had their minds set on spices. These had the great advantage of being very highly priced for their bulk, and were therefore ideal for small cargo ships on long voyages. The Dutch held the East Indies, but took a fancy to the Indian cottons, so a triangular trade was established early in the seventeenth century: bullion was sent out from England, cotton was bought with it in India and then traded for spices in the East Indies.

Then, in the 1640s, direct trading of cotton goods to Britain began. They were first sent from the port of Calicut and given the name 'calico', with various spellings. At first, they proved a trifle too exotic for British buyers, and the London office issued instructions in 1643 that local designs should be adapted to Western tastes:

> Those which hereafter you shall send me desire may be with more white ground, and the flowers and branch to be in colours in the middle of the quilt as the painter pleases, whereas now the most part of your quilts come with sad red grounds which are not equally sorted to suit all buyers.[4]

By the 1660s, the popularity of the new materials was sufficiently well established for patterns to be sent out to India for copying. The Indian craftsmen, however, could make little sense out of European patterns, which

An eighteenth-century petticoat border of painted and dyed cotton from Madras, with scenes showing European domestic life in India.

soon developed into something far more exotic and bizarre than ever their originators intended. What was to become the most popular motif of Indian cloth, the flowering tree, was born out of the mixture of styles from two continents. These new materials caused great consternation among the British authorities given the task of assessing the nature of the cloth made from India's strange, sheepish vegetable, as Samuel Pepys noted in his diary for 1664:

> Sir Martin Noell told us of the dispute between him, as farmer of the additional Duty, and the East India Company, whether callico be linen or not: which he says it is, having ever been esteemed so: they say it is made of cotton woole, and grows upon trees, not like flax or hemp. But it was carried against the Company.[5]

But whatever the nature of the cloth, it was soon clear that the strange and exotic was becoming the fashionable and popular. Aristocratic taste was beginning to favour light, easily-cleaned clothing, and cotton admirably suited that taste. From being a mere curiosity, the new cloths began to appear as a threat to the British textile industry. Defoe attacked the importation of cottons, using his complete armoury of literary weapons, starting with scorn for the fashion:

> The general fansie of the people running upon East India goods to that degree that the chintz and painted calicoes which before were only made use of for carpets, quilts, &c, and to clothe children and ordinary people, become now the dress of our ladies; and such is the power of a mode as we saw our persons of quality dressed in Indian carpets, which but a few years before their chambermaids would have thought too ordinary for them.[6]

He also set out the economic arguments. Money was being taken away from Britain to buy goods abroad, and now the goods that the money bought were being sent back home to ruin the local manufacturers. The British were, he declared, 'cutting their Throats with their own Knife'.[7] And if there were any who argued against that proposition they must be either fools or knaves.

> If this Cause meets with Enemies; if any one Man can be found in Britain, who would not have us leave off Painted Feathers, and stick to our own Manufactures; I say, if one man can be found so prepossess'd, it must be either a Man perfectly ignorant in Matters of Trade, and so not worth talking to; or it must be some Callico-Printer, or his Employer and Dependent, who, finding his Account in the Mischief, acts upon the corrupt Principle of being willing to get Money, tho' at the Expense of the Ruin of his Country.[8]

Like all the best propagandists, Defoe combined this withering attack on his opponents with a vigorous statement of his own position. It was wool and only wool that had brought and would bring prosperity to the people of Britain. 'Heaven bestow'd the Wool upon them, the Life and Soul, the Original of all their Commerce; he gave it to them, and have it exclusive of all the Nations in the World; for none comes up to it.'[9]

There were many commentators ready to argue the contrary case – though few who could bring the literary skills of Defoe to the task. One very popular argument stated that it was not the solid, woollen trade that would be affected by imported cottons, but only the luxury silk trade; and as the latter was as dependent on foreign yarn as was cotton there was no reason why the silk merchants should expect preferential treatment. The cotton traders had just as good a case if they chose to complain about silk imports. Either way, none of it would make the least difference to genuine home-based industry.[10]

The arguments rattled backwards and forwards, and whichever had the better logic, it seemed the protectionists had the louder voice. Excise duty was laid on Indian cotton in 1712 and raised in 1724. There was a total ban on printed calicoes, but plain cloth was allowed in as British printers had established a profitable business of their own. As a Swiss commentator, Jean Rhyiner of Basle, sardonically noted: 'All the world knows this people, whose industry and plodding patience in overcoming every kind of difficulty exceeds all imagination. This nation cannot flatter itself with having made many discoveries, but it may glory in having perfected all that has been invented by others.'[11] The criticism had some justice at the time, though it was not to remain true for very much longer. In the meantime, the cotton trade went into a temporary decline and wool remained triumphant. Yet even Defoe, the most vociferous supporter of the wool trade, had to concede that Britain also owed a good deal of her prosperity to international trade. She was a maritime nation, and if her ships were to be denied cargoes from the East, then they must be supplied with alternatives. Defoe looked westward across the Atlantic to the colonies of North America and, ironically, the trade he proposed was to do more to bring his hated cotton to Britain than anything the East India Company ever achieved. But to understand the significance of Defoe's solution, we have to look a little closer at the nature of Britain's colonies and her policy towards them; and look at the place of cotton in the pattern.

Britain was involved, at the beginning of the eighteenth century, in a complex colonial system, but not one in which an international trade in cotton would seem to have an important place. In Britain it was seen as an unwelcome rival to the old, well-established woollen industry. In India cotton was grown, spun and woven as it had been for centuries to meet local needs. In America it was not considered at all. Yet already there were factors at work that were to lead to dramatic changes in the next half century.

Colonial India could scarcely be said to exist at this time. Indeed, India itself had no sort of coherent identity. Rather there were a lot of different Indias – the India of the decaying Moghul empire, Hindu India, Muslim India and that of the native princes, and in among them a spattering of settlements that made up European India. There were the Portuguese who were becoming increasingly obsessed with creating a Christian India; a policy which kept them busily occupied in their own region of Goa, where they remained, having little effect on the rest of the country until the second half of the twentieth century. Then there were the French and the British, who came to trade. Britain's policy was clear – the interest of the home country came first, and they were there to make trading profits not to settle the land. They saw the natural resources of the country, and saw that they included the cotton plant, but had no interest in developing either the land or the cotton. Even if it had seemed a good idea, they would have had little chance of succeeding. They were a small minority in a very big country. Later, forced into belligerence to protect themselves from the various Indian factions, the British were to stumble into Empire. But by then policy was set along different lines, and the will to develop resources was lacking.

Things were very different for the Europeans who went to North America. There they found a vast country, very thinly populated. There was very little to be gained from trade. There was none of the gold and silver of South America, but there was an abundance of potentially good agricultural land. The British soon ousted the early settlers, the Dutch, from their colony

19

of New Netherlands and set up a string of colonial settlements along the eastern seaboard. In the North, the settlers found a land rich in game and fish, with good arable land and a climate not very different from that of Europe. It was an obvious lure to the independent-minded; the yeomen prepared to stake out a patch of land, clear it and work it. Further south there was also good agricultural land but a very different climate, quite foreign to the north Europeans. It was cold in winter, but hot and humid in summer. The land was often swampy and tropical diseases took their toll among the settlers. It was potentially rich, but few Europeans were enthusiastic about the notion of hard, physical labour in such conditions. Why work in the heat of the South when you could do just as well in the North?

The South may have been unattractive to the yeoman farmer, but it was very appealing to the wealthy landowner who could employ others to work the rich land for him. A plantation system was established similar to that set up farther south by the Spanish and Portuguese. Virginia, Georgia and the Carolinas were soon busy supplying Europe with its tropical grocery list of rice, sugar and tobacco. But there was still the labour problem to be solved, and it was this labour shortage that supplied Defoe with his answer of where to look for a profitable trade to replace the calicoes of India: slaves.

The slave trade to America began with the Dutch in the seventeenth century, but the British soon joined in and, with the ousting of the Dutch, achieved a monopoly. In 1660, with the formation of a chartered company, the Royal Africa Company, the monopoly was made official. But the trade was lucrative and the trade routes impossible to police. Free enterprise soon took command. By the time Defoe was writing, the triangular route – cash to Africa, slaves to America and trade goods back to Britain – was firmly established. The British Government took little notice of breaches of the monopoly. Any ships could carry slaves as far as they were concerned, provided they were British. The Royal Africa Company disappeared. The Government also took no notice of the conditions in the slave ships. The terrible years of the Middle Passage had begun. Later, when the trade had ceased to be necessary or profitable, the British became the most vocal and ardent opponents of the slave trade, but in the early eighteenth century even a man as intelligent and sensitive as Defoe could not see beyond the profit and loss accounts. The slave was, in his eyes, a 'produce of the British Commerce'.[12] Thanks to British enterprise in exploring Africa, this useful commodity could now be bought for 30s to 50s, carried across the Atlantic and sold again at anything from £25 to £30. There were other advantages to the trade too. The profits made in the sale could be used to buy tropical groceries for sale in Britain, while the planters, in their turn, had cash to pay for goods that Britain wanted to export. Defoe estimated that the trade could be carried on at a rate of some forty to fifty thousand slaves per annum.

Slaves were the making of the South, fundamental to its very existence, and the system suited the British admirably. It was not merely the trading accounts that appealed. The American South was becoming established as an area with its own colonial identity, and it was an identity that appealed to Britain. Here was a quiet, acquiescent, semi-feudal society which, in contrast to the independent-minded, self-confident North, was unlikely to cause any trouble. The system seemed ideal – provided always that there was a major cash crop that could be sold in the European market. The planter could own vast acres of land and huge numbers of slaves, but without that crop the land was useless, the slaves an expensive liability. As the South grew, so the search for the right crop was to become more and more urgent. One potential crop was cotton, but for the potential to be realised there had to be a market in Britain. Was there a demand for cotton? In spite of all the protectionist arguments and legislation, there was. Defoe might deplore it, but he was enough of a realist to recognise the strength of that demand. As he wrote, dictates of Parliament do not always stand out against the dictates of fashion:

> All the Kings and Parliaments that have been or shall be, cannot govern our Fancies: They may make Laws, and shew you the Reason of those Laws for your Good, but two Things among us are too ungovernable, *viz.* our Passions and our Fashions ... Should I ask the Ladies, whether they should dress by Law, or clothe by Act of Parliament, they would ask me whether they were to be Statute Fools, and to be made Pageants and Pictures of? They claim English liberty, as well as the Men, and as they expect to do what they please, so they will wear what they please, and dress how they please.[13]

John Kay

John Kay of Bury, inventor of the flying shuttle.

The Flier and the Jenny

There was a growing demand in Britain for the new cotton cloths. There were sources of raw material in the Middle East and India, and a potentially more important source in America. None of this, however, was enough to produce the cloth. There had to be machines and workers to tend them. Britain had the population: her inventors were to produce the machines.

One of the first essentials for any expansion of the industrial area of society is that workers can be fed. In a primitive society, food supply involves virtually the whole population. There is very little surplus. Agriculture in Britain had long since advanced beyond that basic position, and was gradually increasing in efficiency, so that fewer workers could produce more food. That does not mean that there was any desire on the part of the population to leave the land and move into industry. Land has a powerful appeal, and the peasant is not easily moved from his plot. In Britain, however, he had little choice. The movement away from peasant smallholdings to large estates, with landowners employing wage-earning labourers, was well advanced. It was hastened by the spread of enclosures which, while they improved agricultural efficiency, removed grazing and gleaning rights from the country's poor. The hunt for agricultural improvement had thus produced, as a side effect, one of the other requirements for a shift towards industrial work – a large population of unemployed.

The total population of the country was subject to fluctuation. In Europe as a whole, a rising swell of numbers had been replaced by a trough, with population declining. It was a familiar story: increase had brought overcrowding and that, in turn, had brought disease and an increase in the death rate to cancel out the rise in births. Britain, for reasons that are not at all clear, was spared the trough. There was now a problem, which eighteenth-century commentators generally referred to as surplus population. It did, however, have a solution. Some of the landless poor could be sent off to the colonies. You then lost a problem and created a customer. Empire would buy what Britain could make. There was thus an opening for the rest of the surplus population to be set to work making export goods. It was all as neat as an annual balance sheet, and there was a future profit to be read in the figures. Men of wealth began to think that there might be something in the proposition that their capital would be better employed in financing trade and manufacture than in building bigger and better country houses. Men with ideas began to think that they might make a fortune by designing new machines. Fortunes were made – but seldom by the inventors. John Kay of Bury[1] was the first in a succession of men whose ideas were to revolutionise industry and who were to see others claim the profits.

Kay came from Bury in Lancashire where, as a child, he was apprenticed to a reed maker. These reeds were used in the loom. They were split and suspended in the frame and the warp threads passed through them. They were then moved by the foot treadles, so that the alternate warp threads were raised and lowered. Kay, being an imaginative man, began to apply his mind to the improvement of the hand loom and started with the reeds. He realised that the fragile, natural reeds were not ideal for the job and he replaced them with more durable wire. He set up business on his own, and if it did not exactly make his fortune, it kept him very comfortable. He might have stayed that way, and earned himself a modest place in posterity as a footnote in histories of the textile trade, if he had not decided to apply his inventiveness to other parts of the loom. His gaze lit on the shuttle.

The broad loom still required two operatives. The work was, according to the poet Dyer, a thoroughly delightful occupation for the weaver:

He chuses some companion to his toil.
From side to side, with amicable aim,
Each to the other darts the nimble bolt,
While friendly converse, prompted by the work,
Kindles improvement in the op'ning mind. [2]

Some minds were no doubt opened, but others were numbed by the endless repetition of the one, simple task. More importantly, to an inventor looking for a fortune, it was an expensive waste of manpower. Kay considered the problem. If the shuttle could be kept in a straight line then there was no reason why mechanical hands could not replace human hands. A suitable shuttle run already existed in the form of the heavy wooden batten which was used to push the weft threads close together after each throw of the shuttle. He put wheels on the shuttle and the shuttle on the batten. Now all he had to do was put little wooden boxes at the ends of the run, each containing a wire 'hand' that could be jerked by a string. The master weaver only had to pull the string that dangled down in front of him to send the shuttle racing to and fro across the loom at far greater speed than the two men had ever been able to manage. The productivity of the loom had been doubled, and at very little cost.

Kay took out a patent and prepared to make his fortune. He was soon to learn his first unhappy lesson. Having the brilliant idea is one thing, profiting from it another. To the master clothiers who employed weavers as wage-earners, the flying shuttle was an economic miracle. One man could now do what two had done before. It was, in fact, much too good a miracle to be shared with a reed maker in Bury who was demanding royalties. Kay's invention was pirated throughout the textile districts. The law, when called in by Kay, very properly fined those offenders who were brought to court. They responded by forming 'Shuttle Clubs' to pay the fines. Pirating remained more profitable than paying the inventor.

The flying shuttle in use in Ireland. The weaver is jerking the handle to his right in order to send the shuttle across the loom from the left.

The flying shuttle looked less attractive to many weavers, especially to those who had earned their living catching and throwing the shuttle. Throughout the manufacturing regions, there were sporadic, and quite spontaneous, outbreaks of machine breaking. Kay's home at Bury was attacked in 1753, his loom was broken and he himself only just escaped in time. Kay found his hopes of wealth and fame disappearing under these two onslaughts. He might not have been too surprised to find that the unemployed weavers did not take too kindly to his efforts, but he must have expected the merchants who profited from his invention to reward him with something other than brazen piracy. He gave in and set out to look for fairer treatment across the Channel. He died, disillusioned and poor, in France in 1781.

Kay's invention opened a crack in the doorway to the future, through which men could glimpse a prospect of vast industrial advances. But it was not enough to say that the same number of men could now produce twice as much cloth as before. They could – provided there were twice as many

25

looms, fed by twice as much yarn. Even then there would have been no point unless there was a market for all that extra cloth. The success of the flying shuttle made men aware of the vast potential for economic advance that even the simplest invention might hold; but whether it would ever be realised depended on the possibilities being matched by the right set of circumstances. In Britain, in the eighteenth century, they were.

It might not have been easy to increase the amount of wool being passed to the weavers, but with the new demand for cotton goods a simple alternative was immediately available. The extra weaving capacity could be used for the manufacture of cotton cloth. But between the weaver and the supplier of raw material there was a bottleneck – the spinner. Before Kay's shuttle had begun to fly, at least five spinners had been needed to supply each loom. The new shuttle had both speeded up the individual loom and led to an increase in the number of looms. With existing spinning wheels, each spinner could only produce the one thread wound onto the one spindle. What was clearly needed was a device which would enable each spinner to produce several threads. The solution to that problem was to culminate in one of the decisive shifts in the pattern of human life.

The answer could well have appeared in 1738, when Lewis Paul took out a patent for a machine for spinning cotton thread. It could have made his fortune: it could have attracted a hundred copyists. It did neither, and Paul's career, and that of his machine, is surrounded by mysteries. It depended on the principle of rollers moving at different speeds being used to draw out the cotton into a thinner and thinner thread. The idea was sound, as we shall see later, but for reasons which we can now only guess at, it failed in practice. Or, to be more precise, it failed commercially. The authorship of the invention is in some doubt. It was claimed by John Wyatt, a Lichfield man and a relation of the celebrated Doctor Samuel Johnson. Certainly Wyatt and Paul communicated on the subject of the machine, and Wyatt himself claimed it as his own. 'I am the person', he declared firmly, 'that was the principal agent in compileing the spinning Engine.'[3]

The most likely explanation is that Wyatt did invent the machine, but being short of funds he allowed Paul to patent and develop it. From that point, at least, the story becomes clearer. Paul was sufficiently confident to install a full-scale version of the machine in a building in Birmingham in about 1741. It was circular, with a central drive shaft that turned the various rollers and the bobbins set around the perimeter. Donkeys were used to turn the shaft while two women tended to the bobbins. The very first cotton-spinning mill had been established. Doctor Johnson himself called in, viewed the concern with great interest, pronounced it an unqualified success and with his blessing bestowed, left. John Dyer was on hand to praise it in verse:

A circular machine of new design
In conic shape; it draws and spins a thread
Without the tedious task of needless hands.
A wheel, invisible, beneath the floor
To every member of th'harmonious whole
Gives necessary motion.[4]

But in spite of the plaudits of literary men, the invention was not a success. A few machines were installed, Wyatt and Paul enjoyed their disputed glory, then faded from view. Again the records are vague, but since the machine was practical, the failure was probably due to poor commercial management. The problem of machine spinning had been solved, but the solution had gone unrecognised and, for all practical purposes, it simply ceased to exist.

As the second half of the eighteenth century got well into its stride, and the flying shuttle came to be accepted, so the demand for a new spinning machine grew. In 1761, the Society of Arts put up a prize for a machine that would 'spin six threads of wool, flax, hemp or cotton at one time, and that will require but one person to work and attend it'. The award certainly acted as an incentive for inventors, and numerous proposals were put to the committee. When, however, a completely successful machine was developed, the inventor kept the information to himself, presumably reasoning that he would do better by personally exploiting the machine than he would by handing it over to others. The inventor was James Hargreaves, the machine the spinning jenny.

With Hargreaves we take a large step forwards towards the industrial age. As with many new ideas, a mythology has grown up concerning its beginning. There seems, however, to be little truth in the story that Hargreaves had his inspiration when he saw a spinning wheel accidentally knocked on its side. Before he ever turned to the problems of spinning, Hargreaves had already produced a successful machine for use in the earlier process of carding. He was encouraged to continue his researches by a neighbouring farmer and manufacturer, Robert Peel, who was to go on to found the family fortune in cotton, while his grandson was to become Prime Minister. With the encouragement of a successful and ambitious entrepreneur, and with his carding machine successfully at work, Hargreaves needed no accident to persuade him to turn his mind to the problem of spinning by machine.

Hargreaves worked on his invention at his home in the tiny Lancashire village of Stanhill, halfway between Accrington and Blackburn. The essence of it was that a wheel, turned by hand, was used to turn a number of spindles – at first eight – placed at one end of a frame. The thread was held in a clasp and the clasp was moved back to draw out the thread. Then, in a separate operation, the drawn thread was wound onto bobbins. The name 'spinning jenny' is no more than a simple corruption of 'spinning engine', and not a romantic dedication to an old love. A number of jennies were built and several installed in Peel's mill. At first, the use was on a very small scale, but word soon got round that there was a new machine that would enable one spinner to do the work of several. To the cottagers, whose livelihood depended on the spinning wheel, the news brought with it fear of unemployment. In 1768, Hargreaves' house was attacked and a score of jennies smashed. It was the John Kay story all over again. Hargreaves had to make his getaway as best he could, but this time instead of fleeing the country he was content to put a safe distance between himself and the Lancashire spinners. He headed for Nottingham, the centre of the hosiery industry, where there was a steady demand for yarn. He went into partnership in a spinning mill and enjoyed a moderate success. Rather belatedly, in 1770, he attempted to take out a patent, but never gained the protection or the royalties that might have made him a wealthy man.

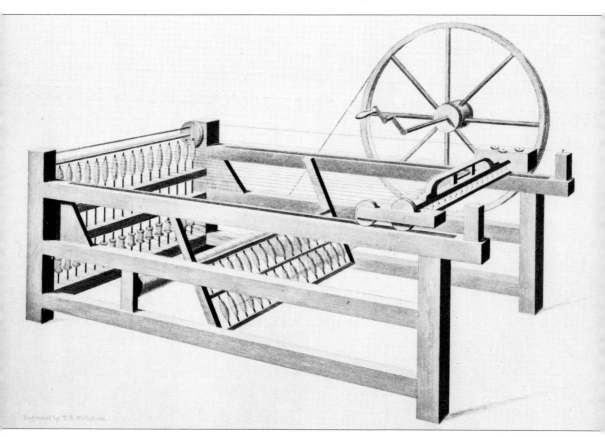

James Hargreaves' spinning jenny. One operative turning the handle on this machine could spin on sixteen spindles at once.

The jenny was, in fact, accepted quite quickly, for it was soon realised that it could be used in the home as a sort of super-efficient spinning wheel. Others were installed in workshops, and either powered by the operatives or by horses and mules. At last the supply of yarn was beginning to catch up with the capacity of the improved looms, but neither the flying shuttle nor the spinning jenny required any reorganisation of the traditional industry. They had increased the efficiency of the cottagers' work, but the pattern of life remained largely unchanged. The same could not be said of the next major innovation in the textile industry – Arkwright's water frame.

Sir Richard Arkwright by Joseph Wright of Derby. A model of the water frame stands on the table.

Arkwright of Cromford

Andrew Ure, a great enthusiast for the new cotton industry, wrote of Richard Arkwright as a man of 'Napoleonic verve and ambition' who forced through a textile revolution in the face of 'prejudice, passion and envy'.[1] Matthew Boulton, the famous manufacturer of steam engines, accused him of 'tyranny and an improper exercise of power'.[2] Both agreed that in Richard Arkwright the world was seeing a new phenomenon: the factory owner as absolute ruler over his workforce.

Arkwright[3] began his working life as a barber and wig maker; a strange beginning, perhaps, for an inventor of textile machinery, but he did work in Lancashire and the barber's shop is traditionally a great centre of gossip. No doubt Arkwright heard his share of the speculation about new spinning machines. In 1761, at the age of twenty-nine, he married a girl from Leigh, and it was there that he began to work at his designs. In 1768 he persuaded a local clock maker, John Kay (no relation of flying shuttle Kay), to help him produce a working model. They had use of a room in the Free Grammar School at Preston, and by now Arkwright was so convinced of the success of his work that he gave all his time to the venture. The family were reduced to extreme poverty, but fortunately he was able to talk a local innkeeper called Smalley into financing him. This, however, was the year when news of Hargreaves' spinning jenny reached the spinners of Lancashire and the inventor was forced to flee to the safety of Nottingham. When, in the following year, rumours of Arkwright's work began to spread, he took no chances. In 1769 he followed Hargreaves on the road to Nottingham.

Premises once used by Richard Arkwright as a barber's shop.

In Nottingham, Arkwright met two successful hosiery manufacturers, Samuel Need of Derby and Jebediah Strutt of Belper, both of whom were sufficiently impressed by the model to enter into a partnership. Smalley, who had provided the initial finance, was allowed in as a junior partner. Strutt, in particular, was receptive to new ideas, for his own fortune was

Part of Arkwright's original cotton mill at Cromford. Though the buildings remain, the water wheel has gone.

built on an improvement which he had devised for the knitting machine, which allowed it to be used for ribbed stockings. With the new partners' capital behind him, Arkwright was at last able to give his machine its first full trial. A building was rented and the machinery installed. It consisted, as with Paul's machine, of a set of rollers moving at different speeds, which pulled out the thread, and turning spindles, which collected and twisted the yarn. Horses were used as the source of power. The experiment was a success and now the partners set about looking for a site where they could begin work in earnest.

The spot they chose was Cromford in Derbyshire. No more than a tiny hamlet, it had everything Arkwright wanted. It was tucked away among the Derbyshire hills, and its very remoteness was one of its main attractions. There were no spinners working in their cottages among those hills and there was no one to raise complaints when Arkwright began building his mill and the town that was to be home to the mill workers.

Cromford and its mill represented something quite new. The mill itself was, by the standards of the day, enormous. It stood six storeys high, with machinery filling every floor, all powered by one big water wheel. This was more than a mere change in scale from what had gone before: it forced a whole new way of working onto the industry. Men no longer began to tend the machine at their convenience: the machine now demanded their presence. Once water began to flow through the sluices, turning the wheel and setting the rollers and spindles moving, then the workers had to be at their places. There they stayed, stopping only when the great wheel stopped. The factory bell rang out over Cromford announcing when work was to start. It rang again to announce the end of the working day. With the establishment of the mill at Cromford, the factory age had arrived.

From the first, Cromford attracted a good deal of attention. Wealthy tourists paused in their browsings around the hills of the Peak District to gawp at the buildings. One visitor – physician, man of letters and amateur scientist, Erasmus Darwin – celebrated it in verses which combined classical allusions with a working guide to the operations of the machines:

> Where Derwent guides his dusky floods
> Through vaulted mountains and a night of woods
> The nymph *Gossypia* treads the velvet sod,
> And warms with rosy smiles the watr'y god;
> His pond'rous oars to slender spindles turns,
> And pours o'er mossy wheels his foaming urns;
> With playful charms her hoary lover wins,
> And wields his trident while the Monarch spins.
> First, with nice eyes, emerging Naiads cull

From leathery pods the vegetable wool;
With wiry teeth *revolving cards* release
The tangled knots, and smooth the ravell'd fleece:
Next moves the *iron hand* with fingers fine,
Combs the wire card, and forms th' eternal line;
Slow with soft lips the *whirling can* acquires
The tender skeins, and wraps in rising spires:
with quicken'd pace *successive rollers* move,
And these retain, and then extend, the *rove*;
Then fly the spokes, the rapid axles glow,
While slowly circumvolves the labouring wheel below.[4]

Gossypium is the family name of the cotton plant, and all the processes involved in turning the raw cotton into thread are sketched into the poem. The workers removed the cotton lint then sent it to be carded, not on the old hand cards but by machines. The action of pulling the wool between cards studded with wire was imitated in the new machine, where the fibre was passed between similarly studded rollers. The cotton was then roughly twisted to form 'rovings' which were passed to the rollers of the principal spinning machine. This, because it was governed by the 'pond'rous oars' of the water wheel, was named the water frame. The mention of glowing axles is no flight of fancy. Friction in the moving parts of the mill was considerable and mill fires became commonplace.

An eighteenth-century water frame preserved at Higher Mill, Helmshore.

The economic importance of the Cromford mill was soon apparent. To begin with, such a mill was expensive. Estimates based on insurance valuations suggest a cost of not less than £3000 for the mill itself.[5] On top of that there was the cost of supplying water. Then, even after the mill was paid for, a new town had to be built to house the workers who were to come to the mill. There was a lot of cash tied up in Cromford and Arkwright wanted a quick return. He was, by all accounts, an overbearing and impatient character, but he was above all an ambitious man. Here was no inventive genius looking only for public acclaim: he wanted a cash return for a cash investment, and he was determined to avoid the fate of other inventors. He had made a start by setting up his works in neutral territory, and now he set about guarding himself against the other possible attackers on his profit. Well aware of the piratical habits of his fellow manufacturers, his first concern was for secrecy. After all, the mechanisms themselves were quite simple, well within the power of any competent craftsmen to construct. It would be a simple task, for example, for just the sort of men for whom he advertised to build his own machines at Cromford:

> Wanted immediately, two Journeymen Clock-Makers, or others that understand Tooth and Pinion well: Also a Smith that can forge and file. – Likewise two Wood Turners that have been accustomed to Wheel-making, Spoke turning, &c.[6]

That very simplicity made piracy all the easier, so we find him writing to his partner Strutt:

> Desire ward to send those other Locks and allso Some sort of Hangins for the sashes he & you may think best and some good Latches & Catches for the out doors and a few for the inner ons allso and a larger Knoker or a Bell to First door.[7]

The preservation of his monopoly was one aspect of Arkwright's search for wealth; his determination to exploit the new machines to the uttermost was another. They had to be kept going for as long as possible throughout the working day, and for this to be achieved there had to be a new attitude towards the workforce.

Arkwright recruited most of his workers locally, bringing whole families in to occupy the new houses which he had built – and built well. They were glad enough to exchange destitution for work and decent housing. The women and children formed the bulk of the workforce in the spinning mill, while the men were either set to the loom or employed in stocking making. Originally, there were looms at the mill, but Arkwright soon got rid of those and concentrated on spinning. The men continued to work in the workshops which occupied the top floors of the village houses.

The many observers who came to Cromford saw little beyond the miracle of technology. If they watched the women and children at work, they passed no comment. Certainly, few gave any indication that they were witnessing a major social revolution. Many years were to pass, and Arkwright himself was to be dead, before the cost of the miracle was spelled out in any detail. Arkwright's son, also called Richard, gave evidence before the Peel Committee of 1816, set up by Parliament to investigate the conditions under which children worked in the new factories. He described conditions in the early days. The workforce was mostly children, he said, aged from seven to thirteen, who worked a thirteen-hour day. He maintained that their health was in no way affected by the work, though he did add, as an apparent afterthought, that some of them had become deformed as a result of the poor design of the machines. The spindles carrying the thread were set very close

Houses for the workers in North Street, Cromford. Note the long windows on the upper floors where the men had their workshops.

to the ground and the children whose job it was to change the bobbins and to mend the threads, spent much of their time bent double. Some never quite managed to straighten up again. The fault might not, in fact, have been due to the machines at all but might have been brought on by disease caused by malnutrition. In either case it makes nonsense of the claim that they enjoyed good health.

Within the confines of Cromford, Arkwright lived the life of a feudal lord. The mill was his castle, as carefully guarded as any fortress, to which only his retainers and a few privileged visitors were admitted. He controlled the lives of his subjects, supplying them with work, home, provisions and every village amenity from church to inn. There are no figures available for the wages paid in those early days, but in the late 1780s Arkwright's spinners were earning an average of from 3s 3d to 3s 6d a week. At this time, the mill was working day and night and the night shift earned slightly more, from 3s 11d to 4s 7d.[8] Arkwright received a fortune in profits, the full extent of which became apparent at his death when the estate was estimated to be worth at least £600,000.[9] He also received the deference of the workforce. He played the lord of the manor to the hilt, handing out annual prizes to the butchers, bakers and grocers whom he considered had best served the town. The villagers acknowledged the favours with hymns of praise to the bountiful master:

> Come let us all here join in one,
> And thank him for all favours done;
> Let's thank him for all favours still
> Which he hath done beside the mill.
>
> Modestly drink liquor about,
> And see whose health you can find out;
> This will I chuse before the rest
> Sir Richard Arkwright is the best.[10]

Those lines were posted on the inn door at prize-giving time. The paternalist received his due.

Jebediah Strutt was unlike Arkwright in almost every way. Where Arkwright was irascible, Strutt was calm-tempered. Arkwright was scarcely literate, while Strutt was not merely literate, but quite stylish. For a time as a young man he lodged with the Wollatt family of Findern and his letters to the daughter of the house, Elizabeth, whom he later married, show a rhapsodic turn of phrase. 'Ye Findern groves & bowers', he lamented, during a temporary absence, 'who haunts your shades now I'm away or hears your warblers sing?'[11] There was also a difference in attitude towards business that was far more important than any difference in temperament.

Until the establishment of the mill at Cromford, Arkwright's life had been one of struggle and poverty. In 1771, when business began, he was nearing his fortieth birthday and as yet had very little to show for his life's work. His drive towards ever greater profits was remorseless. Strutt, on the other hand, was already a man of means. He had left farming to establish a hosiery business in Derby, where his ribbed-stocking machines were in-

Strutt's North Mill at Belper, dwarfed by the later East Mill.

stalled. His promotion of machine spinning was aimed at least as much at ensuring a steady supply of cheap yarn as it was at quick profits. The two men had frequent disagreements, and Smalley, the original backer of the scheme, also fell foul of Arkwright's temper. He had been appointed mill manager at Cromford, but was soon applying to Strutt for help in easing his quarrels with Arkwright. Strutt could offer little comfort. 'I said what I could to persuade him to oblige you in any thing that was reasonable & to endeavour to live on good terms at least ... you must be sensible when some sort of people set themselves to be perverse it is very difficult to prevent them being so.'[12]

Strutt too must have found Arkwright a difficult partner. In 1778, he built his own mill at Belper and three years later when Need died, the partnership between Strutt and Arkwright was dissolved. Strutt was content to build on a local basis, leaving Arkwright to bustle in the world at large. In Belper, Strutt established a similar system to that at Cromford, building houses for the workforce and supplying them with the necessities of life. The work of building town and mills was continued by his son, William, who added the first of a new style of building to Belper – the fireproof mill. It was one of the first of this new – and badly needed – type of building to be constructed. The houses at Belper were, like those at Cromford, built to a very high standard. They were in long terraces or in square blocks, forerunners of the back-to-back houses which were to predominate in the cotton towns of the nineteenth century. The existence of the little cottage hospital, run by Mrs Strutt, provides further evidence that Strutt's paternalism was indeed benign.

The wage books for the Belper mills[13] show very clearly the way in which whole families were involved in the work. The Cotterills, for example, at one time had nine members of the family in the mill. The father, John, was mainly employed as a labourer, whose average earnings were rarely more than 10s a week. But he was still the principal wage-earner. The pay for the rest of the family was on a descending scale, ending with his young daughter, Hannah, who never made much more than 2s a week. All told, when the entire family was at work, their weekly income was just over £2. Other family incomes followed a similar pattern. The bulk of employment went to the lowly-paid women and girls, who outnumbered males in the works by more than two to one. However, there were advantages to working for the Strutts, of which good housing was by no means the least. The rent for excellent houses such as those of Long Row, which still stand, was only in the region of 2s a week. These wages, which were for the years 1801–5, were not high, but they compared very favourably with those paid to the agricultural labourers in many parts of Britain. Sir Frederick Eden carried out a personal survey at the end of the eighteenth century[14] and found many

39

families throughout the country sunk deep into the most degrading poverty, from which, it seemed, no efforts of their own could ever extricate them:

> No labourer can at present maintain himself, wife and two children, on his earnings: they have all relief from the parish, either in money, or in corn at a reduced price. Before the present war, wheaten bread, and cheese, and about twice a week, meat, were their usual food; it is now barley bread, and no meat: they have, however, of late, made great use of potatoes ... Labourers' children, here, are often bound out apprentices, at 8 years of age ... A very few years ago, labourers thought themselves disgraced by receiving aid from the parish; but this sense of shame is totally extinguished.

These miserable Devon labourers were earning no more than a shilling a day, so that they were reduced to begging from the parish to make up their income to the point where they and their families could keep from actual starvation. And these were not the worst. Others had no work at all and had to rely entirely on the pitifully inadequate parish relief. If any of them heard of the promise of work, pay and a good home offered up in Derbyshire they must have thought they were hearing of an invitation to paradise.

The mills of Arkwright and Strutt were unquestionably improvements over the poor-houses, but, from the earliest days, there were social critics who compared Arkwright's personal prosperity with the working conditions of those on whose labour that prosperity was built. Arkwright, 'from being a poor man not worth £5, now keeps his carriage and servants, is become a lord of a manor, and has purchased an estate of £20,000; while thousands of women, when they can get work, must make a long day to card, spin and reel 5,040 yards of cotton, and for this they have *four-pence or five-pence and no more.*' There was also criticism from the old aristocracy who disliked the prospect of a rising class of men who made their money from trade and manufacture. They scorned the pretensions of the *nouveau riche*, and mocked their possessions. Viscount Torrington viewed Willersley Castle, the house being built for Arkwright at Cromford:

> Went to see where Sr R. A. is building for himself a grand house in the same castellated stile as one sees at Clapham, and *really* he has made a *happy* choice of ground, for by sticking it up on an unsafe bank, he contrives to overlook, not see the beauties of the river, and the surrounding scenery. It is the house of an overseer surveying the works, not of a gentleman wishing for retirement and quiet. But light come, light go, Sir Rd has honourably made his great fortune; and so let him still live in a great cotton mill![15]

There were grumblings, too, among the workforce. There was resentment at the more niggling aspects of factory discipline. The complaint was not against long hours and hard work – the poor were well accustomed to those – but against the strictness that was seen in all aspects of mill work. Some of the fines in the forfeit book at Belper seem bizarre until you recall that 'the workers' being penalised for such offences as 'calling thro' window to the Soldiers' or 'Terrifying S. Pearse with her ugly face' were mere children, perhaps not more than seven years old. (Among the apprentices subjected to those disciplines was Samuel Slater, who at the end of his apprenticeship emigrated, taking the details of cotton spinning with him, to begin a new career which was to earn him the popular title of 'Father of the American Cotton Industry'.) These conditions were tolerated, in spite of grumbles, because the Derbyshire workers had chosen mill life as an alternative to destitution. Memories of worse days were still with them. But success meant expansion and expansion, in turn, brought the mills into direct competition with an older way of life. Mutterings were to give way to shouts of anger.

Arkwright extended his empire after the success of Cromford: Masson Mill, Matlock Bath.

The success of Cromford encouraged Arkwright to widen his business activities. He began to build more mills in Derbyshire, and he also allowed other manufacturers to install his machines under licence, and in some cases entered into partnerships with them. He was beginning to move away from his home base and into the traditional textile heartland of Lancashire, and a new mill was begun at Chorley. One question now remained to be answered: how would the local workers react? Would Lancashire take to the new mills as peacefully as Derbyshire had done, or would the reaction be as violent as that which had driven out Kay and Hargreaves?

Arkwright had chosen a bad time to open his Lancashire mill. The War of American Independence which had seemed at first to be no more than a local affair, involving the suppression of a few colonial malcontents had, by 1779, grown into a full-scale international conflict. France had joined in on the American side and was attacking British shipping; and the Spaniards were blockading Gibraltar. Inevitably this had an effect on overseas trade. Work in the textile industry was slack, and workers were in no mood to accept new mills where one machine could do the work of many hands.

In October 1779, the Lancashire textile workers rose in their thousands and marched on the mills. The potter Josiah Wedgwood, visiting Lancashire at the time, wrote this account of the events to his partner, Thomas Bentley:[16]

> I wrote to my dear friend from Bolton, and mentioned the mob which had assembled in that neighbourhood, but they had not then done much mischief; they only destroyed a small engine or two near Chowbent. We met them on Saturday morning, but I apprehend what we saw were not the main body, for on the same day in the afternoon a capital engine, or mill, in the manner of Arcrites, and in which he is a partner, near Chorley was attacked, but from its peculiar situation, they could approach to it by one passage only, and this circumstance enabled the owner, with the assistance of a few neighbours to repulse the enemy, and preserve the mill for that time. Two of the mob were shot dead upon the spot, one drowned and several wounded. The mob had no fire arms and did not expect so warm a reception. They were greatly exasperated and vowed revenge: accordingly they spent all Sunday, and Monday morning, in collecting fire arms and ammunition and melting their pewter dishes into bullets. They were now joined by the D. of Bridgewater's colliers and others, to the number, we were told, of eight thousand, and marched by beat of drum, and with colors flying to the mill where they met with a repulse on Saturday. They found Sir Richard Clayton guarding the place with 50 Invalids armed, but this handfull were by no means a match for enraged thousands; they (the invalids) therefore contented themselves with looking on, whilst the mob com-

pletely destroyed a set of mills valued at £10,000. This was Monday's employment. On Tuesday morning we heard their drum at about two miles distance from Bolton, a little before we left the place, and their professed design was to take Bolton, Manchester, and Stockport in their way to Cromford, and to destroy all the engines, not only in these places, but throughout all England.

An army was on the march, storming through Lancashire, leaving behind the ruins of the mills. Arkwright retreated to Derbyshire and prepared to withstand the siege. The newspapers reported his preparations.[17] 'Fifteen hundred Stand of small Arms are already collecting from Derby and the neighbouring Towns, and a great Battery of Cannon ... besides which upwards of 500 Spears are fixt in Poles of between 2 and 3 Yards long.' Strutt took similar measures to defend the mills at Belper, and one can still see the gun embrasures cut in the bridge which runs across the main road from the mill. They waited for the worst and the worst failed to appear. The Lancashire army had no real leaders, no carefully formulated plan of campaign. Men who were ready enough to remove the menace from their own doorsteps were less eager to march across the country to Derbyshire, a place as remote to most of them as the coast of Coromondel. They were Lancashire spinners: let the men of Derbyshire look to their own livelihoods. They had achieved what they set out to achieve and with Sir George Saville now encamped in the area with three companies of the York Militia, they saw little point in courting further dangers. So they went back to their homes and the old ways of working. If they looked for any reaction in Derbyshire then they were disappointed. There the mills were no threat to old ways, rather a novelty, an additional source of employment. The revolt was over.

The Derbyshire mill owners relaxed. Strutt continued the steady development of his Belper base, adding more and grander buildings. For Arkwright, the burning of Chorley Mill was a setback, but no more. He set about increasing his Derbyshire empire still further, and then set out to other parts of Britain in search of fresh partners. He dashed furiously around the country in a coach and four, and in a journey to Scotland in 1783 he met a Glasgow merchant, David Dale. As a result of that meeting a new mill was built beside the Corra Linn Falls on the Clyde. The site offered many of the advantages that had first attracted Arkwright to Cromford. It had a plentiful and assured supply of water to turn the machinery, and it was remote from any likely arsonists. So the mill was built, tenements constructed to house the workers and the town was named New Lanark. It was to achieve fame in later years as the centre of a series of experiments in social organisation by its manager, Robert Owen. Owen told the story of how Dale set about finding and training a workforce.

This however was no light task; for all the regularly trained Scotch peasantry disdained the idea of working early and late, day after day, within cotton mills. Two modes then only remained of obtaining these labourers; the one, to procure children from the various public charities of the country; and the other, to induce families to settle around the works.

To accommodate the first, a large house was erected, which ultimately contained about five hundred children, who were procured chiefly from work-houses and charities in Edinburgh. These children were to be fed, clothed, and educated; and these duties Mr. Dale performed with the unwearied benevolence which it is well known he possessed.

44   *The mills and mill village of New Lanark on the Clyde.*

To obtain the second, a village was built, and the houses were let at a low rent to such families as could be induced to accept employment in the mills: but such was the general dislike to that occupation at the time, that, with a few exceptions, only persons destitute of friends, employment, and character, were found willing to try the experiment; and of these a sufficient number to supply a constant increase of the manufactory could not be obtained.[18]

Though the business might not have prospered to quite the extent some would have wished, it was a powerful concern which, together with Arkwright's other ventures, had turned the former barber into an exceedingly wealthy man. But Arkwright was greedy. He pushed through still more patents, even more dubious than the original patent for the spinning machine. Other manufacturers were less than enthusiastic about the prospect of handing over any more of their profits to Arkwright in the form of royalties. The end of the American war in 1781 had brought a revival in trade, and with the revival there was a cautious return to mill building in Lancashire. It had been a costly business, and now they determined to challenge Arkwright in the courts. In 1785 they opposed the patents in the Court of King's Bench.[19] John Kay, who had helped Arkwright in the earlier days and a friend of his, Thomas Highs, claimed authorship of the design. Others declared that the spinning machinery was no more than an adaptation of Lewis Paul's. At the end of the day, Arkwright found all his patents overturned and he left the proceedings in a high rage, swearing revenge on 'those Manchester rascals'. He threatened to publish the details of all his machines and send them to overseas competitors, but in the end he did nothing and the loss of the patents did little to diminish his increasing prosperity. He died in 1792 a wealthy man and with his importance officially recognised by a knighthood. The loss of his patents had done little to harm Arkwright and had worked wonders in the British cotton industry. The door was wide open for all and sundry, provided, of course, they had the capital, and provided too that they could obtain the cotton to spin.

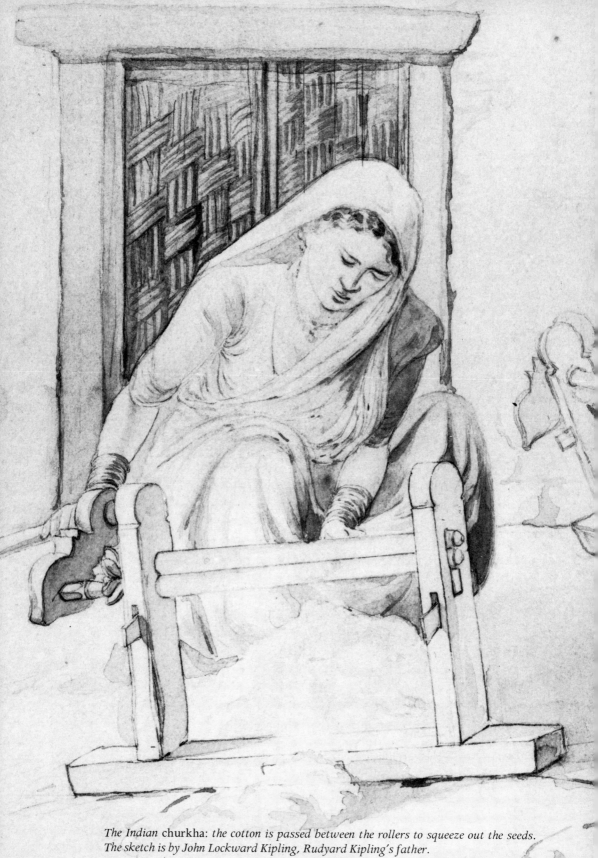

The Indian churkha: *the cotton is passed between the rollers to squeeze out the seeds. The sketch is by John Lockward Kipling, Rudyard Kipling's father.*

Failure in India

4

By the end of the 1780s, there were just over one hundred cotton mills in Britain; fifty years later they had increased more than tenfold and the value of manufacture had gone up from one million pounds per annum to over forty million. And even these dramatic figures tell only part of the story, for while the total value of cotton yarn produced had risen, the cost of the yarn had fallen from 36s per pound to around 3s.[1] This meant an incredible increase by a factor of nearly five hundred in the quantity of yarn coming out of British mills, and a corresponding increase of raw cotton going in. Estimates vary,[2] but it was generally agreed that by the 1830s imports of cotton were running at nearly four million tons per annum. For cotton to be supplied in those sorts of quantities, changes had to be made elsewhere as great as any seen in the North of England.

There was no shortage of potential suppliers. Egypt, with its long tradition of cotton growing, could provide a small but reliable crop. Plantations were also established in the New World in Brazil and, to a much greater extent, the West Indies. The latter grew the native Sea Island cotton, famous for its long staple, creamy-white colour and strong, silky fibres.

Sea Island cotton. On the right the cotton is being picked from the tall plant while on the left seeds are removed using rollers and the cotton is being pressed into bags.

Sunderland Point on the river Lune where the first American cotton was landed in Lancashire.

From the earliest days of settlement on the southern mainland, cotton from the West Indies had been included in a list of possible crops. An expedition was sent in 1669 by the Lords and Proprietors of Carolina which was to found the settlement that was eventually to become Charleston. They received clear instructions on this point:

> Mr West, God sending yo^u safe to Barbados, yo^u are there to furnish y^rselfe wth Cotton Seed, Indigo seed, Ginger Roots ... Yo^r Cotton & Indigo is to be planted where it may be sheltered from ye North West Winde.[3]

West, who was the leader of the expedition, was later to report back to the proprietors that:

> The winter here doth prove something sharpe and colde, soe y^t I feare this will not prove a Cotton Country, but our new Commers like it very well, and say they believe it will produce any commodities y^t the Charibbe Islands doe, as Cotton, Ginger, Indigo, &c.[4]

In this the Barbadians were to prove more accurate judges than Joseph West. For a long time, however, the cotton did no more than serve local needs and very little found its way across the Atlantic. Indeed, American cotton was so rare that when an American ship landed eight bales at Liverpool in 1784, British customs officials seized the cargo on the grounds that such a vast quantity had never been grown in that part of the world.[5] But still the obvious place to look for the bulk of supplies was India, the home of cotton. There appeared to be every advantage in looking in that direction, for British influence was growing apace. The few, small trading enclaves had expanded vastly to fill the vacuum left by the collapsing Moghul empire, while the main trading rivals, the French, were virtually finished. European wars had been transplanted to the East and the British had come out as victors after the fall of Pondicherry in 1761.

The first years of British rule boded ill for the country. Bengal was taken over and systematically stripped of its wealth, with administrators jostling and pushing each other to see who could acquire the largest fortune in the shortest possible time. The country was bleeding to death, and the neglected East India Company was hurtling towards bankruptcy. In 1786, Cornwallis was appointed Governor-General and he took the decisive step of forcing a complete separation of administration from trading. Men had to choose between the two: the days of using public office for private gain were over. Unfortunately, in solving one problem, Cornwallis begat another. In the neat division between the trader hoping for a quick profit and the administrator working for his salary, there was no space left for the encouragement of native production. So, the planting and growing of cotton was left where it was, just one small part of the subsistence economy of India. The small planters grew what they could, sold what they could and paid those taxes that were forced upon them. There might still have been hope for the Indian planter to take advantage of the new demand for cotton, but under British rule, a subtle yet decisive change was made in the old pattern.

Under the old Moghul system, the peasant had paid his taxes to a *zamindar*, who retained a percentage as his own profit as tax collector. It was in everyone's interest to ensure that the peasants did the best they could. It kept them above the starvation line, ensured a profit for the *zamindar* and provided the revenue for the Government. If the *zamindar* failed to pay up, he was sent for, given a beating and sent back with a warning to do better next time. The beating was passed on down the line, and after that everyone got back to work and hoped for better times to come. This was not the British way. A tax collector who failed to deliver the correct amount of taxes was not beaten – that was barbaric. Instead, he was dismissed for incompetence, to be replaced by an incorruptible bureaucrat looking steadfastly towards the proper implementation of the law. The peasant, faced by tax demands,

49

had either to meet those demands or account for his actions before a court run by foreigners he did not know, arguing in a language he did not understand. The best he could hope to do was to find some way of satisfying the new masters. If the authorities required so much cotton lint, then they should have it – and someone else could worry about the quality. But who was to do the worrying? Not the middlemen. Like the peasants, they had to supply so much bulk, and if that bulk was made up of inferior produce, well that too was someone else's problem. The administrators were not too concerned. They were there to balance their books: so much cotton demanded, so much cotton received. The shortcomings only really appeared when the cotton reached distant England. There people cared, but by then it was too late. Who could trace the faults back through the labyrinthine dealings that had begun in a remote field in India? And to make matters worse, the Indian cotton was, in any case, a short staple plant, not best suited to the machines of industrial revolution Britain. It had done well enough for the local weavers, but they too were beginning to suffer under policies decided in far-off Europe.

'Awaiting an offer' by Kipling. Indian farmers patiently wait for someone to buy their cotton.

The restrictions on cotton-cloth exports to Britain had done little to help local weavers, and now that the British controlled all trade, exports were effectively cut to other parts as well. New legislation made matters even worse for the local workers. Taxes were imposed on cloth movements inside India, which produced the absurd situation that it was actually cheaper to buy Manchester yarn and Manchester cloth than it was to buy local products. Everywhere the Indian textile trade was in retreat before the incursions from Lancashire. Not surprisingly, this was deeply resented, as officials of the East India Company pointed out when yet more taxes were added in the nineteenth century:

> The duty of 10 per cent levied in this country on the Cotton Goods of India is felt by the natives as a very great grievance. They do not expect that if the duty were reduced, or even abolished, they could compete with the manufacturers of England, but it is felt an unreasonable aggravation of their natural disadvantages that their hand-manufactured goods should in this country be burdened with a duty of 10 per cent, while the machine-made goods of England, if imported in British ships, are admitted to supersede the manufactures of India on their own soil, at a duty of little more than one-third that amount.[6]

British rule was hampering and hindering development of all sections of the India cotton trade. Lancashire cried out for more raw material. India could have supplied it, if only someone could set the country on the right path.

Looking through the reports of the East India Company, one can chart the progress from optimism to disillusion.[7] In December 1790, the Directors gave approval for Company ships to carry a two-way trade – convicts out to Botany Bay, cotton back to England. Twenty years later, that trade was being described as 'a ruinous and unproductive burthen upon the Company and private importers.' The problems were recognised and accurately analysed:

> The cultivators in small farms ... have barely the means of providing for their families and paying their rents; they are incapable of enjoying any satisfaction which arises from new and successful pursuits; and it would be difficult to persuade them to hazard even the miserable provision they are now certain of, in the hope of obtaining a better one by any new or speculative undertaking.[8]

So, the natives could not be expected to speculate in cotton and, in the absence of a system that could promise a large return on capital, Europeans were equally loth to put money into production. Methods of cultivation were antiquated, rewards small, and the arguments always came back to the same basic problem. Desperately poor cultivators were at the mercy of the middlemen. Faced with food crops on which they depended for their very existence and cotton crops from which they hoped for a tiny profit, the cultivators had no doubts about where their priorities lay. The cotton crop was left until last, and if in the meantime some of the plants had rotted in the field, then there were ways of coping with that:

> The good Cotton is separated from the seed; and the bad stuff, which had been taken away from the good, is beaten with a stone to loosen up the rotten fibre from the seed, and then it is passed through the churka (rollers used to separate out the seed). The good Cotton and this bad stuff are both taken into a little room, six feet by six, which is entered by a low door, about eighteen inches by two feet, and a little hole, as a ventilator, is made through the outer wall. Two men then go in with a bundle of long smooth rods in each hand, and a cloth is tied over the mouth and nose; one man places his back so as to stop the little door completely, to prevent waste, and they both set to work to whip the cotton with their rods, and to mix the *good and bad together* so thoroughly that a very tolerable article is turned out.[9]

The Court of Directors of the East India Company trumpeted their complaints. 'No excuse will hereafter be admitted by us for the foulness, dirt, and seeds, which are suffered to remain mixed with the cotton; and it is our positive order, that the commissions be not paid to any commercial resident whose provision of cotton shall be faulty in this particular.' [10] They complained, but nothing much happened.

Of course, there were ways of improving efficiency, but too often they fell foul of administrative inefficiency. A local resident was sent the latest product of advanced technology, a machine for separating the seed from the fibre. Unfortunately, he reported, 'it was not accompanied by any directions, and after cleaning it and carefully examining every part of it, I have failed to discover how it is to be worked.'[11]

Cotton production became caught in a vicious circle. Dirty cotton would not sell in Lancashire. There was no incentive to produce clean cotton in India. The merchants, who were the ones who would possibly gain from an expanded cotton trade, turned instead to a new crop, one which promised to offer far fewer problems. They set out to satisfy a newly-developed British taste. They turned from cotton to tea.

The story of cotton in India in the nineteenth century is a story of missed opportunities. Yet there was no shortage of men who could see the obvious and could express it forcibly and with clarity:

Certainly, without any exaggeration, the most astonishing thing in the history of our rule in India is, that such innumerable volumes should have been written by thousands of the ablest men in the service on the mode of collecting the land revenue, while the question of a thousand times more importance, how to enable the people to pay it, was literally never touched upon.[12]

Meanwhile, the British looked elsewhere for their main supplies of cotton. The Indian chance was gone.

Cotton picking in America in the 1890s – a scene that could have been taken from any time in the nineteenth century.

The Slave States

'The Peculiar Institution' of slavery marked off the Southern American states from their Northern neighbours more absolutely than any geographical or national boundary could ever have done. The difference lay only partly with the morality of slavery: the response of Northerners to the free blacks amongst them, not to mention their actions towards the native North American, gave them very little right to claim a place on a high moral pedestal. What the acceptance of slavery did for the South was ensure that it followed a totally different pattern of development from that of the North.

The first slaves were brought to North America by the Dutch in the early seventeenth century. There is some doubt about the status of the first blacks, for it has been claimed that their position was really that of indentured servants. This legal nicety of definition could have had little meaning to the African, carried from his homeland in the stinking hold of a small ship, set down in a foreign land among strangers. In any case, whatever the initial situation, slavery soon became established and legalised in the South – and in some parts of the North as well. But it was in the South that slavery dug the deepest, most pernicious, roots. The big plantations formed on the banks of the navigable rivers drew in the slaves and sent out their crops of rice, indigo and tobacco. But the slave was more to the white planter than a mere labourer: he was a symbol of wealth and a marketable asset. And the more slaves who came in, the harder it became to envisage any alternative to the system.

The plantation South fed on slavery. From the earliest days the South offered a different way of life from that of the North. The European immigrants who had made the long and difficult journey to start a new life saw little to attract them to a South, which, with its semi-feudal society, seemed only to offer Europe transplanted. They looked instead to the North, where change and progress seemed to be the watchwords. The poor who might have provided a workforce turned away and the slaves were left to tend the fields. And once the work was accepted as slave work, it became virtually impossible to employ white labourers. They could not be brought in to take on work that set them on the same footing as the slaves, and the masters could not, in any case, have employed them. The whole edifice of slavery rested on a theoretical foundation, which proclaimed black inferiority, white superiority. It was essential, then, that the roles be kept distinct. The fact that as one descended the ladder of white prosperity, one reached workers whose conditions of life were, in practice, little different from those of the slaves resulted in some of the most bitter forms of racial oppression. It was those at the very bottom of the ladder who felt the strongest need to impose a rung below that on which they themselves stood. The fact that this superiority had no basis in reality had to be hidden behind an elaborate screen of pretence, half-truth and dubious morality.

The first justification offered by slave holders was that slavery had always been part of the African way of life. The Africans themselves bought and sold slaves. But, even if it was rational to argue that an act can be justified on the grounds that someone else does it – a catch-all morality that could be used to condone any crime – the argument would still have little force. Black slavery in America was of a very different kind from black slavery in Africa. For the slaves it meant permanent exile to an alien land, perpetual bondage not only for themselves but for their children and their children's children for untold generations to come. There was not even the promise of escape, for they carried with them the indelible badge of their slavery – their black skins. To bring that state of affairs within the bounds of any acceptable morality required a neat twist of logic. The black skin that marked a slave for permanent bondage was itself taken as justification for that bondage. The black skin proved inherent inferiority. The argument was put crudely by crude men, subtly by learned men, but its essence remained the same. Here, from among the hundreds of different statements of the same line, is just one 'proof' of African inferiority:

> The African has never reached ... a higher rank than a king of Dahomney, or the inventor of the last fashionable *grisgris* to prevent the devil from stealing sugar plums. No philosopher among them has caught sight of the mysteries of nature; no poet has illustrated heaven or earth, or the life of man; no statesman has done anything to enlighten or brighten the links of human policy. In fact, if all that negroes of all generations have ever done were to be obliterated from recollection for ever, the world would lose no great truth, no profitable art, no exemplary form of life. The loss of all that is African would offer no memorable deduction from anything but the earth's black catalogue of crimes.[1]

From this argument only one conclusion could be reached:

> 50,000,000 of blacks have not been placed on this magnificent globe of ours for no purpose; it is therefore our duty, by wise legislation to utilize this large mass of human beings. They must be dealt with from no sentimental viewpoint, but from a knowledge of their nature and characteristics, discarding at once the theory of equality ... One section must govern the other.

The argument of white superiority could be buttressed on all sides. There was scientific mumbo-jumbo:

> The negro's brain has in a great measure run into nerves ... From the diffusion of brain, as it were, into the various organs of the body, in the

shape of nerves to minister to the senses, every thing from the necessity of such a confirmation, partakes of sensuality, at the expense of intellectuality ... The great development of the nervous system, and the profuse distribution of nervous matter to the stomach; liver and genital organs, would make the Ethiopian race entirely unmanageable, if it were not that this excessive nervous development is associated with a deficiency of red blood in the pulmonary and arterial systems, from a defective atmospherization or arteriolization of the blood in the lungs.[2]

Such views might seem self-evidently absurd, but their author, Doctor Cartwright of New Orleans, took them seriously and they were widely quoted as solid scientific evidence in other publications. If you were not impressed by the musings of modern science you could always turn to the most unimpeachable source of all. The Bible turned out to be full of texts to support the view that God was on the side of the white race. The black races were the sons of Ham, and had not Noah cursed him and his family: 'a servant of servants shall he be unto his bretheren'.[3] And if black was bad, there was ample evidence that white was good. John's vision of the Second Coming could scarcely be plainer: 'His head and His hairs were white like wool, as white as snow.'[4] Blacks, then, were intrinsically inferior: the white man was doing them a big favour by bringing them out to enjoy the fruits of civilisation. What was more, he was offering them the Christian religion, which was so powerful it could turn the blackest skin white. But not, of course, in this life:

> Here lies the best of slaves,
> Now turning into dust.
> Cesar, the Ethiopian, craves
> A place among the just.
> His faithful soul is fled
> To realms of heavenly light,
> And, by the blood, that Jesus shed,
> Is changed from black to white.[5]

This elaborate justification was applied to slavery because slave traders and slave owners found the system profitable. It was also highly speculative and the traders looked to get profits where and how they could. That might include a little privateering as a side line, but the bulk of the profits came from a triangular trip: trade goods to the slave coast, slaves to America and the produce of the Americas back to Britain. The slave ship, *Hawke*, sailing out of Liverpool in January 1779, took £3000 worth of trading goods, mostly beads, brass, ironmongery and cloth. With these the traders bought an unspecified number of slaves, of whom 386 survived to be sold for over £17,000. At the end of the voyage, after paying wages and other expenses, the owners declared a profit of over £7000. The following year, she was even more successful, clearing £11,000 which included £3700 for privateering, taking the *Jeune Emelia* as a prize on the way home. In 1781, however, the tables were turned. The *Hawke* was captured and over £6000 lost. Even then, the profit for three years' trading was over £12,000.[6] It could well have been higher but for the final misfortune. It was a trade that seemed worth the effort of justification.

Needless to say, many never made any conscious effort at self-justification and fewer still took the trouble to spell out their views at length. Nevertheless, it was a necessary process. It enabled men to live comfortably within a climate of general approval, and when the system came under attack from outside it created a sense of a community acting on an agreed morality. The

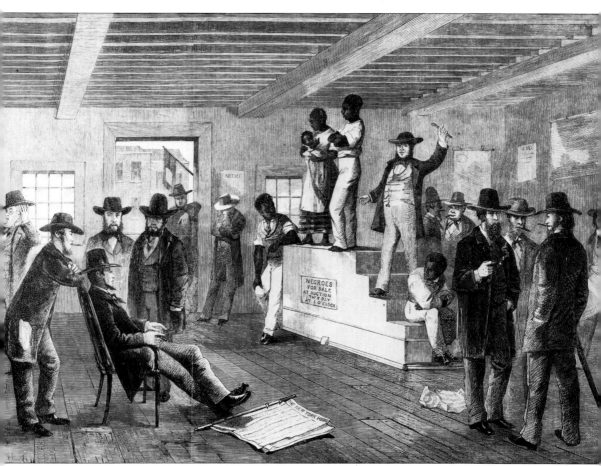

A slave auction in Virginia.

pro-slavery arguments had to sit as uncomfortable neighbours to the realities of slavery. The high moral tone that stated that slavery was 'improving' for the African had little in common with the tone of the auction block:

> Abraham Seixes,
> All so gracious,
> Once again does offer
> His services pure
> For to secure
> Money in the coffer.
>
> He has for sale
> Some negroes, male,
> Will suit full well grooms
> He has likewise
> Some of their wives
> Can make clean, dirty rooms.
>
> For planting too,
> He has a few
> To sell, all for the cash,
> Of various price,
> To work the rice,
> Or bring them to the lash.[7]

The slaves themselves, herded around the country like cattle, seemed not to appreciate the favour that was being done to them in introducing them to civilisation. A traveller journeying through the South wrote this description of a gang he chanced upon:

> It was a camp of negro slave-drivers, just packing up to start; they had about three hundred slaves with them, who had bivouacked the pre-ceding night *in chains* in the woods ... It resembled one of those coffles of slaves spoken of by Mungo Park, except that they had a caravan of nine waggons and single-horse carriages, for the purpose of conducting the white people, and any of the blacks that should fall lame, to which they were now putting the horses to pursue their march. The female slaves were, some of them, sitting on logs of wood, whilst others were standing, and a great many little black children were warming them-selves at the fires of the bivouac. In front of them all, and prepared for the march, stood in double files, about two hundred male slaves, *manacled and chained to each other*. I have never seen so revolting a sight before![8]

59

He noted that the gangs were constantly on the look-out for ways of escape, and he reported hearing of a recent incident where a slave had managed to get his hands on an axe, killing many of the overseers while the rest fled. Such accounts make nonsense of the often repeated view that the black slave was essentially a submissive, docile creature, happy to accept his allotted place in life.

These traders were only one link in a chain of men, passing on the slaves and each taking their profit. Profit was made by those who brought them to America; by those who sold them at auction; and by those who carried them around the countryside. The firm of Templeman and Goodwin, for example, had their headquarters in Richmond, Virginia, and from there they made frequent expeditions into the Lower South. Their book-keeping was meticulous:[9]

1849   Cost of Negroes taken

Nov 15th	Martha	cost	580	Sold to Absalon Dukes	625
	Isaac		675	Sold to Andrew Berry	825
	Caroline		655	Sold to Robt. F. Henderson	700

And so on. Within that month, they sold nineteen slaves for a total of $12,950 and a profit of $2395.

At the end of all this trading, the slave had become an expensive commodity, and a valuable part of his owner's property. Now, like any other capital investment, he had to be turned into a profit. But, however much the slave owner might wish to regard the slave as a mere chattel, in the reality of everyday life he was no such thing. In theory, the owner could do with him just as he pleased but in practice, as we shall see later, the slave could impose limitations. There were also other, intrinsic, limitations to the freedom of the owner wishing to turn his merchandise into a money maker. Work needed to be found, and agriculture provided the great bulk of the work. There were to be later attempts to turn slaves towards manufacturing industry, just as the poor in Britain were being drawn into the factory. But the slave owner had problems that the mill owner never had to face. Responsibility for the slave was totally his, and the slave's well-being was essential for the protection of his investment. Mill hands could work for low wages and be left to fend for themselves as best they might; there was no money tied up in their persons, only in the machines they worked. The slave was different. He had to be kept healthy, fed, clothed, housed, kept in check and kept in work. The factory would not answer: the plantation would. Here the slaves could grow the crops to feed themselves and their masters, and after that all that was needed was a suitable cash crop to provide the profit which was the mainspring of the whole plantation machine. Unless the owner could find profitable use for his slaves, the whole complex machine would start to run down. The slave might be, and was, a status symbol, but these status symbols had to earn their keep. Ambitious owners wanted something more than bare subsistence. They wanted cash in their pockets and the leisure to spend it.

The main crops for the South were indigo, rice and, most importantly, tobacco. Tobacco from Virginia and the surrounding states found a ready, but not infinitely expandable market in Europe. Prices fluctuated wildly. Planters grew so much tobacco that they were forced, at times, to burn their crops in the field to keep prices high. It was a good cash crop, but the demand was just not high enough to support the entire plantation system of the South. So the South looked for an alternative, and their gaze turned to the hungry mills of industrial Britain. Cotton seemed to be the answer to all their problems.

The attractions of cotton were plain. It suited the conditions, there was a ready and expanding market and it was ideal for the big fields of the plantations. Cotton fields were planted along the seaboard and soon spread inland. The West Indies planters, faced by the new competition, simply shifted their ground. They had a new crop, sugar, which promised to do well for them, and they were content to leave the cotton growing to the South. There was, however, one obstacle to unlimited expansion. To be acceptable to British manufacturers, the cotton had to be supplied in good, clean condition, free of its seeds. It was failure to meet this condition that had led to the decline of the Indian trade. Cleaning seeds from cotton was no easy business – they clung hard to the fibres. They could be pulled out by hand, but this was a tedious and time-consuming business. They were also removed by 'bowing', a process in which a bow was vibrated in the cotton, sending the seeds flying out. But none of these methods was especially efficient nor were they suited to the shorter staple cotton which was beginning to find favour in the South. The answer was clearly to be found in some kind of machinery, for if cotton could be spun by machine it should not be beyond man's ingenuity to find some way of cleaning it by machine. And so it proved, but the solution was not found by a native Southerner, experienced in the handling of cotton, but by a visiting Yankee.

Eli Whitney,[10] son of a Massachusetts farmer, arrived in the South, having graduated from Yale in the autumn of 1792. He came to Savannah, Georgia, and from there travelled up-river to stay on the plantation of Mrs Greene, widow of General Nathaniel Greene, who had been awarded the plantation for his gallantry during the Revolutionary War. Young Eli Whitney, during the same war, had shown that he had a taste for mechanics as well as school mastering. He had set up his own small forge and worked as a nailer. Settled in his new home, he could not have avoided hearing the locals discuss the problems of cleaning cotton, complaining that it could take as long as a whole day to get one slave to clean just one pound. It was a problem that appealed to his mechanical ingenuity and he established a small workshop to see if he could find an answer. He found it, but, as ever, posterity has preferred the romantic story of accident to the reality of perseverance. Whitney, it was said, was watching the farm cat trying to get its paws on the chickens. It sat waiting for a chicken to get near the wire frame, then shot out a claw. Result: one nude chicken, one cat with a claw full of feathers. That is the story, and it is certainly the principle of Whitney's invention. Cotton was picked up on a roller studded with metal teeth which carried it round to a metal grill. The cotton was scraped off, the seeds dropped away. An improved version, by Hogden Holmes, replaced the studded roller with a circular saw blade. Simple and effective, it was named the cotton gin and was the making of the South. Now one slave, turning a handle, could do the work of a dozen. On large plantations, the water wheel could be used instead and the gin could do the work of hundreds. The solution had been found: Whitney prepared to receive his reward.

The Whitney gin, a simple hand-operated machine that revolutionised the cleaning of cotton.

The prosperous plantation followed on from the invention of the Whitney gin.

The story of Whitney's gin is strikingly similar to that of the other inventions in Britain: the sequel also followed a familiar pattern. Whitney went into partnership with a man named Phineas Miller and attempted, through patents, to gain a monopoly on ginning throughout the South. Their prices were high, yet the machine was simple. Planters much preferred to spend the cash on building their own gins, and there were far too many imitators for Whitney to challenge them all. Eventually, the State stepped in and paid $50,000 to buy out Whitney's patent. Whitney went back north where he devised a system for manufacturing muskets from standardised parts, the base from which modern mass production has developed. It was a major technological advance, but was of little interest in the South. They already had what they wanted from Whitney. The way was now open to apparently unlimited growth. King Cotton had set off for his Coronation.

Samuel Crompton, inventor of the spinning mule.

Towards the Factory Age

6

Cotton supplies to Britain seemed assured, and the impetus given to production by the invention of the water frame and the establishment of cotton mills on the Cromford pattern was given a powerful boost by yet another invention in the textile industry. The yarn from Arkwright's spinning machines was coarse; for fine yarn, manufacturers still had to turn to the far less productive jenny. Samuel Crompton[1] improved that situation when he introduced his spinning mule. A weaver, born into a moderately well-off family, Crompton hit on the idea of combining the principles of the spinning jenny and the water frame into one machine: hence the name 'mule' for the new hybrid. It used rollers to draw out the yarn, which was then wound onto spindles mounted on a moveable carriage. As the carriage retreated from the rollers, so the thread was stretched. Then, as it returned, the thread was wound onto the bobbins.

Crompton built his machine at his home at Hall-i-th'-Wood, near Bolton, and it was originally known as the Hall in the Wood Wheel. The first model was completed in 1779, just at the time that the spinners of Lancashire were rampaging through the region, burning mills and smashing machines. He decided, reasonably enough, that that was not the ideal time to present his new invention to the world at large. He took the precautions of dismantling the prototype and hiding the pieces. Once the trouble had subsided, he reassembled the mule and began to set it to work. At this time his idea was simply to establish an advantage over his neighbours by supplying fine yarn at low cost, without mentioning the mule at all. The idea was doomed. For one man to produce such thread in such quantities had to mean a new machine. Manufacturers were soon hammering on his door, promising a fortune if only he would pass on his secret. The familiar inventor's tale was about to be re-enacted.

Crompton listened to his tempters, believed what they said and offered his invention to the world at large. The local manufacturers promised compensation, but neglected to put any figures to the offer. Eighty-five of them entered into the agreement with Crompton, and when all the subscriptions were gathered in they reached a grand total of just over £72. Crompton struggled on, watching others make fortunes from his invention and at last petitioned Parliament in the hope of getting some reward. Many leading manufacturers gave evidence of the usefulness of the invention when they appeared before the Select Committee of the House of Commons. Crompton's hopes began to rise, for he had an ally on the Committee, the manufacturer, Sir Robert Peel. His luck seemed really to have changed when, as he was talking to Peel in the lobby of the House, they were approached by the Chancellor of the Exchequer, Spencer Perceval. He passed on the splendid news that Parliament looked certain to award Crompton £20,000. The date was 11 May 1812: the day that Perceval was to be assassinated. Parliament was dissolved and poor Crompton's hopes dissolved with it. He died, as did many of the inventors whose work helped to make the industrial revolution possible, an embittered man. The ideas were his, the profits went to others.

As the eighteenth century ran its course, so the pace of development quickened – and continued to quicken. The manufacturers now had it within their power to supply any quality of yarn by means of new machines installed in factories. Once the turmoil of 1779 died down in Lancashire, the mill builders returned with new enthusiasm, until every stream that could be harnessed to turn a wheel was lined with new buildings. And, as the pressure on water supplies grew, so manufacturers spread out to new regions – to Scotland and to the English Midlands, where the growing hosiery trade provided a ready market for the yarn. It was soon clear that this new industry was here to stay. With each new mill that was built, more workers were pulled into the factory system and yet more crowded round them to get their share of the expanding trade. Weavers jostled for space around the spinning factories; transport systems grew to feed in the raw material and take out the finished products; canals were cut and roads were improved and both were busy with traders. Hamlets grew to villages, villages to towns and the shopkeepers, innkeepers and other tradesmen moved in to serve the new communities. Travellers to the north came back with stories of a world that was changing at a pace that had never been imagined before, let alone seen. Some saw the changes as a great march, striding off on the road to Utopia. It was improvement all the way: 'Get rid of that dronish, sleepy, and stupid indifference, that lazy negligence, which enchains men in the exact path of their forefathers without enquiry, without thought and without ambition, and you are sure of doing good.'[2] Others looked on less happily at the destruction of the old order in which they had held a place made comfortable by centuries of use, and its replacement by a new world which threatened the old traditions. 'Every rural sound is sunk in the clamour of cotton works: and the simple peasant is changed into the impudent artisan.'[3]

Whether they applauded or condemned the changes, all commentators were agreed that the changes were momentous. They also had one other characteristic in common – they viewed the changes from a fairly lofty position. They offered the rich man's view. They tended either to be aristocrats concerned about the status quo, or rising industrialists, beginning to shout for a say in the nation's affairs. The latter applauded the end of the old stagnation and looked forward to a new, dynamic economy creating fresh wealth, fresh opportunities. The wealth was not, however, available to all. The one area where the old aristocracy and the new middle class found common ground was in their approach to the lower orders of society. The aristocracy, shaken by the revolution in France, viewed the lower classes with distrust, if not actual fear. They had to be kept in their place, and that included keeping them poor. The new class had no argument with that view. 'Everyone but an idiot knows that the lower classes must be kept poor or they will never be industrious.' The status quo of wealth should be preserved at the upper end of the scale, and, with luck, the poor would be too preoccupied with work and the new demands of the industrial world to have time to follow the example being set for them across the channel.

Viewed in one light, the status quo was maintained. The poor remained poor, though they were marginally less poor with the industrial régime than they would have been without it. Looked at from another point of view, the old order had been slung out of the window when industry came in the door. If man cannot live by bread alone, then his well-being cannot be measured only in terms of the food on his plate. To understand the vastness of the changes brought about by industrialisation, we have to look a little more closely at the lives of the ordinary people before and after the transition.

It makes no sense to begin talking about life for the worker in the cotton mill unless you have some sort of picture of what that same worker might have been doing if the cotton mills had never existed – and what his contemporaries were doing in other parts of the country. To talk of wages, even in terms of what they would buy, means little unless set against wages in other jobs. It helps to place everything in context if one takes even a brief look at what was still the greatest employer of labour – agriculture.

Spinning mules at work: note the small girl under the machine.   67

Throughout the period of violent change in industry, an almost equally dramatic change was being made in agriculture. The land was being improved, producing better and better crops. Cattle were getting healthier and fatter – the average weight of cattle sold in London's Smithfield Market in the 1790s, for example, was more than double that of the 1710s. But improvement was bought at a price, and much of it was paid in the movement towards enclosure. What had once been common land passed into private hands. Fences were erected and behind them the landowner could set about bringing in new and better crops. There was surplus food available for the new towns, and that surplus brought new profits. The enclosure movement proved its value and, once started, fairly galloped along. In the first half of the eighteenth century, 115 Enclosure Acts passed through Parliament; in the next half that number rose to 2015.[4] Compensation was, of course, paid to those who could establish rights to the land. But what of those whose only rights lay in the unwritten tradition of centuries of use? The matter was decided in law, and the law is notoriously harsh in regard to unwritten tradition. The rights of common grazing and gleaning may have played a comparatively small part in the lives of those who already drew their main income from working as labourers for the big landowners, but in a subsistence economy that small part could be crucial. The dispossessed had to fight their battle as and when they could. The men of Cheshunt, for example, made their view plain in a letter sent to Oliver Cromwell, Squire of Cheshunt Park in 1799:

> Whe right these lines to you who are the Combin'd of the Parish of Cheshunt in the Defence of our Parrish rights which you unlawfully are about to disinherit us of ... Resolutions is maid by the aforesaid Combind that if you intend of inclosing our Commond fields Lammas Meads Marshes &c Whe Resolve before ... that bloudy and unlawful act is finished we have your hearts bloud[5]

The men of Cheshunt were able to win some reparation; others were less fortunate. The independent yeoman of folklore became the unlanded labourer, working from dawn to dusk for a pittance that all too often fell short of even the demands of subsistence. Paid less than a living wage, the labourer and his family were forced into the humiliation of begging relief from the parish. Eden's report on the conditions of the poor (see p. 39) gave wages for the farm labourers as low as one shilling per day. And what would that shilling buy after the worker had set aside the money for his rent? Eden noted that meat was $4\frac{1}{2}$d to 5d a pound, wheat 12s a bushel, butter 13d a pound and cheese 4d. The shilling, it seems, would buy very little, and the magistrates at Speenhamland laid down a rule that a subsistence level should be agreed,

The rural poor were seldom depicted by painters except as here when they were intended to show the results of indolence: in fact conditions for the industrious were often far worse.

and where wages fell below that level, the parish would make up the difference. They meant well, no doubt, but it was a direct incitement to employers to pay low wages. It was a harsh rule that stripped working men of their dignity. It was a bad rule, yet sensible men saw it in operation, noted its results and failed to condemn it. They offered instead the cheerless doctrine of hierarchies which said that some were born to rule, others to serve, and it was a blasphemy to attempt to interfere with this divine order:

> The Poor have nothing to stir them up to labour but their wants, which it is wisdom to relieve, but folly to cure. The maxim is not less calculated for the advantage of the Poor, than it appears for the benefit of the Rich. For, among the labouring people, those will ever be the least wretched as to themselves, as well as most useful to the Public, that,

69

being meanly born and bred, submit to the station they are in with chearfulness; and contented that their children should succeed them in the same low condition, inure them from their infancy to labour and submission, as well as the cheapest diet and apparel.[6]

The author of those fine sentiments then proceeds to lecture the housewife on just what that 'cheapest diet' might consist of:

A pound of good beef or mutton, 6 quarts of water, and 3 ounces of barley, are boiled till the liquor is reduced to about three quarts: one ounce of oat-meal, which has been previously mixed up with a little cold water, and a handful, or more, of herbs, are added.

This, he claimed, would last a large family for three days. These conditions were not even the worst that could be found. In Scotland, for example, in the 1790s, that cash wage of a shilling a day was the top rate. In the impoverished Highlands things were often worse and even in the Lowlands, where the labourer was given food at work, his wages were reduced to a mere 8d. In all regions, lower rates were paid in winter than in summer.[7]

70   *Calico printing: machine printing in Britain imitated the hand painted cottons of India.*

There is no real need to go on making the same point. Life in the fields was brutish and hard, with starvation an ever-present threat. At best the labourer might earn his keep; at worst he was forced to go cap in hand to the parish. And when that occurred, he was liable to find himself faced with the break-up of his family, the children being bound apprentice. Many of those apprentices found themselves headed for the new mills. This was the climate of opinion in which the conditions of the mill were set by the owners; this is the gloomy picture against which those conditions must be judged. It is well to bear this in mind as we turn to the factories themselves.

Children employed at Coat's of Paisley, in the late nineteenth century.

Mill Children

The children who came from all over the country to serve in the new mills were mainly parish apprentices. Some were orphans, others children of those labourers who could not afford to feed and keep their own families. Because the mill controlled all aspects of their lives they provide a perfect gauge for measuring the attitudes and principles of the employers. The children were completely in their charge, their welfare their entire concern. The records of one mill, in particular, give a very complete account of the way of life of these children.[1] It was generally recognised as being one of the best and most humanely organised mills in the country.

Samuel Greg of Belfast came to the hamlet of Styal in Cheshire, just a few miles south of Manchester, in 1784. There he built a large mill on the banks of the Bollin, and a short distance away he built a village to house the workers he would recruit for the new factory. The adult workers signed up for varying periods of time. James Stretch of Morley came along for three years 'at the wages that the said Mr Greg gives to other spinners'; and if he left before the time he agreed to pay Greg one guinea 'for learning to spin'. Others had a more dubious background. Daniel Bate, a clockmaker from Middlewich, was no doubt glad enough to get out of the Manchester House of Correction to work for five years at 15s a week – though first he had to earn the guinea that Greg paid to get him released. Whole families arrived and whole families signed up for work, often borrowing money from Greg to help them get started in their new homes. Most of the families came from Cheshire or the neighbouring counties of Lancashire and Staffordshire. Some of the children who came as parish apprentices were local, but many came from far away. Two popular sources were the poor-houses of Chelsea and Liverpool. The parishes were only too eager to unload their surplus children:

> The thought has occurred to me that some of the younger branches of the poor of this parish might be useful to you as Apprentices in your Factory at Quarry Bank. If you are in want of any of the above, we could readily furnish you with Ten or more at from nine to twelve years of age of both sexes.

On being offered this useful commodity, Greg replied, setting out his terms:

> I am much obliged by your attention and find we have room at present for about 12 young Girls of from 10 to 12 years old ... the terms at which we take them are:
>
> Two guineas each will be expected from the Parish, and clothing sufficient to keep the Children clean,
>
> Say 2 shifts   2 Frocks
> 2 Brats or aprons
> and 2 guineas to provide them other necessaries.

The parish must have thought it was doing well to be rid of the expense of keeping the children for a few guineas, while Greg in his turn was pleased enough with the bargain. Indentures were drawn up, setting out responsibilities on both sides:

It is this day agreed by and between Samuel Greg, of Styal in the County of Cheshire, of the one part and Sarah Irwin Daughter of John Irwin of Newcastle of the other Part, who Agrees to the terms as follows: That the said Sarah Irwin shall serve the said Samuel Greg in his Cotton Mill, in Styal, in the County of Chester, as a just and honest Servant, Twelve hours in each of the six working days, and to be at her own liberty at all other Times; the Commencement of the Hours, to be fixed from Time to Time by the said Samuel Greg, for the Term of four years at the Wages of one Penny p week allso Sufficient meat drink apparal lodging washing and other things necessary and fit for one in her situation.

Further clauses specified that if she was ever absent from work Greg 'may abate the Wages in a double Proportion' and that Greg could get rid of her 'for Misbehaviour, or Want of Employ'. Agreement reached, the young apprentice was brought to Styal and given a new home in the apprentice house. 'Here are well-fed, clothed, educated, and lodged, under kind superintendence, sixty young girls, who by their deportment at the mill ... evince a degree of comfort most creditable to the humane and intelligent proprietors.'[2]

That description was by the Pangloss of the factory system, Andrew Ure, who, if he ever saw anything the least amiss in any mill in the land, neglected to record the fact. The children themselves, far from home, working among strangers for twelve hours and more a day, wrote no books to express their views. They could – and did – make their feelings known more directly. Joseph Stockton, a-penny-a-week apprentice from Newcastle in Staffordshire, was signed up in 1796 for an eight-year apprenticeship. On 12 May 1799 he ran off and was tracked down in Newcastle. A warrant was issued and he was hauled back to Styal on 10 June. Next day he was off again and was caught by the constable on the Newcastle road. On 13 June 'he promised to mind his business and give us no further trouble in future and was again set to his work'. He lasted just over a month this time and then, on 22 July, he ran away for the third time – and this time his name was to disappear for ever from the Styal records. Why did he run away? The records do not say. What happened to him? Again, no answer. Perhaps he got away, more likely he found himself in gaol. Two other runaways, however, give us rather more information about life in the mill. Joseph Sefton and Thomas Priestley ran away to London, in Joseph's case because

74

Cruikshank's view of brutality in the mills.

he wanted to see his mother. They were caught and hauled up in front of the magistrates in August 1806. In their evidence, they gave a very complete picture of their way of life:

Joseph Sefton. I am 17 yrs of age this August. My father I am informed deserted me or went for a soldier when I was about 2 yrs old. His name was John Sefton. I have been told that I was born in Clerkenwell I had been in the workhouse of the Parish of Hackney from an infant about $3\frac{1}{2}$ yrs I consented before the magistrates at this office Worship St to be bound apprentice to Samuel Greg cotton spinner and manufacturer. There were 8 boys and 4 girls of us bound at the same time. We went to Styal and were employed in the cotton mills of Mr Sam[1] Gregs which are a short distance. I was first employed to doff bobbins . . . I used to oil the machinery every morning. In fact I was employed in the mill work. I did not spin. I liked my employment very well. I was obliged to make over time every night but I did not like this as I wanted to learn my book. We had a school every night but we used to attend about once a week (besides Sundays when we all attended) . . . I wanted to go oftener to school than twice a week including Sundays but Richard Bamford would not let me go . . . I have no reason to complain of my master Mr Greg nor Richard Bamford who overlooks the works there were 42 boys and more girls apprenticed. We lodged in the Prentice House near the Mill. We were under the care of Richard Sims and his wife. The boys slept on one side of the house and the girls on the other. The girls all slept in one room. The boys in three. There was a door betwixt their apartments which was locked of a night. Our rooms were very clean, the floors frequently washed, the rooms aired every day, whitewashed once a year. Our beds were good. We slept two in a bed and had clean sheets once a month. We had clean shirts every Sunday. We had new clothes for Sunday once in two years. We had working jackets new when those were worn out and when our working trousers were dirty we had them washed. Some had not new jackets last Summer but they were making new ours when I came away.

On Sunday we went to church in the morning and to school in the afternoon after which we had time to play.

On Sundays we had for dinner boiled Pork and potatoes. We had also peas turnips and cabbages in their season.

Monday we had for dinner milk & bread and sometimes thick porridge. We had always as much as we could eat.

Tuesday we had milk and potatoes.

Wednesday sometimes Bacon and Potatoes sometimes milk and bread.

Thursday If we had Bacon on Wednesday we had milk and bread.

Friday we used to have Lobs couse.

Saturday we used to dine on thick porridge.

We had only water to drink, when ill we were allowed tea.

Thomas Priestley was thirteen years old, and two months before he ran off he suffered one of those accidents that were all too common among the unguarded machines of the mill. 'I was working and there was a great deal of cotton in the machine, one of the wheels caught my finger and tore it off. ... I was attended by the Surgeon of the factory Mr Holland and in about 6 weeks I recovered.' His deposition gives more details of the working day:

Our working hours were from six o'clock morning Summer and Winter till 7 in the evening. There were no nights worked. We had only 10 minutes allowed us for our breakfasts which were always brought to the Mill to us and we worked that up at night again – 2 days in the week we had an hour allowed us for dinner, while the machines were oiled, for doing this I was paid $\frac{1}{2}$d a time, on other days we were allowed half an hour for dinner. When the boys worked over time, they were paid 1d an hour.

In August 1806, there were ninety apprentices in the apprentice house, which today is a comfortable home for one family. The numbers frequently rose above this level. Life at Styal was considered easy by the standards of the day, and other apprentices have left even bleaker pictures of their time at

Litton Mill in Derbyshire, where Robert Blincoe served his apprenticeship.

other mills. Robert Blincoe described how he was taken from the St Pancras Workhouse in London at the age of seven to work as an apprentice in a mill in Derbyshire. In 1815, at the age of ten, he was one of a hundred apprentices, boys and girls, in 'the 'prentice House' at Litton Mill, Derbyshire, established by Ellis Needham in 1780.[3] There was no resident supervisor and the house was like a prison, surrounded by a high stone wall, kept locked at night.

> We all ate in the same room, and all went up a common stair case to our bed chamber; all the boys slept in one chamber and all the girls in another. The beds were in rows along the wall, a second tier being fixed above the first. The beds were thus made double by a square frame work – one bed above, the other below. This was done to save room. There were about twenty of these beds, and we slept three in one bed. The girls' bed-room was of the same sort as ours. There were no fastenings to the two rooms and no one to watch over us in the night or to see what we did.

We went to the mill at five o'clock without breakfast, and worked till about eight or nine, when they brought us our breakfast, which consisted of water porridge with oatcake in it and onions to savour it with, in a tin can. This we ate as best we could, the wheel never stopping. We worked on till dinner time, which was not regular, sometimes half-past twelve, sometimes one. Our dinner was thus served to us. Across the door way of the room was a cross-bar like a police bar, and on the inside of the bar stood an old man with a stick to guard the provisions. These consisted of Derbyshire oat-cakes cut into four pieces, and ranged in two stacks. The one was buttered and the other treacled. By the side of the oat-cake were cans of milk piled up – butter-milk and sweet-milk. As we come up to the bar one by one the old man called out 'Which'll 'ta have, butter or treacle, sweet or sour?' We then made our choice, drank down the milk and ran back to the mill with the oat-cake in our hand, without ever sitting down. We then worked on till nine or ten at night without bite or sup. When the mill stopped for good, we went to the house to our supper, which was the same as breakfast – onion porridge and dry oat-cake.

78   *A child mixes colours for the block printer.*

It makes Styal sound almost idyllic, and it was not the worst. There were mills where work continued day and night. As in so many other matters, Arkwright's Cromford mill led the way, introducing gas light at a very early date. As one group of apprentices fumbled their way out of bed, another set were on their way back, exhausted. It was in such mills that the old saying was born: 'The beds of Lancashire never grow cold.'

Some relief was offered by the Peel Act of 1802, which gave protection to the pauper apprentices. It was an acknowledgement that someone knew of the conditions and was prepared to do something, but little more. The paupers were only one portion of the apprentice population, and the passing of an act means little when there is no one to take on the job of enforcing it. John Moss, an overseer at the apprentice house of Beckbourn Mill, near Preston, gave evidence before the Committee set up in 1816 to enquire into the working conditions of factory children. His evidence told of children working from five in the morning to eight at night, or even longer if there was time to make up. An hour out of the day was set aside for meals. Their only rest came on Sundays, when they only had to work from six in the morning to noon, cleaning the machinery. The conditions matched the hours in breaking all the new rules, and as the questions and answers continued, the sad story was told:

> Did the children sit or stand at work? – Stand.
> The whole of their time? – Yes.
> Were there any seats in the mill? – None.
> Were they usually much fatigued at night? – Yes, some of them were very much fatigued.
> Where did they sleep? – They slept in the apprentice house.
> Did you inspect their beds? – Yes, every night.
> For what purpose? – Because there were always some of them missing, some sometimes might be run away, others sometimes I have found asleep in the mill.[4]

When asked why he had so blatantly disregarded the conditions set down in the 1802 act, he replied quite simply that he had never heard of it, and there is no reason to suppose he lied. Many another overseer must have gone on in the old ways, either ignorant of the new law or certain that there was no one on hand to enforce it.

By 1816, the act was already not only ineffective but largely irrelevant. Manufacturers were moving away from the apprentice system towards the more straightforward alternative of hiring children as ordinary wage-earners.

It could be argued that this shift was a direct result of the Peel Act, an attempt to get round the restrictions on working hours. It seems, however, much more likely that the mill owners were discovering that the apprentice system was too expensive. Samuel Greg of Styal calculated that, in 1790, the weekly cost of keeping an apprentice was 3s 6d and by 1822 this had risen to 5s. Wages were a lot cheaper than that, and by making the change the owner gave up any bothersome responsibilities for the children's welfare. However, the decline of the apprenticeship system brought no noticeable improvement in working conditions.

Within this picture of gloom, there were bright patches and the brightest was to be seen in Scotland, where a novel doctrine was being put forward. Robert Owen of New Lanark, one of the most important manufacturers in the country, addressed these words to his fellow industrialists:

> Will you then continue to expend large sums of money to procure the best devised mechanism of wood, brass, or iron; to retain it in perfect repair; to provide the best substance for the prevention of unnecessary friction, and to save it from falling into premature decay? Will you also devote years of intense application to understand the connexion of the various parts of these lifeless machines, to improve their effective powers, and to calculate with mathematical precision all their minute and combined movements? And when in these transactions you estimate time by minutes, and the money expended for the chance of increased gain by fractions, will you not afford some of your attention to consider whether a portion of your time and capital would not be more advantageously applied to improve your living machines?
>
> From experience which cannot deceive me, I venture to assure you, that your time and money so applied, if directed by a true knowledge of the subject, would return you not five, ten, or fifteen per cent of your capital so expended, but often fifty and in many cases a hundred per cent.[5]

Owen put forward this revolutionary view, that the humans in the mill mattered, in his book *A New View of Society*, which was based on his experience as manager of the New Lanark mill. This was the mill that had been established by Arkwright and David Dale. Owen arrived in 1798, fifteen years after its foundation. As at Styal, the workforce was divided between the families housed in new tenement blocks, let out by Dale at a very low rent, and some five hundred pauper apprentices, mostly from Edinburgh. He found that village and villagers fell some way short of the ideal. 'The population lived in idleness, in poverty, in almost every kind of

The streets of New Lanark, c. 1900. The workers' tenements line the street that leads up to the counthouse.

crime; consequently in debt, out of health, and in misery.' At first sight, the condition of the children was far better:

> The benevolent proprietor spared no expense to give comfort to the poor children. The rooms provided for them were spacious, always clean, and well ventilated; the food was abundant, and of the best quality; the clothes were neat and useful; a surgeon was kept in constant pay to direct how to prevent or to cure disease; and the best instructors which the country afforded were appointed to teach such branches of education as were deemed likely to be useful to children in their situation. Kind and well disposed persons were appointed to superintend all the proceedings.[6]

Appearances were deceptive. The authorities insisted that Dale take the children from the poor-house as young as six years of age, and Dale found it necessary to work these little children from six in the morning to seven at night. He might offer them educational opportunities, but what use was that after thirteen hours crippling labour in the mill – 'many of them became

81

dwarfs in body and mind, and some of them were deformed.' It is an appalling indictment of the system that that was the end result of the best efforts of one of the most kindly of employers.

Owen set about a vigorous improvement campaign. He took over the role of benign despot, cajoling, instructing and demanding cleanliness, sobriety and honesty. Housewives would find Owen on the doorstep demanding to inspect their handiwork. The worst of the ale houses were closed, and Owen endlessly preached the virtues of temperance. But his great emphasis was on education. No building was so important, in Owen's eyes, as the school he set up – the New Institution. Here adults as well as children could be educated. But how was this achieved by Owen when Dale had already failed? Owen had his answers. Children under ten years of age were to be sent to school; they would not be allowed into the works. If the public charities refused to pay for pauper children to come to New Lanark, then so be it. There would be no pauper children. But could adults and other children be expected to benefit from education when they ended the day almost as tired as the little ones who were now to be spared? They could not. Therefore their working hours must be reduced to the point where they were not exhausted at the day's end.

These were wildly controversial views, and they did not go unopposed. Owen's partners in the works viewed with alarm the prospect of being pulled willy-nilly along the road to bankruptcy by this passionate reformer. But Owen was not an easy man to dissuade. Which was better for the long-

The children of New Lanark putting on a dancing display for visitors to the New Institution, c. 1825.

term good of the concern, he demanded to know, a healthy, hard-working employee or a wretched hand, demoralised and dishonest? The experiment was tried and it worked. Owen could demonstrate that shorter working hours produced better and more goods, and he had the evidence to prove it. A healthy individual would do what Owen had always said he would do – produce more than a worker who was permanently on the brink of exhaustion.

Such views were greeted with disbelief when Owen was called to give evidence to the Peel Committee of 1816. They kept on asking the same question over and over again: how did he explain the rise in productivity? Surely, they kept insisting, he must be speeding up the machine. No, replied Owen, healthy alert operatives make fewer mistakes so there are less stop-pages, fewer delays. The Committee simply could not accept the explanation. 'Do you', they demanded, 'as an experienced spinner, or a spinner of any kind, mean to inform the Committee that the machine which you employ for throstle and water spinning can produce an additional quantity from any other cause whatever but the quickening of the motion of the machine?' Owen could only repeat his answer, and the Committee kept repeating their question until at last Owen was forced to reply, rather tetchily that 'it is far from my wish to deceive the Committee.' At the end of the day, the Committee were no more convinced than they had been at the beginning and Owen's fellow manufacturers were equally sceptical.

The experiment at New Lanark remained an isolated affair, a bright example which few wanted to follow. Not, of course, that everything at New Lanark was beyond reproach. Owen wanted to see an industrial society that reflected what he judged to be the best aspects of the previous age. He wanted harmony between master and men, all working together for the common good. Co-operation was the key word, but co-operation along lines that he would draw. He was an autocrat, demanding obedience from his workforce not merely in their work but in their private lives as well. Not every rule he laid down was ungrudgingly accepted; nor obviously to the advantage of the workers. Owen was a fanatical believer in the virtues of music and dance and his tenants were dragooned into playing their parts. One women eventually packed up and left, complaining that Owen 'had got a number of dancing masters, a fiddler, a band of music, that there were drills and exercises and that they were dancing together till they were more fatigued than if they were working.'[7] But whatever his quirks, it was by his treatment of the children of New Lanark that Owen should be judged. Among the literally thousands of visitors who came to see this fascinating experiment was the poet Robert Southey, who watched the scene in the infants' playground with obvious pleasure. 'It was really delightful to see how the little creatures crowded about Owen to make their bows and their

83

curtsies, looking up and smiling in his face; and the genuine benignity and pleasure with which he noted them.' 'The shouts and laughter of the children were,' he declared 'worth all the concerts of New Lanark, and of London to boot.'[8] In this, at least, Owen's despotism found its justification.

In reading the seemingly endless accounts of overwork, brutality and near enslavement of the mill children, one question inevitably demands to be answered – why did almost no one take up the cause of these children? In part, one can find an explanation in the ethos of the age which argued that the greatest benefit society could convey on the poor of whatever age was to keep them at work. A gentleman tourist[9] visiting a carpet factory at Penrith recorded that 'tears of pleasure gushed upon the eye' when he saw the pauper apprentices at work. By that work they were 'saved from the hands of destruction and vice, rendered useful members of society, and happy in their industry and innocence'. The manufacturer, thinking perhaps more in terms of a quick return on his capital, was happy to receive this justification from the old order. The landowners were, in any case, not very well positioned to mount a critical attack on the use of children in manufacture, for they themselves were perfectly happy to employ children in the fields. The child of a farm labourer soon found it had to earn its crust. As soon as they were old enough they were set down beside a gate at the end of the lane

> ... there through long solitary days they pick up a few halfpennies by opening it for travellers. They are sent to scare birds from corn just sown, or just ripening ... They help to glean, to gather potatoes, to pop beans into holes in dibbling time, to pick hops, to gather up apples for the cider-mill, to gather mushrooms and blackberries for market, to herd flocks of geese or young turkeys, or lambs at weaning time; ... and then, they are very useful to lift and carry about the farmyard, to shred turnips, or beet-root – to hold a sack open – to bring in wood for the fire, or to rear turfs for drying on the moors, as the man cuts them with his paring shovel, or to rear peat-bricks for drying. They are mighty useful animals in their day and generation, and as they get bigger, they successively learn to drive (a) plough, and then to hold it; to drive the team, and finally to do all the labours of a man.[10]

Were factory children then any worse off than farm children? It is tempting to answer with an immediate 'yes'. At least, the farm children were out in the open air, not stuck away in a dark, unhealthy mill. But the image of open air life is of fields in the sunshine, and it is easy to forget February mornings when frost turns the ground to iron, or November mists when the clinging damp chills to the bone. But whatever the hardships of rural life, and they were considerable, a close comparison of the two ways of life must come down on the side of the farm labourer.

Children were beaten in factories, and no doubt they were also beaten on farms; factory children worked long hours, but so did those on the land; both were touched by the diseases and miseries of poverty. Yet crucial differences remain. The factory child was taken from a familiar environment, clamped within an iron discipline and a régime that was untouched by the movement of the seasons. Winter was as summer, the working day was measured by the tick of the clock not the movement of the sun. Each day was as the last – no time of sowing, no harvest home. And in every minute of every working day the machines ground on, determining the rate of work, giving no room for personal decisions and choices. Removed from his family, the factory child was at the mercy of the overseer who, too often, was forced to keep the children at work for all hours by whatever means he could devise.

> After the children from eight to twelve years had worked eight or nine or ten hours, they were nearly ready to faint; some were asleep; some were only kept to work by being spoken to, or by a little chastisement, to make them jump up. I was sometimes obliged to chastise them when they were almost fainting, and it hurt my feelings; then they would spring up and work pretty well for another hour; but the last two or three hours were my hardest work, for they then got so exhausted.[11]

It was an experience that was as bitter and dehumanising to the overseer as it was to the children. Parliament was eventually to legislate against the worst abuses of the system of child employment, but by then the factory system had already been in operation for more than sixty years. For generations of children, the legislation came too late. And all the time, the industry was spreading, more and more mills were being built. To the economist it spelled economic growth, to many others it was misery spread still wider. But to the poorest section of the community in England, Scotland and especially Ireland, it spelled hope. Here was a chance to rise above starvation level and they crowded to the textile districts. Mills became larger, towns grew bigger and the slums became deadlier.

Mills along the Irwell. Squalid housing was squeezed in between the tall factories.

Cotton Towns

The cotton manufacturers armed with water frame, jenny and mule might seem to have all they needed for an unopposed advance towards a previously unimaginable prosperity. But there were still a few difficulties to be overcome. There were manufacturers in plenty ready to put their money into new mills, but first they needed somewhere to put their mills. The ideal site would be close to one of the improved main roads or, better still, one of the new canals, but there was one other criterion to be met. The site had to have a reliable water supply to turn the wheels, and such prime sites were disappearing fast. Mills were being forced away from the main transport routes and the centres of population in the search for water. As new rivers could not be built, a new means of turning the machinery had to be found. It soon was.

The steam engine, in one form or another, had been in use in British industry since the beginning of the eighteenth century. At first it had been limited to working as a pumping engine in the mines, but, thanks to the improvements brought in by James Watt, its use was being extended. The engine was able to turn a shaft as well as lift pump rods. It could, in other words, replace the water wheel and in 1778 the first steam engine was installed in Robinson's mill at Papplewick in Nottinghamshire. Here was good news not just for prospective mill builders but also for existing manufacturers who, in the past, had often found work halted for lack of water in a dry spell. At Styal, for example, one of the new engines was rapidly installed. Here, as in many other mills, it was a belt-and-brace operation – if one source of power failed, there was another ready to take over. It was comforting to have a steam engine if a drought came – and it was equally comforting to have the good old reliable water wheel in case this new-fangled thing broke down. If the introduction of the steam engine had meant no more than this, then it would just have been another useful addition to the mill's battery of machines, but in fact it was to have far greater significance.

The new steam-powered mills could be put virtually anywhere, and manufacturers knew just where they wanted them: in the middle of the town, with the workforce literally on the doorstep. No need now for horses to plod down miry tracks to reach a distant mill; no need either for workers to waste precious time – and energy – in tramping between home and factory. Everything could be gathered together in the one place, neat and convenient. So the cotton towns grew up around the new mills – Bolton, Bury, Blackburn, Oldham and the rest. By 1811, there were forty-two spinning mills in Oldham alone, and around these the new houses were clustered in mean, shabby streets and airless courtyards. Whatever the faults of the older country mills – and in terms of harsh discipline they were among the worst – at least their setting was clean. The operatives leaving the

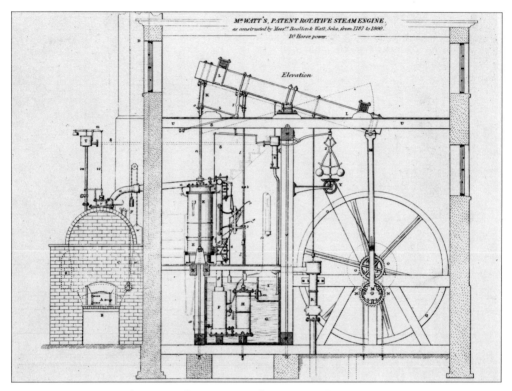

James Watt's rotative beam engine of 1787: one of the first steam engines capable of powering a mill.

mill breathed fresh air. In the towns all that changed. Smoke rose from the tall chimneys to settle as soot on the surrounding houses. Dye works sent out their waste to pollute the rivers. There was no proper drainage, no sewers. The new mills of Oldham brought prosperity of a sort, but it did not show itself in the streets of the town. A *Morning Chronicle* journalist described how he saw it in 1849:

> The whole place has a shabby underdone look. The general appearance of the operatives' housing is filthy and smouldering. Airless little backstreets and close nasty courts are common: pieces of dismal waste-ground – all covered with wreaths of mud and piles of blackened brick – separate the mills.[1]

The bankers and merchants who formed the bulk of the mill owners had their houses on the outskirts of the town: solid stone villas, kept well clear of the slums developing in the centre. The pattern was changing. At Cromford and Styal, the owners had built their houses to overlook the works. In the towns, the owners withdrew, forming their own enclaves of prosperity. The mill workers were left to fend as best they could among the jerry-built terraces. And all the time the pressure of numbers grew. As more yarn came from the mills, so more gathered round, setting up looms wherever a space could be found. Nowhere was the pressure greater than in the capital of cotton, Manchester:

> An idea of the immense population of the country in the environs of Manchester burst upon the mind on a sudden, when we reached the summit of a hill about two miles without the town, where a prodigious champaign of country, was opened to us, watered by the Irwell, filled with works of art; mansions, villages, manufactories and that gigantic parent of the whole, the widely-spreading town of Manchester.[2]

Manchester was both the mercantile and industrial centre of Lancashire cotton. It was important even before the industrial revolution wrought its changes. At the beginning of the 1770s, the trade directory listed, for example, 87 fustian manufacturers and 50 check manufacturers, 30 printers and dyers, 18 yarn merchants and 6 cotton merchants.[3] Altogether there were some 1400 entries. To turn on a hundred years is to see an astonishing change.[4] The 1400 entries had grown to nearly 30,000, and there were some 500 cotton manufacturers, more than 400 printers, a whole new group of engineering firms, manufacturing machinery for the textile industry, and scores of cotton merchants, agents and brokers. Expansion on this scale suggests a vast population increase, and that there was. In the late 1780s, the population was estimated at around 40,000. Fifty years later it had more than trebled. Many of the new workers came over from Ireland, others from the poorer parts of England, but all were drawn by the rumours of boom-time prosperity. Wages for hand-loom weavers rocketed – though the European wars sent them plummeting down again with equal speed. But in peacetime the weavers were the new élite and there was a rush of recruits to their ranks. The great problem, however, remained. Where were they all to live? The only answer seemed to be in insanitary slums.

John Ferriar, physician to the Manchester Infirmary at the end of the eighteenth century, wrote a dispassionate account of the conditions he discovered.[5] His matter-of-fact tone makes it seem all the more chilling. He offered 'a few observations on the means of opposing the production and progress of infectious fevers, in cellars and lodging houses, where they reduce great numbers of the Industrious Poor to extreme distress, and often nearly destroy whole families.' It is worth quoting at some length, for it is the accumulation of Ferriar's drily noted facts that makes the pamphlet so telling.

1   In some parts of the town, cellars are so damp as to be unfit for habitations ... I have known several industrious families lost to the Community, by a short residence in damp cellars.

2   The Poor often suffer much, from the shattered state of cellar windows ... the consequences to the inhabitants are of the most serious kind. Fevers are among the usual effects.

3   I am persuaded, that mischief frequently arises, from a practice common in many back streets of leaving the vaults of privies open ... fevers prevail most, in houses exposed to the effluvia of dunghills in such situations.

4   In Blakely-street, under No. 4, is a range of cellars, let out to lodgers ... They consist of four rooms, communicating with each other, of which the two centre rooms are completely dark; the fourth is very ill lighted, and chiefly ventilated thro' the others. They contain from four to five beds in each, and are already extremely dirty.

5   The lodging houses, near the extremities of the town, produce many fevers ... The most fatal consequences have resulted from a nest of lodging houses in Brook's entry ... In these houses, a very dangerous fever constantly subsists, and has subsisted for a considerable number of years. I have known nine patients confined in fevers at the same time, in one of these houses, and crammed into three small, dirty rooms. ... Four of these poor creatures died, absolutely from the want of common offices of humanity ... The horror of these houses cannot easily be described; a lodger fresh from the country often lies down in a bed, filled with infection from its last tenant, or from which the corpse of a victim to fever has only been removed a few hours before.

On he goes through a catalogue of horror. Ferriar continued his investigations, and thirteen years later found things were no better.[6] Slum houses were being built with windows that were never intended to open, and even the supposedly well-off operatives employed by mighty McConnel and Kennedy, the most powerful of cotton manufacturers, lived in back-to-backs with no water supply, no yards or gardens and no paved roads. Pamphlets were written but no one, it seemed, heeded the warnings. Fever struck in 1796 and again in 1832, when cholera spread through large parts of the city. John Fielden, Member of Parliament for Oldham, and himself a manufacturer at Todmorden, rounded on his fellow manufacturers. Here was none of the calm analysis of Ferriar, but an impassioned outburst:

We were panic-stricken; we knew our sins; we recollected the fevers of 1796; we knew the 'squalid homes' of those who made our wealth; we knew the malignancy would fix on them, and that this would endanger ours. It was there that we flew, not from charitable motives, but to save ourselves: we subscribed, we visited, we scoured, we whitewashed (would to God we could whitewash ourselves!): we did all that men could do – to save our own! We found hunger, nakedness, bare earthen floors and unfurnished houses with unwhited walls: what of that! neither of these was catching. Ah! but pestilence was! We sought out pestilence where we were sure to find it; we did not carry charity where we always knew it was wanted. We were moved exactly as we were in 1796, not by the love of our neighbours, but by fear of the visitations of God.[7]

Of all those who came to investigate conditions in Manchester in the first half of the nineteenth century, none gave a more detailed description, nor more vehemently denounced what he saw, than the twenty-four-year-old son of a German cotton manufacturer, Frederick Engels. *The Condition of the Working Class in England* is one of the key works in Marxist literature and, probably for that reason, it has had no shortage of either critics or defendants. One must, however, be wary of one thing – putting the Marxist cart before the Engels horse. Engels did not set out to blacken Manchester to bolster up his communist doctrine – rather that doctrine grew as a result of the conditions he discovered in Manchester. He obtained much of his material from observation and a good deal from Mary Burns, the Irish mill girl who lived with him as his wife until her death in 1863. From his descriptions of walks around the poorest districts of Manchester and Salford it is clear that what he saw disgusted him and there seems little doubt that he described what he saw as accurately as he could. Here, as one example, is his view of the River Irk and its surroundings:

At the bottom flows, or rather stagnates, the Irk, a narrow coal-black, foul-smelling stream, full of debris and refuse, which it deposits on the shallower right bank. In dry weather, a long string of the most disgusting, blackish-green, slime pools are left standing on this bank, from the depths of which bubbles of miasmatic gas constantly arise and give forth a stench unendurable even on the bridge forty or fifty feet above the surface of the stream. But besides this, the stream itself is checked every few paces by high weirs, behind which slime and refuse accumulate and rot in thick masses. Above the bridge are tanneries, bone mills, and gasworks, from which all drains and refuse find their way into the Irk, which receives further the contents of all the neighbouring sewers and privies. It may be easily imagined, therefore, what sort of residue the stream deposits. Below the bridge you look upon the piles of *debris*, the refuse, filth and offal from the courts on the steep left bank; here each house is packed close behind its neighbour and a piece of each is visible, all black, smoky, crumbling, ancient with broken panes and window-frames. The background is furnished by old barrack-like factory buildings. . . .

Above Ducie Bridge, the left bank grows more flat and the right bank steeper, but the conditions of the dwellings on both banks grows worse rather than better. He who turns to the left here from the main street, Long Millgate, is lost; he wanders from one court to another, turns countless corners, passes nothing but narrow, filthy nooks and alleys, until after a few minutes he has lost all clue, and knows not whither to turn. Everywhere half or wholly ruined buildings, some of them actually uninhabited, which means a great deal here; rarely a wooden or stone floor to be seen in the houses, almost uniformly broken, ill-fitting windows and doors, and a state of filth! Everywhere heaps of debris, refuse, and offal; standing pools and gutters, and a stench which alone would make it impossible for a human being in any degree civilized to live in such a district.[8]

The mills along the Irwell might have been gloomy, but they brought a new prosperity to Manchester seen in fine buildings such as the Exchange.

Engels dwelt on one side of Manchester life, others looked and saw only the pathway to a glorious future. They saw Manchester businessmen at the very heart of the movement that was dragging Britain from a static past towards a dynamic future. Their key words were not 'squalor, filth, degradation' but 'progress, expansion and trade'. The great mills and warehouses stood as tall and proud as palaces or stately homes. The homes of the manufacturers were the epitome of solid values and respectability. It was a city of contrasts, but whatever the filth spawned in the new slums, however much dirt might drift and fall from factory chimneys, the manufacturers could always point to the other marks of progress, the statistics of increase. Cotton manufacture went up and up – a million pounds a year in the 1780s, 6 million by 1800, over 20 million pounds in 1820 and up to 30 million by 1830. And all the time prices were falling. There seemed to be no reason why it should not go on for ever.

Yarn was exported around the world and there never seemed to be enough weavers to handle the outflow of the mills. The next step was inevitable. Once it had been the weavers who had been held up by lack of yarn. That problem had been solved by mechanical spinning. Now the time had arrived for the power loom to replace the hand loom. The answer was, in fact, found quite early in the history of the development of mechanisation in the industry. The man responsible was the least likely of all our inventors. He was the Rector of Goadby Marwood, Dr Edmund Cartwright, and the circumstances surrounding the invention sound equally implausible.[9] The story goes that Cartwright was at a dinner party at which one of the guests mentioned that no one had ever produced a power loom and, what was more, no one ever would. The thing was impossible. Cartwright rose to the challenge. He had never in his life seen any sort of loom, and he was almost as ignorant of conventional weaving techniques when he completed his experiments as he had been when he started.

Cartwright's first effort at a new loom was powered by two local men, who turned the handle for two hours before collapsing, exhausted. It was a crude device, but Cartwright had made his point – the thing was possible. Cloth had been woven on a machine without the services of a skilled weaver. It was a very odd machine. The warp was held in a vertical frame, and the shuttle was sent across by a spring which, in the inventor's own words was 'strong enough to have thrown a Congreve rocket'. Odd it might have been but it worked well enough for Cartwright to start taking it rather seriously. He decided it was time he went to see a normal loom at work, and after that he returned to work on his power loom in earnest. In 1786 he took out a patent and his mind began to ruminate on the pleasant prospect of profits. He went to Manchester and tried to arouse the interest of local manufacturers. No one seemed especially impressed, so he set up on his own. He bought a mill at Doncaster in Yorkshire and began building looms. Other manufacturers viewed these antics with some amusement. They found it rather difficult to take a weaving vicar – and a poetic one at that – seriously.

> Mr Cartwright was once Professor of Poetry at Oxford, & really was a good Poet himself – But it seems he has left the Barren Mountain of Parnassus & the fountain of Helicon for other mountains and other vales & streams of Yorkshire, & he has left them, to work on the wild Large & Open Field of Mechanics ... you say not a word about the probability of success, likely to attend his weaving Invention. Can this new automaton perform the wonders in weaving so confidently & so flatteringly held out to the world? do let us have your most candid opinion & distinguish between what is Visionary & what may be practicable in this new Michaine Machine.[10]

A number of people came to see this latest marvel of technology, including the inventor's friend, the poet George Crabbe, who brought his wife along to share the experience. Her son later described her reaction: 'When she entered the building, full of engines thundering with relentless power, yet under the apparent management of children, the bare idea of the inevitable hazards attendant on such stupendous undertakings quite overcame her feelings and she burst into tears.'[11]

Others were less sensitive and the sight of the factory at work inspired one Manchester manufacturer to begin work on a new mill, with five hundred looms powered by a steam engine. No more than twenty looms had been set to work when the building was mysteriously burned down. Was it accident or arson? No one knew, but local manufacturers had their own ideas. There was no great stampede to install power looms, and there was little to encourage them to take the chance, if they looked across to Doncaster. In 1793, Cartwright's mill closed, leaving the inventor heavily in debt. Perhaps the fault lay in the machines themselves, but more likely it could be put down to the inventor who, like so many of his ilk, lacked the necessary business acumen to turn his invention into profit. But the power loom worked, and it could now only be a matter of time before looms began to appear beside the spinning machines in the cotton factories.

In 1770 every part of the cotton manufacturing process had been carried out by hand workers, many of them working in their own homes. Twenty years later, manufacturers had it in their power to transfer all the processes from home to factory, to machines powered by water wheel or steam. The transformation was astonishing. It was not, as we shall see, universally

Power looms driven by steam.

welcomed. Nevertheless there was a huge increase in production. One writer, looking back in 1835, expressed perfectly the sense of awe and wonder felt by many who viewed the industrial scene:

> It is by iron fingers, teeth, and wheels, moving with exhaustless energy and devouring speed, that the cotton is opened, cleaned, spread, carded, drawn, roved, spun, wound, warped, dressed, and woven ... Men in the mean while, have merely to attend on this wonderful series of mechanism, to supply it with work, to oil its joints, and to check its slight and infrequent irregularities; each workman performing or rather superintending, as much work as could have been done by *two or three hundred men* sixty years ago. At the approach of darkness the building is illuminated with jets of flame, whose brilliance mimics the light of day ... When it is remembered that all these inventions have been made within the last seventy years, it must be acknowledged that the cotton mill presents the most striking example of the dominion obtained by human science over the powers of nature, of which modern times can boast.[12]

Statistics[13] don't often make exciting reading, but the statistics of the cotton trade tell a dramatic story. In 1787 there were 119 cotton mills in Britain. Half a century later there were 1791, providing employment for over a quarter of a million. More mills devoured more cotton and what was true of

Lancashire loom shed; Roe-Lee Mills, Blackburn in 1905.

Manchester was true of the cotton districts as a whole. The first part of the nineteenth century saw the consumption of cotton in British mills doubling almost every decade: 56 million pounds in 1800, 123 million in 1810, 152 million in 1820, 263 million in 1830, 572 million in 1840. As the Empire expanded so new markets were opened up. As an American commentator put it: 'There is not a battle that England has fought in India, Afghanistan or China ... that did not extend the consumption of cotton.'[14]

By the middle of the nineteenth century, the pattern of the cotton boom was fairly set. Each passing year saw the British manufacturers increasing their dependence on America as the supplier of raw material. By the 1840s, more than 80 per cent of all cotton spun in Britain came from the American South. As that demand grew, so the cotton fields spread across the Southern States. Where in the 1790s cotton was seen only in South Carolina and Georgia, by the 1830s it had spread to nine States, reaching as far east as Arkansas. Production rose from 2 million pounds a year in 1791 to more than 400 million pounds in the 1830s. Not that all this cotton found its way to Britain.

Samuel Slater's Pawtucket Mill, the first cotton mill in America.

Pawtucket and After

The British, having established a lead in the new factory age, were, not surprisingly, anxious to maintain it. They passed legislation banning the export of textile machinery, and models and designs of machinery, and, to make doubly sure that the methods remained secret, they also banned any person who had worked in the new mills from emigrating. Secrets, as the inventors had already discovered, are not that easily contained, especially when there were gentlemen in plenty across the Atlantic prepared to pay out hard cash. Industrial espionage on a large scale is no modern concept. A Philadelphian by the name of Tench Coxe almost scored an early success when he persuaded English workmen to build models of Arkwright's water frame to be sent to America. But British Customs were equal to the challenge, and the models were duly seized. It was to be a very temporary success.

In 1782, a fourteen-year-old boy named Samuel Slater was one of many youngsters who came to work for the Arkwright-Strutt partnership. Seven years later, seeing the tempting offers being put out by the Philadelphian Society of Artists and Manufacturers, he set off in defiance of the law for New York, and this time no one spotted the departure of the Arkwright secrets. Slater was, in fact, far too nervous of being stopped to risk carrying either plans or models, preferring to rely on his memory and the experience of the years he had spent working in the mills. He found New Yorkers disappointingly slow in using his talents, so he accepted an invitation from Moses Brown of Providence, Rhode Island to make the journey to New England. There he found Brown and his son-in-law, William Almy, ready to finance a mill in which Slater, in exchange for the information he had carried across the Atlantic, was to receive a half share of the profits. Agreement was reached and a site selected by the falls on the Pawtucket River which would ensure adequate water power. Slater lived up to his part of the bargain. Working from memory, he planned the water courses, designed carding engines and constructed a water frame on the Arkwright pattern. It was a small affair, a mere twenty-four spindles, but it worked and America's first cotton mill was ready for production.

There was, however, one obstacle to success. Arkwright and Strutt had been able to tap a vast reservoir of poor families for their labour force. America had no such source of cheap labour. It was a vast country with a small population. Land was there for the taking and there was little shortage of opportunities for those who wanted to make their way in the world. At first the tiny mill was run using child labour – seven boys and two girls constituting the entire workforce. But as the mill prospered it was soon evident that something extra was needed. Slater, having borrowed his notions on mill engineering from Britain, now proceeded to borrow social engineering notions as well. He built company houses just as Arkwright had done at Cromford, offering families a home and guaranteed work for all. It

proved to be sufficiently tempting to attract the workforce Slater needed –
the New England cotton industry was on its way.

At much the same time an apparently unconnected event was to lead to
the next phase of development. In 1792 an enterprising group in Massachusetts
set out a notion for developing a canal that would link the upper reaches of
the Merrimack River to the coast. They formed the Proprietors of the Locks
and Canals on the Merrimack River and set to work constructing a canal to
Newburyport. Unfortunately for them, a second company, the Middlesex
Canal Company, began constructing a route to link Chelmsford on the
Merrimack with Boston. The latter succeeded, the older company failed. But
if it failed in its first objective, the work was by no means wasted; though it
was to be a little while before the endeavour was to bear fruit.

In Britain, textile inventions were leading on to ever greater efficiency
and the same laws aimed at protecting manufacturing secrets still applied
long after Slater had slipped through the protective net. Very efficient they
proved, too, in keeping the physical evidence within the country, but the
human mind is not so easily controlled. Francis Cabot Lowell visited Britain's
textile mills and proved to have a memory equal to Slater's, for he carried
back in his mind the design of the new power looms. Back home in Boston,
with the help of a mechanic called Moody, he reconstructed that design
from memory. In 1814 the first loom was completed and Lowell invited a
local merchant, Nathan Appleton, in to inspect it. Appleton recorded his
first impressions:

> I well recollect the state of admiration and satisfaction with which we
> sat by the hour watching the beautiful movement of this new and
> wonderful machine, destined, as it evidently was, to change the character
> of all textile industry.[1]

America's first composite mill, combining both spinning and weaving, was
opened at Waltham. It was a small-scale affair, a pilot scheme that was to lead
directly to the development of America's first major mill town.

Lowell himself died young in 1817, but his brother-in-law, Patrick
Jackson, together with Appleton and Moody, continued the work and began
hunting for a development site. It was now that the old canal built above the
Pawtucket Falls was remembered and in November 1821 the Bostonians,
together with Kirk Boott, who had been appointed to manage the new
enterprise, visited the site. They liked what they saw and they decided that
it was here that the mill should be built, and that the mill town to be built
around it should be named Lowell, after the man with the photographic
memory who had made it all possible. At the time of the first visit one of the
group remarked that they might live to see the town reach a population of

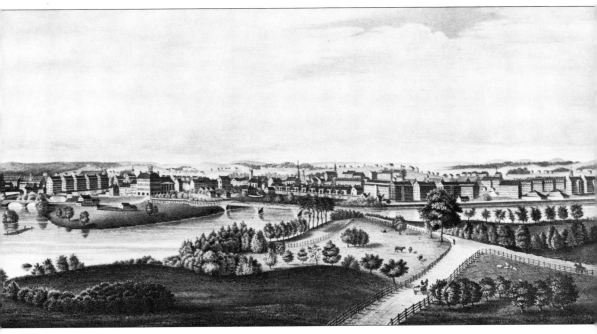

Mills along the Merrimack at Lowell in the 1830s.

twenty thousand: in fact by the time Appleton died in 1861 it had almost reached forty thousand. The old canal was restored to bring water to the new mill and the canal system was to be extended over the years into the most sophisticated example of water power to be seen anywhere, with over five miles of canal distributing water to the various wheels and turbines. That was in the future, but on 3 January 1824, Kirk Boott recorded that '10 bales of goods sent off to Boston – being the first lot sent off from the Merrimack.'[2] The first but not the last: Lowell grew and grew so that fifty years after those first bales were sent out, there were a hundred mills in the town consuming a million pounds of cotton per week.[3] It was to become known as the Manchester of America. The original mill owners, however, were determined that the new town should only comply in part with its English forerunner. Manchester would be matched in productivity and efficiency – but not in exploitation and squalor.

The motives of the proprietors were not entirely attributable to benevolence. The labour recruitment problems that had faced Slater were no less pressing at Lowell. Here, however, a quite new source of labour was noticed. Throughout the region there were what were described as 'solitary women' which meant, in practice, little more than single women. They were women,

101

however, who needed money – as dowries if they were to marry, to pay for their keep if they were not. There were few opportunities open to them beyond the drudgery of domestic employment, the miserable wages of seamstresses and teachers or the depressing prospect of a life spent as the poor relation. Mill work did not offer much in the way of wages – the highest paid women received no more than $4 a week when the mill opened, which was 50c a week less than the lowest paid male – but it was still more than the wage offered by the alternatives. There was, however, one major drawback to be overcome. The idea of good, decent New England farm girls being despatched to the dangers and temptations of an urban, industrial centre was by no means widely welcomed. It was up to the owners to prove to parents – and to the girls themselves – that mill work was respectable, and that the girls would live in a community of unimpeachable morality. In meeting this requirement, the mill owners of Lowell set up a system which

Lowell boarding houses, with the Merrimack Mill at the end of the road.

was to make the town famous not only in America but throughout the industrial world.

The mill owners, in effect, guaranteed the moral welfare of their young female charges by building boarding houses where they were lodged under the care of landladies whose probity and piety matched the most rigorous of even New England standards. As each new mill went up, so the boarding houses went up with it. Here the girls were fed, housed – and controlled. A list of boarding house regulations for the 1840s[4] makes it quite clear what was expected of the landladies. They were not merely moral guardians, but moral narks as well. They were 'considered answerable for any improper conduct in their houses' and were to 'report the names of such as are guilty of any improper conduct, or are not in the regular habit of attending public worship'. The boarding houses acquired a high moral tone which the girls themselves were anxious to sustain, for there was still a whiff of wickedness surrounding the name of mill girl. Concern for moral welfare was more assiduously pursued than concern for physical well-being. The regulations also demanded that 'the buildings and yards about them must be kept clean and in good order', yet many houses were verminous and almost unbearably stuffy, with as many as eight people living in a room. And mill conditions were little, if any, better than those in Britain which were so often and so roundly condemned in America. The girls worked twelve to fourteen hours in a day, and by the time money had been deducted for board and lodging they often had as little as $1 a week for all their labours.

Yet in spite of the hard work, the long hours and the crowded living conditions, the view of the mill girls that has come down to us is of a group which was bright, intelligent, hard-working and, above all, enthusiastically devoted to self-improvement. The girls clubbed together to buy pianos for the houses, attended lectures and even started their own magazine, *The Lowell Offering*. Everyone who visited Lowell, from Davy Crockett to Charles Dickens, spoke of their liveliness and intelligence: though few also noted that all this effort produced little material reward and less status. It is perhaps not too surprising to find some remarkable radicals rising from their ranks: women such as Harriet Robinson who worked for women's suffrage and to improve the life of the mill girls, and Lucy Larcom who went on from *The Lowell Offering* to become a professional author.

In a sense, the story of the mill girls is a success story, but one that was to be short-lived. Lowell in time was to follow the path of the other industrial society across the Atlantic. Work rates were raised, wages lowered and conditions deteriorated to such an extent that the New England girls no longer came down from the farms to work in the mills of Lowell. Others were, however, ready to take their place: refugees from the famines of Ireland and the political revolutions of Europe. For a while it had seemed

The Lowell Offering, *the magazine written and produced by the mill girls.*

that a new kind of industrial society might indeed have been built on the banks of the Merrimack, but the ideas and values of the Old World were now transplanted to the New, just as the machinery had been. The mill girls, pride of Lowell, were no more. The seven-day wonder was over and the visitors no longer came to stare at them and admire, as William T. Thompson of the *Savannah Morning News* had done in 1845:

> They cum swarmin out of the factories like bees out of a hive, and spreadin in every direction, filled the streets so that nothin else was to be seen but platoons of sun-bonnets, with long capes hangin down over the shoulders of the factory galls. Thousands upon thousands of 'em was passin along the streets, all lookin happy and cheerful and neat and clean and butiful, as if they was boarding-school misses just from ther books. It was indeed a interesting sight, and a gratifyin one to a person who had always thought that the opparatives as they call 'em in the Northern factories was the most miserable kind of people in the world.[5]

Thompson's view of factory workers as 'the most miserable kind of people in the world' was shared by many of his compatriots in the South. It was one of the factors that prevented the establishment of a major manufacturing element in the region. Logic suggested that it made little sense to pick the cotton in the South, spend a great deal of money sending it North and then spend still more money bringing it back down South again as cloth. There were attempts at establishing a Southern industry. As early as 1808 there was a notably ambitious scheme begun at Charleston where the South Carolina Homespun Company was formed, largely due to the efforts of Dr John Shecut. He was so convinced of the potential success of the scheme that he named his daughter 'Carolina Homespun', though what the daughter's views of her unusual names might have been must be left to guesswork. She was presumably less than overjoyed at being forever tied nominally to a scheme that proved a disastrous flop. This was true of very many Southern mill enterprises, most of which foundered under bad management. Men who knew nothing of the business hired managers who knew less, simply on the grounds that the latter offered some evidence of once having worked in some mill somewhere.

The mills were largely manned by poor whites, but numerous attempts were made to employ black children too young for field work. Governor David Williams was an early factory owner who trained slave children from his plantation and kept them at the mill until they reached an age when they were reckoned to be worth $20 a year as field hands. Then they were sent from the mill and replaced by other 'little hominy eaters' as he called them.[6] But Williams soon found, as others found, that mill work did not help in the

105

production of good, strong field hands. His human investment was suffering. So, beset by labour problems and ill-management, the South staggered on towards an industry to set alongside the plantation. But even as late as 1860, the South employed a mere 8 per cent of the mill population of America.[7] And America as a whole showed little sign of catching up on the British lead in manufacture. With American cotton finding its way all over the world, Britain still took more than half the crop. Some might complain – and many Americans did complain – but that was the reality of the situation.

There is in reality but one great cotton mill, and that belongs to England, and her agent sits at Liverpool, and sees our labour, in bales of raw cotton, piled up around him till it will cover a ten-acre field. The reports of that market will show a stock, sometimes of a million of bales, that stand in Liverpool unsold: with a knowledge of the fact, that it cannot be taken anywhere else. The grower has no remedy. There are the spindles, and there it must stay.[8]

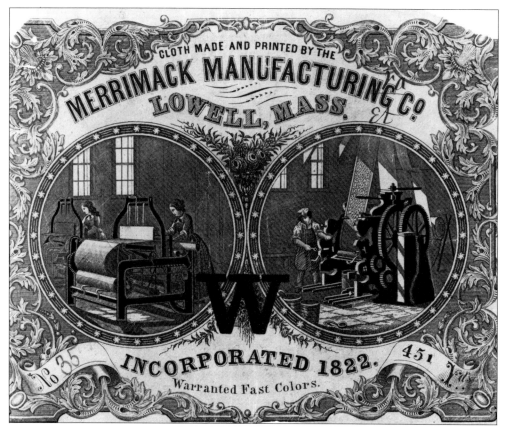

106   *Merrimack Company label.*

On a world scale, the manufacturing capacity of the South was infinitesimal, but its role as a producer of raw material was vital. For better or worse, the fates of Lancashire and the South were tied together. The destiny of an operative in a remote mill or of a slave on a Georgian plantation could each be determined by decisions taken on the Manchester Exchange. Other factors might affect the situation, other countries have roles to play, but it was on this unique link across the Atlantic that the world of cotton ultimately depended.

The wealth of the plantation seen in the Greek Revival home: the Colley-Barksdale house in Washington, Georgia.

The Planter

The spread of the factory system in Britain gave rise to a new social order. Once society had been thought of as a pyramid with the royal family at the apex, descending down through the aristocracy to the gentry and on down to the broad base of the poor. It was a system apparently as solid and inflexible as any pyramid in Egypt. Now, however, men were starting to think of their lives in terms of a new relationship. The division that mattered was between employer and employee, master and worker, bourgeoisie and proletariat, capital and labour – whatever label you preferred, it amounted to a recognisable division. America was too young a country to have established any rigid patterns to match the old hierarchies of Europe, so the pattern imposed by the spread of the cotton plantations did not seem to involve any dramatic conflict with the past. Yet a new type of society was being established, and the changes were as profound as any in Europe. Where Britain was developing a class society, the Southern States were building a society based on racial divisions, on master and slaves. The point is so blindingly obvious that it might scarcely seem worth mentioning at all, but it marks the crucial difference between the experience of industrialisation and the accompanying changes in the plantations. The textile worker in Britain had, in theory at any rate, a prospect of change held out in front of him. This could either be through that beloved doctrine of the Victorian middle classes – self-help – or through the new mass organisations which were to try to speak and act for the whole body of industrial workers. And, however slowly, the position of the textile worker did shift. For the black slave, however, the spread of the plantations was accompanied by the spread of a totally rigid system. There was to be no change, either in his status or his circumstances. Where the spread of cotton was forcing changes in British society, it served only to fix Southern society in its ways. In place of the dynamic of change, the plantation offered near stagnation: cultural, social and technological. The Manchester of 1850 was altogether different from the town of half a century before; yet half a century brought no discernible change to life on the plantation.

The society of the plantations was based on the planter as absolute monarch. There was no such thing as a typical plantation, any more than there was a typical mill, and equally there was no typical planter. Yet a stereotype has persisted, bolstered over the years by novels and later the cinema. The image is of a pampered existence, of big houses and Southern hospitality – of gambling and the code of honour among the men, acquiescence to pretty domesticity among the women. The shock comes in discovering how frequently these unlikely fictions turn out to be based on reality.

John Quitman arrived in Natchez in 1821 to practise law and described a society in which the planters ruled as to the manner born:

The Southern planter and his family.

In the city proper, and the surrounding country, there is genteel and well-regulated society ... The planters are the prominent feature. They ride fine horses, are followed by well-dressed and very aristocratic servants, but affect great simplicity of costume themselves – straw hats and no neckcloths in summer, and in the winter coarse shoes and blanket overcoats. They live profusely: drink costly Port, Madeira, and sherry, after the English fashion, and are exceedingly hospitable.

Life in this society seemed idyllic:

Mint-juleps in the morning are sent to our rooms, and then follows a delightful breakfast in the open veranda. We hunt, ride, fish, pay morning visits, play chess, read or lounge until dinner, which is served at two P.M. in great variety, and most delicately cooked in what is here called the Creole style – very rich, and many made or mixed dishes. In two hours afterward every body – white and black – has disappeared – the siesta of the Italians. The ladies retire to their apartments, and the gentlemen on sofas, settees, benches, hammocks, and often gipsy fashion, on the grass under the spreading oaks. Here, too, in fine weather, the tea-table is always set before sunset, and then, until bedtime, we stroll, sing, play whist, or croquet. It is an indolent, yet charming life, and one quits thinking and turns to dreaming.[1]

Reading through planters' diaries can often seem rather like reading the diary of a character in a Jane Austen novel. A planter[2] reads Johnson's Life of Dryden and finds him 'a prolific author wielding a pen powerful, elegant, majestic' and resolved 'as part of my daily literary employ' to read all the lives of the poets at a rate of one poet per day. He hunts, visits friends and, in the evening, when he has finally run through his catalogue of poets, turns with equal pleasure to Macaulay. Ladies' diaries are, if anything, even more Austenish. Mary Bateman's life,[3] for example, was a round of visits and music lessons, teasing about 'the Judge' and excursions in the family carriage. The young ladies sat listening while gentlemen callers read out loud from the works of Shakespeare and even, rather daringly, Byron. An event such as the arrival of the boat where daguerra-types were taken, was of such major importance that it completely monopolised the diary for three days.

That fine home, however, had to be built in the first place, and even then was not always so fine as tradition would have us believe. Joseph Thompson wrote from Louisiana, where he had gone to start a plantation, to his aunt in Alabama:

> I have undergone some hardships since I left you But notwithstanding my health has been good. I am at this time living in an open Cabin that keeps but little wind out and it is very chilly cold at this time We had ice a plenty this morning The grass had taken a fine start but this change will check ... I found provision hard to get until my friend Ned arrived since I have Faired sumptuously of your kind present the fine barrel of flour ... I am in a country that is full of sharpers and from all parts. There is about 20 new settlers within the limits of six miles around here and more expected daily ... the face of the country is not so level as I thought it to be last fall and the soil is not so dark as I thought it to be But they all say Cotton will grow and that is the main object in this Country.[4]

The English actress, Fanny Kemble, went out to join her husband on a Georgian plantation, and the record of her stay for the years 1838–9 is one of the sharpest, as well as one of the most readable, accounts of plantation life that have come down to us.[5] She has been accused of prejudice and lack of understanding – the fate of all critical foreigners in the country they criticise – but her words ring true. She admitted quite freely that she arrived with a good few prejudices: 'Assuredly I *am* going prejudiced against slavery, for I am an Englishwoman, in whom the absence of such a prejudice would be disgraceful.' But, as she also made clear, her wish to think the best of her husband inclined her to look for what was good in his life, not dwell on what

111

was bad. But on her arrival she found a plantation home that fell a long way short of the ideal:

> It consists of three small rooms, and three still smaller, which would be more appropriately designated as closets, a wooden recess by way of pantry, and a kitchen detached from the dwelling – a mere wooden outhouse, with no floor but the bare earth ... Of our three apartments, one is our sitting, eating, and *living room* and is sixteen feet by fifteen. The walls are plastered indeed, but neither painted nor papered; it is divided from our bed-room (a similarly elegant and comfortable chamber) by a dingy wooden partition covered all over with hooks, pegs, and nails, to which hats, caps, keys &c. &c., are suspended in graceful irregularity. The doors open by wooden latches, raised by means of small bits of packthread – I imagine, the same primitive order of fastening, celebrated in the touching chronicle of Red Riding Hood; how they shut I will not pretend to describe, as the shutting of a door is a process of extremely rare occurrence throughout the whole Southern country. The third room, a chamber with sloping ceiling, immediately over our sitting-room and under the roof, is appropriated to the nurse and my two babies. Of the closets, one is Mr. — the overseer's

112   *The planter's first crude home, at the Callaway Plantation, Washington, Georgia.*

bedroom, the other his office or place of business; and the third, adjoining our bedroom, and opening immediately out of doors, is Mr. —'s dressing room and cabinet d'affaires, where he gives audience to the negroes, redresses grievances, distributes red woolen caps (a singular gratification to a slave), shaves himself, and performs the other offices of his toilet. Such being our abode, I think you will allow there is little danger of my being dazzled by the luxurious splendour of a Southern slave residence.

The life itself was far from healthy. Any plantation diary can be virtually guaranteed to have its descriptions of illnesses; most, not too surprisingly, in the slave quarters. Many of the diseases were associated with poor diet and bad sanitation: stomach complaints were commonplace, dysentery and even cholera by no means rare. Lucian Polk of Mississippi recorded the bald statement that he had lost twenty-seven slaves with cholera 'produced it was supposed by eating soured meat and corn' – which, of course, he had himself supplied. When an epidemic hit, however, it was no respector of colour. White and black, master and slave both fell victim. A South Carolina planter wrote that 'out of about fifty souls, white and black on the plantation not one escaped the fever, and I lost my lovely daughter Thirza'.[6] But disease hit hardest at the slave children, prey to scarlet fever and pneumonia.

The 'second generation' home at Callaway, the wooden federal-style house.

The white masters were also prey to all forms of medical quackery. There were their own patent remedies which, if not beneficial, occasionally do sound quite appetising – blackcurrant cordial, made up to a quart of sweetened juice, to which was added a quart of brandy, would probably produce no worse effect than a bad hangover. It is more alarming, however, to be told that a recipe consisting of a tablespoon of common salt and half a teaspoonful of red pepper is a 'nearly infallible' cure for cholera.[7] Patent medicines were widely peddled, many of them so downright harmful that they probably saw off more patients than they ever cured.

If the plantation home was not always a fine Colonial-style mansion, and if the happy children playing among the magnolias were liable to be struck down by cholera, yet other aspects of the stereotype do still hold. The gambler and the man of honour existed, if in less glamorous forms than romance would have us believe. John Nevitt of Mississippi seems the very prototype of the gambler. His diary[8] is full of accounts of idle days and nights at the card table – and of his lack of success. 'Rode to Natchez done nothing Set up at Dr Gustins playing Eucre lost 70 dolls.' In May 1827 he had six big card games. His best day was the 21st, when he was able to record that he had lost nothing. On the other five days he lost amounts varying from $50 to $150 – a grand total for the month of $435. In December the following year he went to the theatre to see 'The Gambler's Fate' and was, he reported, 'greatly affected'. The effect lasted right through to the next day when he was off to the races, where his view of gambling was much improved by winning $30. Nevitt's life, when he was not demonstrating his lack of skill at the card table, was mainly taken up with immensely complex financial transactions. The financing of many plantations involved a complicated system of debts and credits. Just one entry for one day gives some idea of how tangled these affairs could become:

> Gave Ew^d turner a Mortgage on 75 head cattle 30 horse 5 waggons 2 carts & for his endorsement to my note for 1500 Dolls in two several notes one for 1000 the other 500 Dolls gave Jas. C. Wilkins the one of 500 becoming due on the 15 Decr next for his acceptance for the same amt. disposed of that acceptance to Wm Brun at the rate of 10 pr cent per annum paid my acct. to Brunamt 143 doll purchased meat paid Blackman 25 Dolls to acct of my due bill which he had lost and gave him my due bill for balance 27.25[9]

The property was frequently mortgaged and, in spite of growing debts, credit seemed always to be available somewhere. Notes were handed out to creditors, payable at some specified future date and a good financial manager could keep all his debts and credits permanently on the move, like a juggler

A surviving slave cabin, Boone Hall Plantation, near Charleston.

keeping his Indian clubs up in the air. But even the best jugglers drop a club sometimes. Nevitt dropped his in January 1831. His debts caught up with him and he had to sell off part of his estate, together with nineteen slaves, to pay debts of over $10,000. The whole system was summed up by another planter, living in similar style: 'I am considerably in debt, & it troubles me to think so for I do not feel as free as 'tis pleasant to feel . . . this credit system is so fascinating so inclined to make a man go farther than prudence would dictate that I do here declare that I will not go in debt for anything more this year, except barely for articles to keep my plantation going.'[10]

Gambling, whether at the card table or in terms of selling crops that had yet to be planted let alone harvested, was very much a reality of plantation life. So too was the concept of honour and the duel, though in reality it was frequently very little better than an undignified brawl. In 1839, in Louisiana, Fielding Davis and Henry Moore met at fifty yards with rifles, and Moore was killed at the first shot. The background was less dignified:

> Leigh of Va. challenged Davis for no cause whatever – Moore took the challenge – Davis told him he would answer him in the morning. Moore then observed it was cowardly Evasion – Davis then struck him with his whip – breaking his nose &c. Somewhat of general fight took place – Davis supposing it was all over retired to the Post Office – having found that Leigh intended to kill him armed himself – in a few minutes saw

Leigh coming towards him in a great hurry – he told him to stop or he would shoot him – Leigh rushed at him with a sword cane drawn – Davis snaped both caps of his gun – then with it knocked Leigh down and could have killed him supposing he had injured him very much threw down the gun and started off – but had taken but a few steps before Leigh was at him again – he then retreated 'till he got his pistol out which was Entangled in his breast whireld & fired & hit Leigh in the small of the Back – Leigh had fallen in pursuit of Davis but was getting up when Davis fired – he is expected to die every day, perfectly dead from the wound downwards – Davis is justified in every act.[11]

Superficially the life of the planter might have seemed one of gentility, hospitality and impeccable manners, but behind the facade there was violence, disease and a financial system that was based on debt. The mythology of the South had been stressed because in one vital area the South came to believe its own fiction. It set up a mythology surrounding the relationship between the planter's family and the house servants, then acted as if the fiction was truth.

The house slaves necessarily had a special relationship with their white masters, very different from that of the field hands. They lived in the same

116   *House slaves up for sale in New Orleans.*

house or very close to it. They were intimately concerned with the family and, when it came to bringing up the children, the black servants were often more involved than the white parents. The stereotype here is of the loyal slave, faithful and devoted, who in return was awarded by the affection of the planter's family. Mammy Harriet, a slave on the Dabney plantation in Mississippi, recalled this scene when the mistress of the house went to see an old dying slave:

> Missis put on her bonnet an' went to her jes' as fast as she could. When grannie saw her she could not speak, but she hold out both arms to her. Missis run into her arms an' bust out crying'. She put her arms roun' grannie's neck an' grannie could not speak, but de big tears roll down her cheeks. An' so she die.[12]

Affection was possible between white owner and black slave, and genuine regard too. Everard Baker wrote an obituary in his diary for the slave Jack, who died aged about sixty-five. It is the more moving in that it represents private thoughts expressed in a private diary:

> He has been in my mothers family since he was quite small, served my mother faithfully during her life time, & stood high in her regard. Since I have owned him he has been true to me in all respects – He was an obediant trusty servant to his master & mistress, an affectionate husband & father to his family – I never knew him to steal nor lie & he ever set a moral & industrious example to those around him ... altho' he was not a professing Christian – yet no man white or black that I have ever known was more exemplary in his conduct.[13]

Baker seems to have been aware that there was something odd in this eulogy, but could only conclude, rather lamely, 'He deserves a better reward than can be given in this world.'

While it is easy to see the misery of slavery for the slaves, it is not always quite so easy to see the damaging effects of slave ownership. Fanny Kemble, coming to the system as an outsider, was able to take a more detached view than most. She found the slaves almost overwhelming her with offers of help, and watched with alarm as the same thing happened to her daughter. She noted

> the universal eagerness with which they sprang to obey her little gestures of command. She said something about a swing, and in less than five minutes headman Frank had erected it for her, and a dozen

young slaves were ready to swing little 'missis' ... think of learning to rule despotically your fellow creatures before the first lesson of self-government has been well spelt over! It makes me tremble: but I shall find a remedy, or remove myself and the child from this misery and ruin.[14]

The house slaves were a group apart, with their own privileges. In the cities they dressed in a style that astonished Northern visitors:

To see slaves with broadcloth suits, well-fitted and nicely ironed fine shirts, polished boots, gloves, umbrellas for sunshades, the best of hats, their young men with their blue coats and bright buttons, in the latest style, white Marseilles vests, white pantaloons, brooches in their shirt-bosoms, gold chains, elegant sticks and some old men leaning on their ivory and silver headed staves, as respectable in their attire as any who that day went to the House of God, was more than I was prepared to see.[15]

Not surprisingly such slaves tended to think of themselves as a cut above the rest.

On hand every day, ready and eager to do just what master or mistress demanded, loyal and faithful and genuinely affectionate towards Massa's family – that was how the planter wished to think of his house slaves. It was a creed to which the planters wholeheartedly subscribed. The Civil War brought home a new reality. The South discovered that the drama they had written, in which the blacks had played their parts, was no more than a fiction. Now the play was done. The actors took off their masks. To the whites it was the great betrayal – to the blacks the end of a long pretence.

Edwina and Bertha Burnley looked back with sentimental affection when they remembered many of their old slaves, such as Aunt Dicey:

All the little negroes called her 'Ga Muh'. She took charge of all the babies while their mothers were in the field – each baby had its own cradle with an older child to rock and amuse it. In summer the cradles were under a great spreading oak and scores of children under twelve years playing around them. Some of the little ones lay asleep on the grass and Aunt Dicey would caution us not to step over them – because they wouldn't grow any more.[16]

And there was Uncle Banks, the carpenter who built the cotton gin. When he was ill 'Pa used to see him every day and talked with him. They were friends.' And then came the change, the trauma:

In the first year after the war Pa was sick a good deal, we had no overseer, the negroes got their provisions regularly but worked when they pleased. One morning Cousin Hexzy rode over to inquire about Pa and found us without a stock of wood, the house servants all gone, and me trying to break up pickets with an ax. He took his gun, went to the quarters and ordered out negroes, set them to work cutting and hauling wood and did not leave until there was a winter's supply piled up at the house. I need hardly say that that year's crop was a failure.

It had all been a sham. The planters had wanted the impossible – total obedience and love too. The obedience had been theirs while the slaves had no option; the love now seemed to have been all in their own imaginations. They had invented a character called the faithful slave, hoping that the invention would become a living creature. If there were faithful slaves, then the harsh punishment inflicted on the unfaithful was justified. The same device was in use in the factories of Britain to justify the suppression of discontent. They invented the contented workman:

> I live in a cottage and yonder it stands;
> And while I can work with these two honest hands,
> I'm happy as they that have houses and lands,
> Which nobody can deny.
>
> I keep to my workmanship all the day long
> I sing and I whistle, and this is my song –
> 'Thank God, who has made me so lusty and strong,'
> Which nobody can deny.[17]

The song was a fraud, the author no workman but Mr John Byrom, MA, FRC. Discontent could not be wished away that easily, laid at the door of outside agitators. This was as true of the mill hands as it was of the slaves labouring in the fields.

Loading cotton for Liverpool in New Orleans.

Cotton for Lancashire

However you view the way of life of the planter, it was ultimately dependent on the crops in the fields. Calculation of profit and loss was even more difficult than it was for the mill owner. The latter bought in raw materials and sold finished goods. At its very simplest, the difference between the two prices, once you have deducted the cost of labour and depreciation, is the profit on the capital invested. The same calculations for the plantation looked very different.[1] You could not treat slaves as wage labourers, for they were the property of the slave holder; nor could you treat them simply as property, in the way the mill owner would treat machines, for machines are inanimate. And machines do not reproduce themselves. Looked at in strictly economic terms, a male and a female slave who had children were increasing the value of the owner's property; for the children, like their parents, were part of that property. The owners were very aware of this as plantation rules clearly show: 'Marriage is to be encouraged as it adds to the comfort, happiness and health of those entering upon it, besides ensuring a greater increase. No negro man can have a wife, nor woman a husband, not belonging to the master.'[2] There were other arguments against allowing outside marriages:

> No rule that I have stated is of more importance than that relating to negroes marrying out of the plantation it seems to me, from what observations I have made it is utterly impossible to have any method, or regularity When the men and women are permitted to take wives and husbands indiscriminately off the plantation, negroes are very much deposed to pursue a course of this kind, and without being able to assign any good reason, though the motive can be readily perceived, and is a strong one with them, but one that tends not in the Least to the benefit of the Master, or their ultimate good, the inconvenience that at once strike one as arising out of such a practice are these –
> First – in allowing the men to marry out of the plantation, you give them an ungovernable right to be frequently absent
> 2d – Wherever their wives live, there they consider their homes, consequently they are indifferent to the interest of the plantation to which they actually belong –
> 3d – It creates a feeling of independence, from being, of right, out of the control of the masters for a time –
> 4th – They are repeatedly exposed to temptations from meeting and associating with negroes from different directions, and with various habits & vices.[3]

It is interesting to note that the writer seems not even to have contemplated the possibility of meeting some with better habits and greater virtues! There might seem to be every argument against marriage to a slave on another plantation, but slaves were no more in control of their affections than any of the rest of us. They would wish to marry where their love lay, but if they did so they created a terrible dilemma for themselves. The threat of separation hung constantly over them. The more fortunate were able to get together, provided the two owners could agree terms:

> Dear Sir,
>
> Your negro man Sam states that you wish to know if my Mother will sell his wife (Matilda) and child. She could better spare any other negro she had than Matilda, and does not wish to sell at any price. But Matilda seems as if she wished to go with her husband and under such circumstances she will take sixteen hundred dollars for her and her child.[4]

A plantation rule book reads like an instruction manual for a new engine. It is all quite exact and precise and not the least prone to variation. The Highland Plantation rule book puts it quite clearly: 'A plantation might be considered as a piece of machinery, to operate successfully, all of its parts should be uniform and exact, and the impelling force regular and steady.'

The overseer watching the cotton picking.

But it was not a machine, and all the rule writing in the world would not make it one in practice, whatever theory might say. And what the theory said was that a slave was property. 'I have ever maintained this doctrine', declared David Barrow, a planter from Georgia 'that my negroes have no time whatever, that they are always liable to my call without questioning for a moment the propriety of it.'[5] But that didn't work either. However much the owner might deny the humanity of his slaves, that humanity continually asserted itself. When the account books came to be balanced that human element remained the great imponderable.

Was the slave system essential for a profitable cotton plantation? There is a certain similarity here between the slave system and the apprentice system in the mills. In the latter case, the majority of mill owners decided that they were better off hiring labour for wages than having all the expense and bother of being responsible for the lives of their apprentices. Might the same sort of thing be true of slave labour? The question is unanswerable, for the whole economy of the big plantations was tied as much to the value of the slaves as it was to the value of the crops. They were inseparable. What really matters, however, is that the planters firmly believed that without the slave system, the cotton plantations would collapse. All their efforts were bent towards making that system successful – though often it would be more accurate to say that they relied on others making every effort on their behalf.

'The Peculiar Institution' gave the cotton plantation its unique character, but this apart the planter faced the same problems as any other farmer. He depended on the vagaries of the weather, the healthiness of the crop and the state of the market. The absentee planters, and there were many of them, relied on regular reports from their overseers to keep them in touch with the day-to-day business of the plantations. Many of these reports were barely literate, but they provide the most complete record of the running of the plantations. As in any farm reports, there are good times and bad, but the issue of slavery always provides that crucial difference:

> i have the promisingest Crop that i have had since i have been in the miss   i will finish in a few ours going over the cotton the first time   my negroes and mules is all fat an you think go a hed and i say go a hed and a good Crop is the object.
>
> Thir is a lot of negros to be sold at Coffiville the first of August and for cash and i expect will be barganes to be bought.[6]

Most owners paid regular visits to their plantations, and when things were going well they were cock-a-hoop:

I came here on Wednesday last and I found my negroes all well and every thing seemed to be going on well and prospering – negroes all looking well, seemingly well satisfied, pleased with the overseer and have made me an excellent crop both of Corn and Cotton – fattened and killed seven thousand pounds of Pork & made me between Two hundred and sixty and 270 bales of Cotton weighing each 500 pounds besides Seven of the women have had children since we left & they are all living and doing well so I think if this is not beating Edgecombe it is doing well enough to satisfy a moderate appetite[7]

But bad times, as ever, seemed to keep pace with the good: 'We had the hardest rain Tuesday that I ever saw fallen the Rains Have injured our cotton in this section powerful.'[8]

Nothing good to write about ... the grass caterpillars that were eating the young corn and grass when you were here have eat up all the grass and commenced eating the corn and cotton. They are tearing the cotton and corn all to pieces and cane and peas and in fact every thing that they can crall on to they eat off ... I think they are going away now and I hope in a few days they will all be done They have destroyed a Great

124   *A Mississippi plantation with a steam-powered gin in the background.*

Deal of cotton since they commenced Though they have served us bad enough we have not suffered no loss compared with the people on Flint river below Bainbridge and some above.[9]

A story of ruined crops that could be repeated a thousand times, and one that is all too familiar to any farmer. Equally familiar is the uncertainty over crop prices. The cost of growing cotton varied little from year to year, but the price the farmer might expect from his crop was subject to violent fluctuations. There was, to some extent, a natural evening-out. As with any crop, prices tended to fall in a bumper year and rise in a bad one; but the grower of cotton found himself with a special problem. The price of his crop was being determined by men thousands of miles away – the cotton merchants of Liverpool and Manchester. The grower did have a number of options open to him: he could deal directly with a British agent, or employ a factor at a major port such as New Orleans or Savannah; he could look towards the British market, or he could try and sell to the American manufacturers in the North. But, ultimately, as the major user, Britain set the price. The planter in Georgia or Alabama was generally content to place his affairs in the hands of a factor who understood the intricacies of this international trade.

The Minor family, who had a plantation near Natchez, Mississippi, received a steady flow of letters from their factor, giving the current state of the market. One difficulty they constantly faced was the time lag between the cotton being sent out from the plantation and its arrival in Liverpool. Terms might be favourable when it was shipped out from America, and rather less so by the time it had completed the Atlantic crossing. 'The present vessel has been long delayed by head winds, but as I think there appears some chance of a change I think it necessary to advise you that several vessels are in from Savannah whose arrival with advices of the decline in price in America has damaged our markets & American cottons are down full a halfpenny.'[10]

Each month, the importers sent out a printed bulletin giving current prices and other trading details, and then added a handwritten note to suit a particular client. A bulletin of January 1823 reviewed progress for the previous year:

That the demand for the Raw Material will go on increasing, while prices remain moderate, we have not a doubt; – because the low price at which the manufactured article is brought into the market induces an increased consumption at home, and a more extensive demand for foreign countries; which will be aided by the new markets that have recently been opened to us in South America. In order to meet this demand, new mills are erecting with great rapidity.[11]

This was all very fine for British manufacturers, but the Southern planter found himself faced with falling prices; a prospect which Liverpool greeted with cheerful sanguinity. The fall in price, they assured the world, would not encourage planters to shift to other crops, but would 'have a direct contrary tendency, by stimulating his exertions to extend the cultivation to the utmost of his means, in the hope that an inceased quantity may compensate for a decreased price.'

The view was reasonable when one was looking at the overall picture of the cotton market, but looked less attractive to the individual planter. Manchester and Natchez might be mutually dependent in the long term, but there was no guarantee that their views would coincide at any one particular time. There was even less chance that the individual planter would find things always to his liking. To this uncertainty, the planter could add the risks of delays, damage, bad packing and handling, and a host of other possible misadventures. Faced with that array of problems, many simply opted for a sure price from the American factors – and left them to carry the risks of trading on the British market. In theory, this then left them free to concentrate on their crops, improving the quality and the yield. In practice, many were quite happy to pass that job over as well. They employed overseers and either stayed in the Big House or returned to the towns, which offered more refined pleasures than those available on a remote and unhealthy

The rivers were the main transport routes of the South. Here the stern-wheel paddle steamer America *is being loaded with cotton bales.*

plantation. The real job of running the plantation fell to the overseer: success or failure of the crops could depend on his abilities; happiness and misery among the slaves on his temper.

Owners were well aware of the importance of such a key figure, and in order to try and make sure that everything was run exactly as they wanted during their frequent absences, they laid down complex sets of rules, covering all aspects of plantation life. An overseer who obeyed the strict letter of the law would have been a true paragon of all the virtues. He was expected to set a high moral standard, though the regulation that forbade 'swearing, drinking or any immorality' in one set of rules was only to be applied on the plantation itself.[12] Elsewhere, it seems, he could sin till he bust.

The overseer controlled everything: he decided what work had to be done, who was to do it and even set the length of the working day. His duties continued after work was over, for he was held responsible for the behaviour of the slaves. Within his own domain he was lord and master – and in matters of law, he was judge, jury and executioner. The rule book laid down a full list of punishable offences. Some prohibitions were specific and obvious – running away coming at the top of the list, followed by drunkenness and stealing. Others were concerned with more personal matters, designed to ensure that the slave had little or no say in the regulation of his own affairs. If the overseer deemed the slave's hut to be dirty, then the slave was punished. If he failed to get back indoors by the time the horn blew at the end of the day, he was punished. And there were catch-all rules, such as those dealing with neglect of work. The overseer was sole arbiter over such matters. But the rule makers had a problem. How do you punish a slave? You can sack an employee, but the slave is your property and therefore valuable. You cannot fine him for he has no money; you cannot imprison him without losing the benefit of his work. You cannot even remove privileges where no privileges are given. So you are left with the whip, but still you must act with some caution. You have no wish to damage your property, yet discipline must be maintained. 'They must be flogged as seldom as possible yet always when necessary ... The highest punishment must not exceed Fifty lashes in one Day.'[13]

So, again, it comes back to the personality of the overseer. In some cases he was a member of the planter's family, and in others he worked under the direct supervision of the owner. But, when he was absolute despot, the scope for abuse was enormous. It was in such cases that the worst examples of overseers' brutality appeared. Yet there were limits set, even here, to the overseer's freedom of action. Theoretically, all white men were inherently superior to even the best black man, whose status could never be higher than

Stern-wheelers and side-wheelers lining the Levee at New Orleans, loading cotton for Liverpool.

that of a chattel. In practice, the wish of the owner to see a well-run plantation gave the slave the leverage he needed to use against an unpopular overseer. If things went wrong, the overseer had to have an explanation ready. Even when a slave ran away, the overseer had to be quick to point out that it was not his fault:

> On last munday Gilbert left home and we believe is aiming to git to Dr Caldwell i think you had best come by thir for I have serct the neighborhood and Cannot hear of him i do not no what took him of unless it was becaus he had been stealing i have not struck him one lick in a year nor yet thretend him[14]

Although access to the master was limited, slaves had ways of making their views known. An unpopular overseer might mean poor crops. The overseer could be replaced, but the slaves were a permanent fixture: the wise owner therefore listened to the views of his slaves. Archibald Arrington visited his Alabama plantation and found his overseer avoiding him: 'If he does not come to see me I intend to send for him, for from what my negroes tell me he is a dishonest man.'[15] The chattels had made their point.

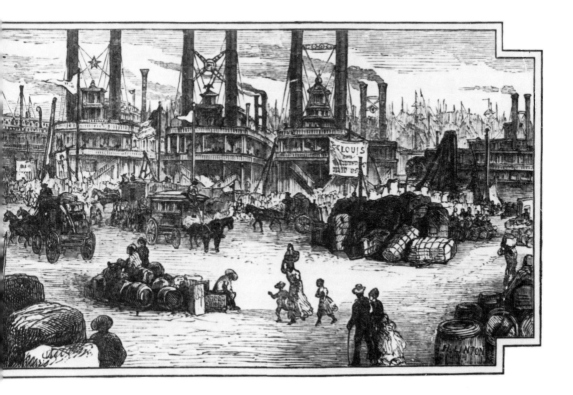

The overseer's position was always anachronistic. He was set up as a member of the superior race, yet the slaves well knew that he was as dependent on the whim of the planter as they were. His life was different from theirs, but not that different. He could not demean himself by working in the fields, yet he always had to be present when they worked in the fields. Their movements were limited, but then so were his. He was tied to the plantation almost as securely as they were. His status could seem at times little higher than theirs:

> The overseer's time is paid for by his employer and belongs to his employer. It is not right for the overseer to use that or anything else that belongs to his employer, in going about, in visiting, or in entertaining, or in any way but for his employer.[16]

The missives that were handed down from absentee owner to overseer were as curt and high-handed as any that passed from overseer to slave. Some owners piled regulation upon regulation in an attempt to maintain long-distance order. The Hugenin Plantation Book sets off in high style with a statement of principles:

In the management of my people I would always demand justice and moderation. But at the same time my people must be kept in perfect order, and if necessary should always be corrected to the extent of the fault or crime committed.

I never allow stealing – getting drunk or any unruly or loud conduct such as quarrelling and fighting Absence from home without permission impertinence in any form or shape as this when allowed is the first step to the disobeying of all the above regulations and finally leads to dissatisfaction On the contrary I should wish the moral conduct and appearance of my people well attended to – I think that negroes on a plantation should always be made to appear at least decent, especially when there appears to be a disposition to the contrary.[17]

Everything was laid down to ensure a perfect order, yet in the following year fresh rules had to be added, and the tone becomes distinctly more strident:

I positively forbid my negroes working out for any person in the neighbourhood. From what I can understand my negroes are very much in the habit of going about the neighbourhood and on Sundays lurking about peoples houses that must also be stoped. My regulations expressly say that there shall be no visiting except by permission from the overseer, who should be as few times from the plantation as possible, especially on Sundays.[18]

Plantation owners and overseer watch over the press where cotton is being screwed down into bales.

New regulations constantly turn up, interspersed with complaints about failure to keep to the old. The overseer, in his turn, no doubt, passed the threats on down in an attempt to meet the demands of his absentee employer.

The overseer is not one of the more lovable characters of history, but his life must often have been a lonely and miserable one, shut away in a plantation with no company but that of the slaves with whom he was expressly forbidden to have any social intercourse at all. As an integral part of the system that denied the common humanity of black and white, he was, in theory at least, set permanently apart. In theory he regarded the female slaves as something less than women: in practice – however brutal that practice might have been – it was as women that he turned to them. Slave owners, as well as overseers, were fathers to children whose skin colour was testimony to their parentage. Nowhere was the essential ambivalence of attitudes seen more clearly than in the case of the mulatto children, born of white fathers and black mothers:

> There is a great deal of talk through the Country about abolition, &c. Yet the people submit to Amalgamation in its worse form in this Parish. Josias Grey takes his mulatto children to public places, &c. and receives similar company from New Orleans, fine carriage & Horses.[19]

Fanny Kemble was one of those who saw the contradiction very clearly. She drew an analogy between the attitude towards marriage and that towards the education of blacks. According to the theory of racial inferiority, the blacks were ineducable – so why were laws necessary forbidding that which was impossible? Similarly with sex:

> Now it appears there is no law in the white man's nature which prevents him from making a coloured woman the mother of his children, but there is a law on his statute books forbidding him to make her his wife; and if we are to admit the theory that the mixing of the races is a monstrosity, it seems almost as curious that laws should be enacted to prevent him marrying women towards whom they have an invincible natural repugnance, as that education should by law be prohibited to creatures incapable of receiving it.[20]

The evidence of racial mixing was there for all to see throughout the South; visible proof that all the law making and rule making could be irrelevant in at least one area of human relationships. What it did not prove was that there was any breakdown in the rigid demarcation between master and slave. And where did the children stand? Did they belong with the white parent or the black? The answer had to be, in general, with the black, since according to the theories under which white society operated they could not exist at all. The children grew up, victimised by the theories. Some observers claimed that the paleness of skin elevated them in the black community. A more realistic view would suggest that it did little more than add to the sense of indignity and injustice that touched all slaves. As one mulatto bitterly pointed out,[21] slavery is bad enough, but it is even worse for those who know they are suffering at the hands of their own fathers.

The white overseer, isolated by an untenable system among the black workers, has become one of the villains of the cotton story. No doubt he was, but he should also be numbered among the victims. Isolation is not necessarily more tolerable for being self-inflicted. James Barth applied for an overseer's job in Alabama, writing from a lonely plantation in Georgia:

> My main cause for coming back to live for one or 2 years is I am yet a single man and do not wish to live single any longer and rather come back to old Georgia to get me a wife and I have a nother cause for quitting is my employer is sutch a hard man to get money out of he has not paid me one Dollar in 3 years.[22]

No dispassionate observer looking at this cumbersome, unwieldy system could have called it sensible or practical, even if they had no wish to condemn it on moral grounds. Yet once begun, the plantation system developed a momentum of its own which carried it over the reefs of absurdity. And, as the demand for cotton grew, so the plantation system spread. In Britain, the spread of cotton mills was part of a dynamic process. New machines brought new methods, revolutionising the lives of the workers. New markets were constantly being won, a new social class was developing. None of this happened in the cotton South. A slave worked in 1850 just as he had worked half a century earlier. Apart from the gin, no new machines arrived to speed the labour. Ploughing, sowing, weeding, harvesting – the life of the fields went on in an unchanging pattern.

Slavery acted not as a spur to change and growth, but as a disincentive. The planters were too often content to count their wealth in terms of human heads. So long as their slave population was increasing then, so they believed, their wealth was increasing. It was a mere illusion of wealth, that could only be sustained as long as the closed world of slavery could be maintained intact. But, for the absentee planter, the illusion was enough. A few chose to look beyond that to the reality of an inefficient agricultural system, dangerously based on a single crop – and that a crop which was mostly sold in a distant land:

Southern planters are getting poorer, every year now, this is acknowledged by all. They own large tracks of land which they plant in one
patch till it is worn out, then another, till all is worn out, never cultivate
the soil and pay enormous tax for labor in supporting their slaves,
which is another cause of their depreciation; crops never will again
bring former prices and if I could (said he) sell my land for any decent
price I would transfer my property to the North. Tell your son-in-law I
advise him to this for the time is short to the abolition of slavery.
Freedom is now spreading her wings and soon will soar and plant her
standard throughout the globe. The people of the earth are now
becoming a thinking and inquiring race. Look at chartism in England,
look at the King of the French, encased in armour, defended by a
numerous armed guard ... [23]

The writer of those thoughts was no abolitionist, but 'almost a hater of
negroes'. How far were such ideas justified by reality? Was freedom spreading
its wings over the South or even over the mill towns of Britain?

Girls in the weaving shed at Holehouse Mill, Blackburn.

Success to the Rising of the Whites 12

The chapter title is taken from John Wade's Extraordinary Black Book,[1] in which he puts forward the views of a rather restrained form of radicalism:

> We are not of that number of those who inculcate patient submission to undeserved oppression. A favourite toast of Dr Johnson was, 'Success to an insurrection of the Blacks'. Shall we say – Success to the rising of the Whites! We should at once answer yes, did we not think some measures would be speedily adopted to mitigate the bitter privations and avert the further degradation of the labouring classes.

Insurrection for the blacks, constitutional reform for the whites: many who viewed the scene on both sides of the Atlantic would have thought the opposite more likely. The British would follow the French revolutionary road, while the chances of an unarmed minority seizing power in America seemed remote. Reality fitted neither expectation, but the white textile worker and the black slave found their own methods of opposition to systems imposed on their lives against their wishes. The methods were necessarily different because the circumstances were so different.

In the early years of the factory age in Britain, the whole movement away from cottage to mill was so rapid that no sort of organisation, except on the most local scale, was possible. The spread of the first mills had been temporarily halted by riot. The same was to happen when manufacturers began to build power looms beside the spinning mills, replacing the old cottage looms. It is tempting to think of the reaction to the new looms as no more than a repetition of the events of the 1770s, but there were crucial differences. The new opposition represented something more than a simple gut reaction, a sudden violent eruption in protection of the traditional way of life. It was organised, systematic and clear in its objectives. Opposition to the looms was not, in fact, based on the burning of the spinning mills, but rather on the actions of the framework knitters of the Midlands.

The knitting frame for making stockings had been in use for two centuries when the main knitting centres of Nottingham and Leicester were the scene of a great outburst of frame smashing in 1811. Bands of knitters went out at night, heading for one particular workshop. Guards were posted outside while their colleagues, armed with hammers and axes, went inside to demolish the frames. It was all carried out like a well-planned military manoeuvre, with a high degree of discipline among the men. They took assumed names or numbers for the night to preserve their anonymity, and the leader took a suitably military name for himself – General Ludd. The followers became known, in time, as Luddites and the whole movement as Luddism. Today, Luddism tends to be thought of as a sort of brainless opposition to progress, a simple antipathy to all machines. There was no

A contemporary view of Luddites.

element of this in 1811. Why should hosiers suddenly turn against the machines which had provided them with a living for generations? The trouble was not with the machines themselves but the way in which they were used. The argument was with the machines' owners.

Theoretically, the hosiery industry was governed by a set of official rules, concerning such matters as the proper employment of apprentices. With the movement of the industry from London to the Midlands, the rules became less and less carefully observed. Apprentices were no longer thought of as boys being trained for a skilled trade, but as cheap labour that could be discarded and then replaced by more young cheap labour. The hosiers looked first to the due processes of the law. In 1778 they took their grievances to Parliament, where they told a sorry tale of hardship and exploitation.[2] They dwelt especially on the apprentices: 'Some boys, who are Paupers, are put to this work at the age of ten or eleven, but they make bad work of it – That the work affects their nerves very much ... the masters of these Boys make them work till Eleven or Twelve o'clock at Night.' They complained about fraud, low payments and, in May 1778, they had to complain that those who had come to Parliament at the beginning of the year had been sacked on their return. Legal rights were demanded, many promises were made, but nothing happened. They met the common fate of most workmen trying to use the law at this period: at best they received empty promises, at worst they found themselves persecuted for their pains. One of the most blatant examples of discrimination in favour of employers occurred in Scotland in 1812. The Glasgow weavers pressed for a minimum wage, arguing their case through the courts. They won, but there was little cause for celebration as the employers simply refused to pay. The weavers struck against this flagrant disregard of the law – and at last the law stepped firmly in. The strike leaders were arrested, tried and imprisoned. The minimum wage was not paid.

It is against this background – of legal methods tried and failed – that Luddism must be seen. The hosiers had to learn to make their own law. In March 1811, the machine breaking began:

> Some hundreds of country framework-knitters assembled in Nottingham Market place, and expressed a determination of taking vengeance upon some of the hosiers, for reducing the established price for making stockings, at a time too, when every principal of humanity dictated their advancement.[3]

The military were called in to break up the meeting, but that night another crowd gathered and sixty-three frames were smashed in Arnold, just outside Nottingham. A pattern for the future was set. Frames were broken at selected workshops by an increasingly well-organised private army. Two magistrates came down from London and set up a secret committee with funds to pay informers, but none came forward. In 1812, frame breaking was made a capital offence, yet General Ludd's army still marched the night streets, and even after more conventional trade unions were formed, frame breaking still took place from time to time as a last resort.

Frame breaking was a direct attack on the employer, not a reaction to new machines and, whatever the morality of Luddism, there can be no denying that it was more successful in achieving redress of wrongs than all the court cases and appeals to Parliament had ever been. Employers had been saying, in effect: 'We are sole arbiters of who shall work, how long you will work, where you will work and how much you will be paid for your work. Accept our terms or look for another job.' As there was often no other job, there was no real choice. But the Luddites put their own, rather different, case: 'If you try to increase your profits out of wage cuts, sweated labour and the like, then we will make sure you have no profits. We shall not just stop

137

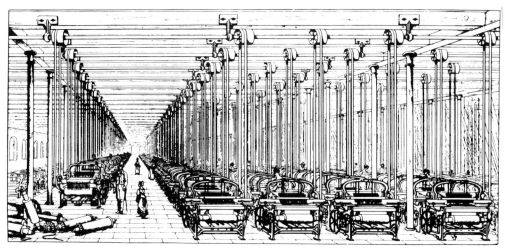

The vast array of power looms at Robinson's, Stockport. They could do the work of literally thousands of hand-loom weavers.

work, for we know you can starve us out. We shall destroy the machines in which all your capital is tied.' It was, to say the least, a crude way of conducting business, but it was not lacking in rough logic.

The case of the cotton industry was not quite that of the hosiery trade, but there were many similarities. Just as Luddism cannot be understood in terms of anti-machine riots, so too the events in Lancashire make nonsense if thought of purely in terms of progressive employers looking to the future, opposed by backward employees longing for the past. The argument was, in the long term, much more dangerous and damaging than that. It was all about how change was to be implemented and who was to benefit from that change. Increasingly, it came to be an argument between two groups whose interests ran in opposing directions. Put at its simplest, the employer saw progress as being, by definition, good, and he felt he could measure progress quite accurately. It was made up of new machines, greater productivity and higher profits. Other considerations were, at best, irrelevant and, at worst, downright damaging to the cause of progress. To employees, progress was felt as a deterioration in the condition of their lives. It is possible to assemble statistics to show that progress did, in fact, mean higher wages and better conditions, but the people on the receiving end of those statistics remained unconvinced. They knew that they were being forced into a way of working they detested. They knew that work that had once supported a family was going to children who would work for a pittance. They saw the growth of slums and at the same time they saw substantial villas being built for their employers. They felt that the gulf between rich and poor was widening, and that the new riches were being bought from the fruits of their miseries. It is possible, with hindsight, to produce a convincing argument to prove that they were wrong, but such an argument is now immaterial. The cotton workers were totally convinced that their position was deteriorating, and they acted on that conviction. That was the important reality. In dictating changes, without taking into account the views of those who would be affected by the changes, the new employers did their bit to establish a new phenomenon that was to bedevil British social and economic life right up to the present day – that phenomenon was class antagonism. The working class found its identity in opposition to the employers, and that opposition was bred in violence.

The spread of the power loom did not, by itself, produce suffering among the hand-loom weavers, who had frequently prospered as more and more yarn came from the new spinning mills. But the role of the power loom became crucial at times of depression. The manufacturer now had capital tied up in his new machines. Stop the loom and you stopped that capital earning its keep. With the hand-loom weaver things were different. They generally either owned their own looms or rented them from the manufacturer – if the former, then that was the weaver's own problem; if the latter, well, rent was not dependent on use. It was payable on bad days as well as good. When the trade wind changed direction, the weaver was the first to feel the cold. In the 1820s the wind was bitter. The weavers told their own story of poverty in the popular ballads of the day:

> Aw'm a poor cotton-wayver, as mony a one knows,
> Aw've nowt t'eat i' th'heawse, un' aw've worn eawt my cloas,
> Yo'd hardly gie sixpence for a' aw've got on,
> Meh clogs us' boath broken, un' stockins aw've none;
> Yo'd think it wor hard, to be sent into th' world
> To clem [starve] un' do best 'at yo' can.[4]

The ballads also sounded the new note of antagonism towards the owners. 'The Hand-Loom Weaver's Lament' caricatured the life of the employer:

> With the choicest of strong dainties your tables overspread
> With good ale and strong brandy, to make your faces red;
> You call'd a set of visitors – it is your whole delight –
> And you lay your heads together to make our faces white.[5]

The chorus to that ballad makes the new militancy clear:

You tyrants of England, your race may soon be run.
You may be brought into account for what you've sorely done.

The conditions that gave rise to such bitterness can be found spelled out in the diary of William Varley, a weaver from Higham, a small village just to the north of Burnley.[6] He was luckier than some, for he had a country cottage with a garden where he could grow his own vegetables and keep a pig and a few hens. Yet he found his standard of living steadily falling in the 1820s. From receiving as much as 3s a piece for his weaving, he found himself reduced to a mere 9d, though even that was better than the periods when there was no work at all. He was reduced to misery and the ignominy of accepting charity hand-outs, and the hardest blow fell when his daughter Elizabeth died of consumption. There is small wonder that he felt bitterness, working all day with his wife, yet quite unable to earn enough from his labours to feed the family. The first entry for the 1820s sets the mood for the whole decade:

The year commences with very cold frosty weather. ... The poor weaver is now very hard put to it, what with the rigour of the weather and the unrelenting hearts of our masters, whose avarice will not allow us above half wage.

It is a story of poverty, death and disease; not a new story, perhaps, but what was new was the sense that some were growing rich amidst all this destitution. Nor was it hidden poverty, unrecognised by authority; but when steps were taken to alleviate the worst conditions, the weavers found the actions were not always generous. An unemployed weaver[7] was given a job so that he could earn his parish relief. He was asked to carry a heavy parcel to a village ten miles away. On the way he met another weaver with another, suspiciously similar, parcel. The two men opened the wrappings and discovered just what it was they were being asked to haul around the neighbourhood – paving stones! They complained of the absurdity to the parish overseer, who roundly abused them both and sent them away with no relief at all. The faces of charity and cruelty could look surprisingly similar.

Varley's diary notes the blackening mood of the weavers in 1826:

March 11th Wm Hargreaves lowers wages 3d. per cut and there is not half enough work so that the whole country is all in an uproar for the poor weaver cannot get bread.
March 14th There is some disturbance at Blackburn this day; the poor people throw stones at the coach and break the windows.

The magnificent engine house at Coat's, Paisley. The ropes wrapped round the fly wheel in the centre of the picture carried the drive to all parts of the mill.

In April there was a further cut in wages. In Bolton[8] cuts were as much as 15 per cent, and the more far-sighted of the manufacturers saw the dangers that lay ahead. They called a meeting at Bolton-le-Moors, at which they deplored the action of those manufacturers who had taken 'an undue and unjustifiable advantage of the deplorable state of the depressed weavers'. Their resolutions had no force – the wage cuts remained. Perhaps a change of heart among the manufacturers would have had some effect, but time and patience had run out. Varley made a brief note in his diary on 24 April: 'This day the country rises in a great multitude and breaks the power looms of Accrington and Burnley and many other places.'

141

The short entry might suggest a howling, uncontrolled mob on the rampage. There was nothing uncontrolled about the events of April 1826. The men had a specific target – the power looms and their associated machinery. Their actions were, predictably, condemned by the press, conservative and radical alike. The former put out the traditional view of the supporters of progress. It was unfortunate, they agreed, that the introduction of new machines brought starvation to the old class of machine operatives, but such was the way of the world. 'There is, there can be, no other test of the intrinsic utility of a new machine, than whether it effects better or more cheaply, the purpose of that which has previously been in use. If it does, it ought to, and what is more, it surely will, force its way.' That view is a logical one, and could fairly be taken as a crude statement of industrial philosophy that extends down to the present day. The radical press, while trumpeting the appalling conditions of the mills, describing mill girls reduced to prostitution and the starvation of the weavers, argued that violence was no answer. That view, too, would be acceptable today. They also hinted darkly at the presence of paid spies and agitators. That seems less convincing. Who would pay them and, given the conditions of the time, who would need to? Few thinking men viewing the events of that April seriously believed that the march of industry could be permanently halted. The machine and the factory were established facts of life. Equally, given the willing support of officialdom for the mill owners, few doubted that the violence could soon be controlled. Was the machine breaking then no more than a futile attempt to turn back the clock? No it was not. To understand just what it was you have to start looking at it from the specific viewpoint of the weavers.

There was, undoubtedly, a strong element of resistance to the change from cottage to factory – and why not? Conditions in many, probably the majority, of mills were wretched. There seems little reason why a man should not object to giving up one way of life for another that was demonstrably worse, even if the latter was deemed to be more progressive. But there was more to the power-loom controversy than that. There was a feeling that the new machines were being installed for the benefit of the few to the detriment of the many. There was no thought for the well-being of the cotton workers. And that too was demonstrably true. Yet, even granting that, was machine breaking an appropriate response? There was no end to the commentators pointing out that it offered no sort of long-term answer to the problem. But the weaver was more concerned with a short-term problem – starvation. The weavers' argument had a simple logic. 'If I break a power loom and leave the spinning machine untouched, the manufacturer will still produce yarn but he will have to send it to me for weaving.' This was precisely what they set out, in their thousands, to do.

'No damage has been done to the spinning part of any of the factories,' reported the *Bolton Chronicle*, 'nor even to the windows, the sole object of attack being the power looms.' The report ended with a note that 'no disposition to commit outrage upon any other property has been manifested'. If this was a riot, then it was one of the most controlled riots in history:

> On Wednesday, about 100 of the rioters assembled between Haslingden and Rawtenstall, about $\frac{1}{2}$ past 8 o'clock in the morning. They gave a shout at the north end of the hill leading to Rawtenstall, and immediately descended into the village, and commenced an active attack upon Mr. Whitehead's factory, which was strongly barricaded on the inside, and occasioned them a delay of half an hour, before they could effect an entrance. On entering they immediately commenced the work of destruction, and in the short space of half an hour they completely destroyed ninety looms – all that the building contained. They did not attempt to injure any other machinery besides the looms. On coming out they gave three cheers, and proceeded to Mr. Thomas King's of Long Holme.

They were clearly a disciplined and organised group, and at times it all sounds almost friendly. After visiting Rawsthorne's factory at Edenfield someone remembered the dressing frame, a machine that had recently been installed to take up the cloth from the loom, so back they went, 'but on Mr. Rawsthorne assuring them that there was nothing but spinning machinery, they retired without doing any further damage.' Not the action of an uncontrolled mob.

The end was inevitable. The military were called in, lives were lost, injuries inflicted. The bitterness and despair of the weavers was seen in full measure. 'Our informant saw a poor fellow lie down before the feet of the soldiers' horses: he said they might trample on him if they liked, he was starving to death, but he would persist in breaking the looms.' The violence was soon over, but it had its effect. The condition of the weavers became a matter of public concern as reports began to appear, describing the conditions that had bred the riots. The papers sent men out to towns such as Colne to see for themselves just what life was like:

> This place, like others mentioned, exhibits one scene of equal distress. Work for weavers is so scarce, that the night before the taking-in day, the weavers come at eight or nine o'clock in the evening, and remain starving with hunger and cold, until eleven or twelve o'clock the next day. The wages which they are receiving are so mean, that you would

143

wonder how the poor creatures could exist. There are employers here who give one shilling and threepence per cut of 30 yards – others one shilling and three-halfpence, and others only one shilling. Report says that the present overseer of this town, made an attempt to live for a week upon one shilling and sixpence (the parish allowance to each person) and it was consumed by Thursday night. His diet was porridge and treacle, and he declared that this allowance could not keep any human being alive for any length of time.[9]

Government relief was sent. Varley received nine pounds of meat from the Government on 23 May, and the next day brought even better news. 'This day I got work of Mr. Corless, so now I hope through the mercy of God I will be able to maintain life a little longer.'

The relief for the individual weavers was limited, but the great explosion of violence that April did at least focus attention on the problems of the textile districts. Parliament came up with one possible solution to the problem – send it away. A Select Committee was set up to consider the possibility of exporting the poor to the colonies. The idea came to nothing, largely because Parliament was unwilling to foot the bill, but the Committee did at least look at local conditions, and some unsavoury facts were brought to light. One point which was brought forcibly home was that the problem was by no means limited to Lancashire. In the Glasgow and Paisley districts, for example, there were estimated to be some 11,000 hand looms, and the average weekly earnings were only 5s 6d.[10] What also became clear in the enquiries was that it was not just the old-fashioned hand-loom weavers who

144   *Cotton operatives clashing with the military in Preston, 1842: two workers died.*

were suffering. Those who were brought in to man the new, sophisticated machines on which the age of prosperity was to be built were little better off. They too lived well below any reasonable subsistence level. Figures spell out the hard facts of poverty. These below applied to a man in a power-loom factory, described by his employers as 'a *first-rate* workman'. Provisions for the year came to just over £23, of which these were the main items:

Meat	£6 10s 0d
Potatoes	£3 18s 0d
Milk	£4 11s 0d
Bread	£2 1s 2d
Soap	17s 4d
Starch	12s 0d
Coal	£1 18s 6d
Oil	16s 6d

On top of that there were items such as rent at £4 10s 0d, medicine, clothes and shoes for the family. The grand total for a year's expenditure came to £32 12s. To set against this was his own income of £26 a year and his wife's pay, a mere £3 18s: altogether £29 18s. It needs no Mr Micawber to point out that the net result of that financial equation is misery. The same story could be repeated in every district in the land where cotton was spun and woven. Things were bad and getting worse. A 'second-rate' weaver could earn £48 a year in 1815; a first-rate man in 1826 had to work sixteen hours a day to make half that amount.

Where was the progress of which everyone talked? Where was the prosperity? It seemed that prosperity for the worker did not follow as an automatic corollary to progress in the trade. The Select Committees sat, pondered and did nothing; the Relief Committees passed out their rations to the hard-pressed families. None of this looked much like a movement towards a new Golden Age. The textile workers were adopting a new attitude, a new philosophy. Employers were not going to give anything as a right. They would not listen to argument, and would be persuaded to part with more pay only if forced to do so. The two sides of industry were moving farther apart, taking up increasingly hostile positions. A working class was emerging, aware of its own identity and increasingly convinced that the only way forward lay through unity and sheer weight of numbers. That awareness, however, did not arrive like a flash of light on the road to Damascus. Rather it was a gradual dawning. Even when the message was clear, it was no easy matter to apply the new philosophy in practice.

The idea of workmen co-operating to help each other through the bad times was not new in the 1820s. Thirty years before, the spinners had banded together in Benefit Societies. They had got together again to petition

145

Parliament about low wages; they gave evidence before Select Committees, produced documents to argue their common cause and sought the support of men of affairs. Parliament listened to these pleas to involve government in the world of trade, carefully documented them all and then did nothing.[11] Parliament was, however, also aware of the growing movement towards more militant workers' organisations and responded with the Combination Acts, forbidding workers to combine to pursue their pay claims. (They also forbade combinations of employers, but where workers who put in joint pay claims were prosecuted, there were no prosecutions of employers who met to fix wages.) The acts were short-lived, and when unions re-emerged from their forced closure in the 1820s they did so with renewed strength. In retrospect it was clear that the Combination Acts had not only failed to stop the growth of trade unionism, but had actually encouraged it. The acts had proved conclusively to many workers that they could look for no help from constitutional reforms – on the contrary, government seemed to be determined to take sides against them. Authority was only seen in the form of troops sent in to back up the mill owners. Government joined the owners on the opposite side of the frontier in the new war. Employees increasingly relied on their own resources.

In 1829, there was a series of strikes against a reduction in wages. The leader of the Lancashire spinners was John Doherty, a thirty-year-old Irishman. That year, he organised the biggest of the strikes in Hyde, near Manchester. It lasted six months, and was marked both by a new bitterness and by a new sense of defiance and purpose. A handbill spelt out the workers' defiance to the owners: 'You are mistaken, if you suppose that 14 weeks' starvation can shew us the propriety or reasonableness of a measure which we could not see before and the mischievous consequences of which we can demonstrate.'[12] The new militancy was apparent in the correspondence between the new working-class leaders. The Chartist Francis Place wrote to Doherty, criticising one of his pamphlets:

> A large portion of the printed address is worse than useless, in as much as it is an appeal to the humanity of the masters, against their interest. The reasons given for the appeal are futile. The manufacturer looks only to his immediate profit, and cares little or nothing for what may be the state of trade hereafter, or what may be the profits of his successor ... Depend upon it the working people never will, as they never have, obtain anything by such appeals. The struggle is a struggle of strength and 'the weakest must go to the wall'. Whatever the people either gain or even retain, is gained or retained, and must always be gained or retained by power.[13]

It seemed a bleak prospect of perpetual struggle, but for all the talk of militancy and holding out forever, the strike failed. Six months of near starvation broke the strikers, but one new lesson had been learned. A single district could not hope to win a strike – combination and concerted effort throughout the industry was needed. If wages were cut in Glasgow, then the Scots should receive help from Manchester and vice versa. In December 1829, the first steps were taken towards a national union when delegates from England, Scotland and Ireland met to discuss the problem.[14] They agreed to form the National Union with Doherty as secretary and passed a series of resolutions, demanding, for example, a reduction in working hours for the under-twenty-ones. Authority listened to their deliberations – for there was nothing secret about the Ramsey meetings – and reacted in panic:

> The combination of workmen, long acknowledged a great evil, and one most difficult to counteract, has recently assumed so formidable and systematic a shape in this district that we feel it our duty to lay before you some of its most alarming features ... a weekly levy or rent of one penny per head on each operative is cheerfully paid. This produces a large sum, and is a powerful engine, and principally to support those who have turned out against their employers, agreeable to the orders of the committee, at the rate of ten shillings per week for each person. The plan of a general turnout having been found to be impolitic, they have employed it in detail, against particular individuals or districts, who, attacked thus singly, are frequently compelled to submit to their terms rather than to the ruin which would ensue to many by allowing their machinery (in which their whole capital is invested) to stand idle.[15]

The authorities over-reacted, and certainly over-estimated the abilities of the cotton workers to form such a united group. Communications between the two major centres, Manchester and Glasgow, were poor, and even in its heyday the union did not include the women and children who made up the bulk of the workforce. By no means all the workers were convinced of the value of unions – and nor were all union officials scrupulous in their methods of recruitment. The darker side of the movement was hinted at in 1838, when five Glasgow cotton spinners were put on trial:

> The cotton spinners of Glasgow have long been noted for the violent and arbitrary proceedings of their confederacy. Early in January, five individuals connected with this body, were indicted at Edinburgh on counts charging murder, attempts at arson, and conspiracy, besides other grave offences of a similar character.[16]

An anti-union cartoon from the 1830s. This was very much the accepted establishment view of the union.

It all sounds most sinister, but after the trial had already begun, the prosecution introduced three new counts: conspiracy, illegal combination and writing threatening letters. Ninety-one witnesses were called for the prosecution, who described 'some curious though revolting details of the practices and formidable organisation of the cotton spinners union of Glasgow'. At the end of the day, they were acquitted on all the serious charges, and only found guilty – and that by a majority verdict – on the three lesser charges hastily introduced during the proceedings. One can only presume that the prosecution sensed they were losing the original case. The accused, who had already served five months in gaol awaiting trial were, in spite of being cleared of all the main indictments, still given the savage sentence of seven years' transportation each. No one in the infant union doubted the significance of the trial: authority was out to hammer them, and it looked very much as if they were succeeding.

The great trial of strength between union and owners came in 1853. 'Preston has become somewhat celebrated', wrote the town's historian, 'as the principal "battle field", where the capital and labour engaged in the cotton manufacture fight in defence of what each deems its respective rights or privileges.'[17] That was how it seemed to men of moderate opinion, and it seems no less a battleground when viewed over a century later.

A trade union banner.

The lead-up to the big strike was long. Wages had been cut in the recession of 1847, but promises had been made to return to the old levels when trade improved. Trade did improve, but against a background of rising food prices. The operatives put in their demand for a 10 per cent pay rise, and here the story becomes confused. Some mills gave the full rise, some argued about the amount and others gave nothing at all. Then, from this confusion, a single, clear issue emerged. The workers demanded 10 per cent for everyone. The masters dug in their heels, stating flatly that no one could dictate terms to them and, in October 1853, closed down their mills. The lock-out had begun. From being an argument over pay the issue had now become that infinitely less tractable problem – a matter of principle:

> The real question at issue in the Preston strike was not one of wages, but of property: not whether the operatives would have more or less money in exchange for their labour, but whether the masters should have the power of saying whom they would employ and on what terms; whether they would be masters within their own just province, viz. within the factories they had built, and among the men who received their money. Their cause was not that of capital against labour, but that of property against communism.[18]

149

The strike was marked by the greatest possible bitterness. From the start, the masters refused any kind of arbitration, arguing that no one had the right to meddle in their affairs. More than twenty thousand workers were laid off, but the mills did not stay idle for long. The 'knobsticks' came to Preston. They were Irish brought over specially, poor men and women recruited from the agricultural districts and a few local people who were persuaded to work during the strike. Their presence did nothing to calm the situation – nor did the authorities who arrested union leaders on conspiracy charges. The strikers sent a deputation to Palmerston who delivered a brisk lecture on laissez-faire economics – wages are determined by supply and demand, morality doesn't come into it – and sent them home again.

The mood of defiance can be heard in the many ballads that appeared during the strike:

> You may see, of a truth, that the people are not dead,
> Though 'tis said they died long ago;
> We've risen from our sleep, a holiday to keep,
> Determined to work under prices no more.
>
> So we've thrown away reed, hook, and comb,
> And hung up the shuttle on the loom;
> And we'll never be content, till we get the ten per cent
> In spite of the 'let well alone'.[19]

The ballads did more than cheer up the strikers. One of the most famous of them, 'The Cotton Lords of Preston', was hawked around the neighbourhood to raise funds:

> So men and women all of you,
> Come and buy a song or two,
> And assist us to subdue
> The Cotton Lords of Preston.
> We'll conquer them and no mistake,
> Whatever laws they seem to make,
> And then we'll get the ten per cent
> Oh then we'll dance and sing with glee
> And thank you all right heartily,
> When we gain the victory
> And beat the Lords of Preston.[20]

The strike lasted for thirty-six weeks, right through the winter, and for all the brave words of the balladeers there was little hope that the operatives could win. Funds became short, and the effect of 'knobstick' labour was felt ever more strongly. Slowly the drift back to work began. The strike leaders had no option but to capitulate. The masters celebrated a famous victory:

It is now surely established, on the basis of experience, as well as reasoning, that, no more than any other commodity, can labour obtain a higher price than the purchaser is willing to give for it. This is a law in which, whatever the consequences may be, we have to acquiesce, just as much as we should have to acquiesce in the law of gravitation ... But happily, it might be demonstrated, that all the results of this economical law, are in perfect harmony with justice and benevolence.[21]

Others, even when they were sympathetic to the masters, saw matters rather more soberly:

The victory obtained by the employers merely demonstrated that which every one previously knew, viz., the strongest party in the end would win. But this is not sufficient to set at rest the mighty question, which yearly throbs with increasing vitality beneath the surging mass of mercantile contention. No one really wins in these struggles. They are essentially productive of loss to all, except in so far as they inculcate lessons of wisdom. It is, therefore, the duty and interest of all that the differences which must occur occasionally between the buyers and sellers of labour, as well as of any other commodity, should be settled in a commercial, and not in a military spirit.[22]

This was certainly one of the lessons that should have been drawn from Preston. Employer and employee were now cast in the roles of victor and vanquished. The great revolution in cotton production had reached its peak, yet this was the result: two sides firmly set in stances of hatred and antagonism. Trade might grow, but the social price was desperately high. The employer chose to regard his human employees much as he regarded his inanimate machines – as commodities to be acquired at the lowest possible price. It was not, in many ways, very different from the attitude of the planter who thought of his slaves as his property. The rising of the whites, it seemed, was not to be. What hope was there, then, for an insurrection of the blacks?

A medallion designed by Josiah Wedgwood: the answer to the question 'Am I not a man and a brother?' in the American South was a firm 'no'.

The Insurrection of the Blacks 13

If the white cotton operatives of Lancashire were faced with apparently insurmountable difficulties in obtaining a decent standard of living and a dignified way of life, then the difficulties faced by the black slaves were even greater. They had no status in law higher than that held by a cow in the meadow or even a chair in the master's house. They were simply objects to be bought and sold. They could no more appeal to the courts for justice than a chair could sue an overweight man that broke its leg. The British operative found the law generally unsympathetic, but the law did exist. The possibility of justice existed as a concept for him. Not so for the slave: for him law was something applied by white men for white men. If the slave was injured then the owner could sue for damages to his property, but if he won the compensation was all the owner's. The possibility of change always existed, at least in theory, for the mill worker. He or she could leave the mill and, as the Victorian preachers of the doctrine of self-help never tired of insisting, make a fortune. Even a dream or fantasy of change could not exist for the slave. The mill worker could, if he was very, very fortunate, rise on the social scale and leave his past behind him. The slave carried the mark of his subjection with him always in the colour of his skin. What hope was there for any change in his life? Could he do anything at all to alter his condition?

The answer that might seem to offer the best possibility of change would be revolt: a rising-up against the planters. Those who wonder why more slaves did not, in fact, rebel have not really thought about the situation from the slave's point of view. Start to add up the obstacles in the way of a slave rebellion and it seems a wonder that there were any revolts at all. The odds were stacked against the slaves from the very beginning. Compare the situation of the mill workers with that of the slaves. The mill workers formed a majority in the regions – the slaves were generally in a minority. The early union organisers had difficulties because communications were bad between Lancashire and Scotland: the slave was lucky if he was allowed to talk to a friend on the next plantation. The British worker could rely on support from his neighbours, even when he was at his most militant. Isolated by the colour of his skin, the slave was surrounded by a unanimously hostile population. The list of difficulties seem endless. Yet revolts there were, and their effect was out of all proportion to their scale.

The largest of the slave revolts is, in fact, the least well known. In 1811 some five hundred Louisiana slaves marched on New Orleans. They put up a brave show, striding along with banners flying. But hoes and axes were no match for swords and guns: defeat came with swift inevitability. It caused little stir. Louisiana had only been purchased from France eight years before, and was still regarded as a foreign land. A few years later it might have seemed more of a threat. There were two other abortive uprisings, led by Gabriel Prosser and Denmark Vesey, but there was one revolt that attracted huge notoriety and prevented many a Southerner from enjoying a comfortable night's sleep long after it had ended. It was the rebellion of 1831, led by a Virginian slave, Nat Turner.

Nat Turner's revolt might seem comparatively unimportant, as even at its height there were no more than a hundred slaves involved. Compare this with the twenty thousand caught up in the Preston strike and it might seem to have affected only the tiniest minority. But its effect was not to be measured in terms of the numbers taking part. The numbers that were taken seriously were the number of white people killed. Sixty whites died in the revolt: one hundred blacks died in the aftermath. Turner himself remained free for two months after the rising had been quelled. He was captured on 30 October 1831. Less than two weeks later he was hanged. He left behind a personal statement, in which many of the elements that typified slave resistance can be seen.[1]

Nat Turner was born in 1800. He gave no details of his parents, though both mother and grandmother featured at the beginning of the story. His father is not named, though we do learn that he ran away and possibly managed to escape to the North – or was captured and ended up in an

Nat Turner discovered in hiding after the collapse of the slave revolt he had led.

anonymous grave. Only one man is named at this period of his life, the man who gave Nat his name, his owner, Benjamin Turner. From the start of his life, Nat Turner, like all slaves, was denied a part of his identity – his name. Even in modern Western society, names are important. Through them, identity is passed on. One of the first targets of the modern feminist movement was the change of name at marriage: they feel that in surrendering their given names they are surrendering part of their identities. The name is a badge of personality – to the slave it was a mark of ownership. The owner was saying, in effect 'I name you "Nat", because I choose to and "Turner" because that identifies you as my property.' Before he could learn to reason for himself, he was awarded this badge of inferiority. Not that all slaves accepted the situation. When the slave Mammy Maria was asked why she called another slave, Henry, 'Mister Ferguson', she replied angrily: 'Do you think 'cause we are black that we cyarn't have no names?'[2]

Religion played an important part in providing the cohesion and identity in the slave community which the laws would have denied. It offered an authority higher than that of the slave owner: a court of final appeal, more powerful than any human court. In coming to share the white man's god, the slave asserted a common humanity. He also followed the white man in other ways: he too found there was no shortage of Scriptural support for his own opinions. In the earlier Vesey conspiracy, one of the slaves, Rolla, gave evidence in court:

> At this meeting Vesey said we were to take the Guard-House and Magazine to get arms; that we ought to rise up and fight against the whites for our liberties; he was the first to rise up and speak, and to read us from the Bible, how the children of Israel were delivered out of Egypt from bondage.[3]

Nat Turner went further than this, claiming a Messianic mission. Reading his own words, one is struck by the obvious depth of his conviction – and by the mixture of older African beliefs with his Christianity. He described how, as a child of three or four years of age, he began to talk about events that had happened before he was born:

> Others being called on, were greatly astonished, knowing that these things had happened, and caused them to say, in my hearing, I surely would be a prophet, as the Lord had shown me things that had happened before my birth. And my mother and grandmother strength- ened me in this my first impression, saying, in my presence, I was intended for some great purpose, which they had always thought from certain marks on my head and breast.

Later he was to claim divine inspiration for the uprising, receiving his orders directly from 'the Spirit'. His questioners looked at Nat Turner in the condemned cell and asked him if he did not now feel that he had been mistaken. He simply replied, 'Was not Christ crucified?' There is no reason to doubt that he believed himself to be divinely inspired and so there is no hint of remorse in his account of the rising itself:

> I took my station in the rear, and, as it was my object to carry terror and devastation wherever we went, I placed fifteen or twenty of the best armed and most to be relied on in front, who generally approached the house as fast as their horses could run. This was for two purposes – to prevent their escape, and strike terror to the inhabitants; on this account I never got to the houses, after leaving Mrs. Whitehead's, until the murders were committed, except in one case. I sometimes got in sight in time to see the work of death completed; viewed the mangled bodies as they lay, in silent satisfaction, and immediately started in quest of other victims. Having murdered Mrs. Waller and ten children, we started for Mr. Wm. Williams', – having killed him and two little boys that were there; while engaged in this, Mrs. Williams fled and got some distance from the house, but she was pursued, overtaken, and compelled to get up behind one of the company, who brought her back, and, after showing her the mangled body of her lifeless husband, she was told to get down and lay by his side, where she was shot dead.

This mixture of Messianic fervour and total ruthlessness shocked the South. It was as disturbing as it was frightening. Every planter saw himself and his family surrounded by Nat Turners. It was also a sharp reminder that the 'slave as property' theory had very real limitations. Once you have accepted a creed that says the slave has the same status as a chair, it is more than a little alarming to find the chair removing itself from under your backside and beating you on the head. There were inevitable repercussions, and many slaves came to resent the trouble stirred up by Turner. 'We poor colored people could not sleep at nights for the guns and swords being stuck in at our windows and doors to know who was here and what was the business.'[4]

Slave revolts were few but that does not diminish their significance. Although the possibilities of revolt were, to say the least, limited, the individual slave had opportunities to mount a form of personal opposition.

A constant complaint made against the blacks was that they were idle, dishonest and stupid. If idleness is seen as a refusal to do more work than is absolutely necessary in conditions where there is no reward for work, and if dishonesty is seen as taking that due reward which the master refuses to you, then perhaps the charge of stupidity has already been answered. On the question of work, it has often been pointed out that the work ethic so strongly recommended by the owners was not one which they chose to apply to themselves. The slave, seeing his master enjoying a life of ease, might be forgiven for feeling that he would be happy to settle for a little less virtue for himself and a greater share of sinful comfort.

Stealing might seem to be a self-evidently immoral activity, but visitors to the slave states noted that the slaves had developed their own morality.

> It is told me as a singular fact, that everywhere on the plantations, the agrarian notion has become a fixed point of the negro system of ethics: that the result of labor belongs to the laborer, and on this ground, even the religious feel justified in using 'Massa's property' for their own temporal benefit. This they term, 'taking', and it is never admitted to be a reproach to a man among them that he is charged with it, though 'stealing', or taking from another man than their master, and particularly from one another, is so.[5]

Stealing from the whites was justified over and over again in the testimonies of former slaves after the Civil War. The whites, they said, were themselves the biggest thieves of all, for they had stolen the people from their homes in Africa. So the slaves 'took' and, if only indirectly, made their protest against the system. They also made more direct protests – they sometimes ran away.

The runaway slaves really fall into two categories: those whose aim was to get clean away, to make it to the North and freedom, and those who left for reasons of their own, often returning of their own free will.

The Underground Railroad was the most famous example of an organization set up to get slaves out of the South and on their way to freedom. They were passed from 'station' to 'station', every movement controlled by agents, some of whom, like the magnificently resourceful Harriet Tubman, became folk heroes. Though many slaves travelled the railroad it could have done no more than touch on the central problem. However, it was very important as a safety valve, relieving some of the worst pressures of slavery. The bitterest part of the system for many slaves lay in the knowledge that they were slaves for life and that their children, and their children's children, would all be bound to their masters for generations to come. Each slave that escaped pushed open the door to a hopeful future just a little wider, allowing some light to fall on an otherwise infinitely gloomy prospect.

For every slave who found a new life, there were countless thousands who made temporary escapes. Some were gone for months, some for a matter of days. Those who left in the hope of getting clear away faced appalling difficulties, as a former slave described:

> No man who has never been placed in such a situation can comprehend the thousand obstacles thrown in the way of the flying slave. Every man's hand is raised against him – the patrollers are watching for him – the hounds are ready to follow on his track, and the nature of the country is such as renders it impossible to pass through it with any safety.[6]

The odds against the runaways were indeed formidable. Many slave owners kept packs of 'nigger dogs' to hunt down escaping slaves, and too often the chase ended with the dogs savaging their prey. Most slave catching

Newspaper adverts for runaway slaves were commonplace.

fell to the slave patrols, made up of local poor whites. As a group, they were universally detested in the quarters, and with every justification for they were noted for their brutality. That brutality became more pronounced as abolitionists became more vocal. The runaway, who had previously been thought of as a special kind of thief of his master's property – stealing himself, as it were – now became a dangerous part of a detested political movement. Repression increased as the abolitionist movement grew.

This, however, was only one, if the most dramatic, part of the runaway story. Every plantation seems to have had its share of runaways – and not all were even attempting the long trek north. For many it was a form of protest, one of the few open to them. The diary of John Nevitt,[7] who owned a cotton plantation in Mississippi, is dotted with accounts of slaves running away, being captured and returning on their own. It is worth studying in some detail because it illustrates just what a complex matter this was for both owner and slave.

Entries are generally brief, with no indication of a slave's motives. These entries appeared in the early part of 1826:

> February 2 – Peter run away in the morning
> April 24 – Peter who ran away 2nd Feby last was Brought home by Mr Dreggs paid him his fee, and whiped and ironed Peter

This is the traditional idea of the runaway, brought back by the slave patrol, punished and placed in irons. The following year there were some very different entries:

> February 28 – Bill ran away
> March 3 – Bill came home last night
> April 21 – Maria runaway
> April 28 – Bill & Jerry catched Maria at Campbells
> April 29 – whiped Maria and put Iron on her leg

Here we have two very different phenomena. Bill awards himself a short, unofficial holiday or, if you prefer, stages a short strike. Maria disappears to another plantation. To meet a lover, to start an escape? We are not told, but after only a week away she is caught, not by the patrols but by fellow slaves, whipped and put in irons. Yet, in contrast with the harsh treatment handed out to Maria we find this reference to John, whose job was carting:

> July 20 – John who ran-away on the 1st Inst came home forgave him and set him to work had his team got in readiness for tomorrow

In spite of the lenient treatment, John was off again two weeks later. Harsh treatment was no more effective in keeping the persistent runaway at home. There was no holding Maria:

> 21 August – Maria who ran away on the 12th was brought home by Rubin gave her a light whiping and set her to making cotton bags
> 28th September – Maria runaway
> 1st October – Rubin runaway
> 2nd October – Rubin came home in the morning sent him out for Maria he returned in the Evening with her forgave Rubin his falt an gave Maria severe whiping
> 9th November – Maria was brought home by Jerry on the night of the 8th had her whiped severely an Ironed with a shackle on each leg connected with a chain

So the story goes on, with both Rubin and Maria regularly running away and regularly being caught. Only once, in March 1828, was it recorded that Maria came home voluntarily, and on that occasion she escaped punishment. There is no hint at the depths of the despair that sent her off time and again in spite of the inevitable punishments. What the bare account does do, however, is point out the old dilemma facing the planter. If the work on the plantation had been done by hired labourers, he could have let them go and

The mule driver: an important man in plantation life.

hired replacements. But Rubin and Maria were not employees, they were property, they were capital investment, just like the machines of the spinning mill. A runaway slave represented a nil return on investment – but then a slave shackled and beaten was not going to be very profitable either. If whipping did not deter the runaways, then what was the owner to do? In the case of Maria, the final answer came on 26 December 1828 when she was sent to Natchez gaol. Whatever that may have meant to Maria it was an admission of defeat by Nevitt. His property was locked away, useless.

The problem of Maria was solved, though that of Rubin remained. His name keeps cropping up right through to 1830:

> Went to the swamp to hunt runaways … several men came from town to hunt runaways the overseer went with them Took little Sal who was in company with Rubin, Sandy

And on 11 June this entry appears:

> Rubin came home having been runaway for two or three months – *did not punish him*

The emphasis is Nevitt's, clearly overwhelmed by his own generosity. It was just one response in a continuing battle between slave and master. The slaves having no legal rights, could only show their opposition by illegal means. Running away was the most common, but more violent methods would also be used:

> January 13, 1827 – This day at 1 Oclock in the morning my gin was destroyed bi fire Supposed to be the work of an incendiary loss about twenty Bales cotton the buildings entire All hand Employed putting out fire and saving what cotton possible the boy Gusty was Burnt in the gin

The culprits were never located, but even if they had been the problem would not have been resolved, for the question of punishment remained. Sometimes the problem was taken out of the owner's hands:

> 27th July 1830 rode to Natchez found that Kate was put in Jail on suspicion of having stolen meat found she had received it of Bill rode out with Mr Armstrong (the constable) and apprehended Bill who after a little flogging confessed that he and Mrs Campbells Sandy had broken into Mr Lyles warehouse and taken from it Bakin & Liquor Mr Armstrong also apprehended Sandy took them both to Jail

Bill was found guilty and sentenced to thirty-nine lashes, but now Nevitt still had to decide what to do with him:

> I left him in Jail for further consideration what to do with him Sandy was used as a witness against Bill and of course forgiven

Which was best – the carrot or the stick? The owners tried both, but never overcame the fundamental contradiction that lay at the heart of all slave problems. The law wished to deny the slave his humanity; the slave wished to assert it. The 'good' planter could be a kind and humane man, yet the very act of acceding to the system made him a party to the process of dehumanisation of the blacks. Others were positively eager to take part in the process, but were notably less willing to show that paternal benevolence which Southern apologists never tired of claiming as the chief characteristic of the planter. Racial hatred spread as a malevolent disease among the poor whites,

The busiest time of the year, and the hottest: picking the cotton.

to such an extent that it brought them into conflict with the planters. A typical example of conflict arose when a ferryman got into an argument with one slave, America, and proceeded to take it out on other slaves. The plantation overseer told the subsequent story to the owner:

> It seems that Mr. Moran either dissatisfied at the escape of America or determined to wreke his vengeance on some of my slaves – took occasion on last Monday to whip with a Wagon Whip & beat with a hand spike another of my men – named Tom – whom I had scnt to my farm – upon being informed of this circumstance on my return from the farm whither I had gone early on the same afternoon I enquired of Mr Moran the cause of such correction – he replied that the slave had 'saucied' him. That he had beaten him, that he intended to beat him again upon his return & would beat him or any other of mine when it pleased him – I remonstrated with him as to the mode of correction, stating that if one of my slaves ever gave me any offence he should be punished severely for it – but that I wished him corrected properly and lawfully – not with bludgeon & hand spike, which might disable him or injure him so as to render him unfit to do his duty – he thereupon reiterated the threat to beat him upon his return & added (with no small insult to myself for protecting, as he termed it, such saucy negroes) that he would beat him with a hand spike or anything he could lay his hands upon. In consequence of this threat & such treatment Tom went by Holts ferry, where the principal part of my crossing has since been done at an expense which I cannot well defray.[8]

The antipathy that existed between master and slave showed itself in many different ways. The slaves could slack over their work, and they often had good reason to do so. Cotton picking was a back-breaking job, and the records often give no more than a hint of the severity of the conditions. 'Commenced picking cotton the 1st day of August 1860. Dry weather. Thermometer at 106.'[9] Even in those temperatures they were able to pick a thousand pounds of cotton per slave per week.

There was some relief from this life of drudgery and from the drabness of the quarters. One great solace was in religion, with its promise of a better life to come. There was a great comfort in the human fate which most of the rest of us dread:

> We're a marching to the grave
> We're a marching to the grave, my Lord,
> We're a marching to the grave,
> To lay this body down.

It says a great deal about the conditions of life that this was a favourite hymn.

The slaves also created their own society, which often seemed comical to white observers. But underneath the mockery, one can still see a picture of a group of human beings attempting to establish their own system of identities and status:

> At a wedding I witnessed here last Saturday evening, where some 150 negroes were assembled, many being invited guests, I heard a number of them addressed as governors, generals, judges, and doctors (the titles of their masters) and a spruce, tight-set darkey, who waits on me in town, was called 'Major Quitman'. The 'colored ladies' are invariably Miss Joneses, Miss Smiths, or some such title. They are exceedingly pompous and ceremonious, gloved and highly perfumed. The 'gentle-men' sport canes, ruffles, and jewelry, wear boots and spurs, affect crepe on their hats, and carry huge cigars. The belles wear gaudy colours, 'tote' their fans with the air of Spanish senoritas, and never stir out, though black as the ace of spades, without their parasols. In short, these 'niggers', as you call them, are the happiest people I have ever seen.[10]

It is interesting to conjecture how far the calling of each other by their masters' names was put on for the watching white man.

It was common for the master to give holidays on 4 July and at Christmas. The latter was a special treat, and considered very important by the masters. 'I have endeavoured to make my Negroes joyous & happy – & I am glad to see them enjoying themselves with such a hearty good will', wrote one planter, adding in his diary three days later:

> I have recommenced work today – I called all hands up last night, told them the work we had before us compelled our holidays to close, & made a few remarks to them as to their duties the following year. They seemed thankful for the favor I had extended to them & eager to commence work I gave them from Thursday last night ... I did all I could to make their holidays pleasant to them & they seem to appreciate my endeavours.[11]

Later in the year, he had another friendly occasion to report:

> Wm & Rachel married last night – I performed the ceremony. Gave them a nice supper, had several of the darkies from around here – I played the violin & they danced awhile, everything passed off pleasantly.[12]

Yet for all this talk of happy slaves, eager to do their master's work, the same diary keeps on telling a very different tale. There are stories of violence, of a slave attempting to stab an overseer, and the more familiar comments on punishment by the lash. The happy holidays and weddings never appear with quite the regularity of the beatings. The scope for resistance for the black was there, but it was desperately limited. For some, faced with the bleakness of life as a slave, there seemed to be only one solution. In too many diaries there are entries such as this: 'Cherry found hanged by the neck.'

Former slave cabin, photographed in Georgia, c. 1900.

Scapegoats

14

The slaves of the cotton plantations were in no position to change the fundamental conditions of their existence. They could, and did, temper those conditions in a variety of ways, but it was totally outside their powers to alter the core of the system – slavery itself. If slavery was ever to be banished, unless there was to be a significant change of heart among slave owners, it would have to come about through the work of white abolitionists and the legislature. The plight of workers in the factories would seem, on the face of it, to be less desperate. They were free members of society who, if they found factory work totally abhorrent, held the remedy in their own hands – they could leave and look for other jobs. As they did not do so in any great numbers, one can assume that they were satisfied with what they had or, more plausibly, that they knew conditions elsewhere in the country were as bad or worse. The latter argument is so often heard in defence of the factory system of the early nineteenth century that it is worth looking at a little more closely.

To decide whether life was better for the textile worker under the new system than it had been under the old is, to say the least, a complex matter. For a start, the industry was subject to violent fluctuations of slump and boom, which makes direct comparison virtually impossible. No one, however, would seriously dispute that, in the long term, life for the average worker became far better as a result of the economic expansion that stemmed from mechanisation. But during the actual transition it did not seem that simple, and if one starts to look at the change in terms other than simple money wages, one finds that the process of change caused serious long-term damage. A gulf developed between masters and men; not just a gulf between prosperity and poverty, but a gulf of mutual incomprehension. There was a total inability on the part of the masters to see the system from the operatives' point of view. Andrew Ure, the chief advocate of the factory world, looked at the new age and saw it already in a state of near perfection:

> The constant aim and effect of scientific improvement in manufactures are philanthropic, as they tend to relieve the workmen either from niceties of adjustment which exhaust his mind and fatigue his eyes, or from painful repetition of effort which distort or wear out his frame. At every step of each manufacturing process described in this volume, the humanity of science will be manifest.[1]

Yet, for some reason, the workers seemed not to appreciate that they were being offered paradise:

> Even at the present day, when the system is perfectly organised, and its labour lightened to the utmost, it is found nearly impossible to convert

167

persons past the age of puberty, whether drawn from rural or from handicraft occupations, into useful factory hands. After struggling for a while to conquer their listless or restive habits, they either renounce the employment spontaneously, or are dismissed by the overlookers on account of inattention.

Modern readers of Ure will probably feel that his first description of the beneficial effects of mechanisation is little more than an account of work from which all interest has been removed, but his failure to understand the reactions of others went beyond this. He later described one of 'our enlightened manufacturers' of Stockport who had introduced this beneficial new system. He shared Ure's enthusiasm for labour-saving machinery and was bewildered by the lack of equal enthusiasm among the workers. It genuinely seems not to have occurred to Ure that one of the great benefits of the new system – 'he would save £50 a week in wages, in consequence of dispensing with nearly forty male spinners' – might produce something less than ecstasy among the forty men thrown out of work.

Ure, if he had thought of such matters as evils, could no doubt have argued that this was the price that had to be paid for progress, for increased productivity and expanding trade. The workers could, and did, argue that they saw no reason why they should be the only ones to pay that price. This brings us to the point which is crucial to any argument about the new system. The argument is not about whether the system itself was good or bad, but about the way in which it was brought in. The factory system was imposed by the few on the many; conditions were laid down which suited the few not the many – the changes were welcomed by the few, not the many. However convincingly you can argue that the changes were for the best, there is no denying that they were unwelcome to the vast majority and pushed through with little or no regard for the effects on their lives. As much as any other factor, it was this method of imposing change by dictat that led to the growing gap between employer and employee. One imposed – the other, with increasing reluctance, accepted. The end result was a general hostility to change.

The resentment felt towards the factory system was not without cause. Hours were long, pay low, conditions bad. Increasingly the worst of the labour fell to women and children. The argument that things had always been bad, or that they were no better in other parts, was largely irrelevant. In an industry supposedly heading full speed towards Utopia, the workers were entitled to ask – why aren't they getting better? Why should bad conditions exist at all? Ure, the apologist, came up with two answers. Firstly, things really aren't as bad as they seem; don't be deceived by appearances: 'Mr Wolstenhome, surgeon at Holton, says that "The health of the factory people is much better than their pallid appearance would indicate".' Where, however, there was inescapable evidence that things really were very bad indeed, then Ure was able to show that it was the workers' own fault. At Anderston, near Glasgow, five hundred operatives were housed in barracks built by the mill owners. There 'they have been frequently visited with typhus fever of the most malignant and fatal type', simply because they had allowed themselves to get dirty and had not kept the barracks ventilated 'in spite of every remonstrance of the proprietor'. The owner saved them from their own stupidity by running metal pipes from the factory chimney to each of the apartments in the building and, at the end of each day, blowing a blast of air right through the barracks. How, with such examples of benevolence before them, could the workers possibly find cause for complaint?

One need not spend too long on such arguments. Conditions were bad, and the rise of the steam mills with their surrounding clusters of jerry-built terraces brought a new squalor to the face of Britain. In 1863, the Home Secretary, Sir George Grey, ordered an investigation into the principal towns in 'the cotton manufacturing districts'. A civil engineer, Robert Rawlinson –

Nineteenth-century Manchester – a city of tall chimneys.

who had just finished a survey of the plumbing at Windsor Castle – was put in charge. His report spells out, in graphic detail, just how wretched were those towns built on the prosperity of cotton:

> Large cotton mills, and other buildings connected with the trade of the district, were from time to time constructed, to be surrounded by new streets set out without plan or level, in which houses were built without control or order, the natural surface of the ground being, in many instances, left to form the road ... As there was no main-sewering in such streets, house-draining was, for the most part, impossible: foul water, and other refuse, consequently added to the evil. Where there was a natural fall, slop and fluid refuse from the houses on the higher ground flowed down and over the surface of adjoining yards at a lower level ... This round of sanitary neglect, producing filth, misery, drunkenness, disease, pauperism, and sometimes crime, is as consequent and certain as any other form of cause and effect.[2]

This, then, was the product of a hundred years of development which, all agreed, had set Britain on the road to previously unimaginable prosperity.

Faced by such conditions, the textile workers had attempted to band together in unions to effect some improvement in their lives. Their successes were, at best, limited. They faced hostile employers, who could call on the force of law to help them. Fundamental changes in conditions, it seemed, depended on fundamental changes in law. Here the workers met a major obstacle. Even after the passing of the great Reform Bill, they still lacked the vote and, lacking the vote, they lacked a direct voice in the deliberations of Parliament. They had to depend on sympathetic supporters to argue their case for them. Their position turned out to be not so dissimilar to that of the slaves, after all. Both found themselves relying on outsiders – and those outsiders found themselves faced with a powerful and active opposition. And it is at this point that the two stories of mill and plantation meet.

Looked at from our position, more than a century later, both mill and plantation can be seen as the homes of evident evils. Those evils were equally evident to some contemporaries. Were mill owners and planters, then, evil men? Not at all, in the sense that they felt all their actions to be justified and justifiable. The mill owner could argue that though he was, admittedly, making a large profit, that in itself was no evil, and he was at the same time providing employment and adding to the general level of prosperity of the whole community. The planter, for his part, could argue that he had taken ignorant savages and introduced them to the benefits of civilisation. Both arguments might, however, look suspiciously like special pleading; thinly-disguised attempts to justify profitable enterprises. Planter and mill owner were no different from any of the rest of us: they wished to be thought well of, to demonstrate their humanity. They needed to show that they too cared about the ills of the world and were doing their bit to fight them. They needed scapegoats – and found them in each other.

If you read through the newspapers, pamphlets, books and journals of the plantation South, you will find two related themes repeated over and over again: conditions on the plantations are positively idyllic in comparison to those of Lancashire mills; British abolitionists who buy slave-produced cotton are hopelessly hypocritical. The Parliamentary Blue Books, such as the reports of the 1833 Commission on conditions in the mills, were seized on with great glee in the South:

> It is shocking beyond endurance to turn over your Records in which the condition of your laboring classes is but too faithfully depicted. Could our slaves but see it, they would join us in lynching Abolitionists ... When you look around you how dare you talk to us before the world of slavery? For the condition of your wretched laborers, you, and every Britain who is not one of them are responsible before God and Man.[3]

The slave owner reading such tracts could reflect comfortably that his slaves were better off than those unfortunate children in Lancashire. No slave owner, he could proudly claim, would dream, for example, of setting a black child to work before the age of ten, though when he turned his attention to manufacturing, the planter was happy to break that rule. In any case, the more thoughtful might have considered that an argument that says that because my neighbour beats his wife every night I am virtuous because I only beat her twice a week, lacks validity. They could, however, take comfort from the thought that they need no longer pay any attention to criticism when the critics were so evidently hypocritical. 'Why beholdest thou the mote that is in thy brother's eye, but considerest not the beam that is in thine own eye' was a favourite text.

The most famous and popular defence of slavery, which found an honoured place on many a planter's shelf, was Elliott's *Cotton is King*.[4] Many of its arguments were directed against the British Anti-Slavery Society. The anti-slavery movement in Britain had begun with Wilberforce's Society for the Suppression of the Slave Trade. The society had succeeded in getting the trade itself banned by law, but only, the cynical noted, after it had ceased to be profitable; when America and the West Indies had all the slaves they needed. The society's medallion, designed by Josiah Wedgwood, showed a slave in chains and carried the motto 'Am I not a man and a brother?' Elliott was quick to point out that there seemed to be nothing that could be described as brotherly in the treatment of the factory children. After the

171

A cartoon of 1832 contrasting the misery of industrial Britain with the 'idyllic' life of the plantation.

trade was banned, the society was reformed as the British and Foreign Anti-Slavery Society. The charge of hypocrisy was reframed. The society had the gall to attack the planter, even though they had a weapon to hand which could destroy him, but would never use it because it would have attacked their own interests:

> As long as all used their products, so long the slaveholders found the *per se* doctrine working them no harm; as long as no provision was made for supplying the demand for tropical products by free labour, so long there was no risk in extending the field of operations. Thus, the very things necessary to the overthrow of American slavery, were left undone, while those essential to its prosperity were continued in the most active operation; so that now .... we may say, emphatically, COTTON IS KING, and his enemies are vanquished.[5]

The argument was a powerful one and difficult to refute. There was a strong feeling among American abolitionists that the British found the Americans a convenient target at which to aim social reformers who might otherwise be pointed at objectives nearer home. The Americans in the society joined in the attack on their British colleagues:

> Who are the Slaveholders of America? – The Planters? – No! – The overseers? The feculent dregs of society? – No! *The Slaveholders of America are in the City of London!* – in the heart of Great Britain! – excuse me – it is *yourselves,* the people of England who are the real slaveholders of America! – *you* hire him to chain, to whip and to work his slaves to death! – *you* stimulate him by your money – by your patronage – by your Commerce! – If Great Britain would buy no slave-raised produce, Slavery would not last one year! – That is the plain unvarnished truth, and you will forgive me for telling you so! – many slave-holders go further, and try to excuse themselves by saying Slavery was entailed upon them by England! that it is not their fault 'because had England not introduced Slaves into our country there would be no slavery here!' *then let England abolish it;* by refusing to partake of the profits of slavery – you *can* do it! ... *Repeal your Corn Laws!* – repeal all duties upon the products of our *free* states – discriminate between Liberty and Slavery! – impose a *duty upon cotton.*[6]

The Corn Laws were in time repealed, because it suited the interests of the new industrialists to have access to cheap food. There was no attempt to impose a tax on cotton imports. This one action was never seriously contemplated, though the Society on other occasions did demand direct action by the British Government. When Texas declared independence from Mexico, they wrote to the Government to try and persuade them not to recognise the new state in which slavery was permitted. 'The government', they wrote, 'should avail itself of so just and striking an opportunity of using its mighty moral influence.'[7] The mighty moral influence was not brought to bear. Texas was duly recognised, and even if it had not been it would have made very little difference to anyone. Americans, north and south of the Mason Dixon line, had a poor opinion of British morality. The British had always held the one effective weapon against slavery and that was the boycott of slave-produced goods. The weapon was never used. The charge of hypocrisy must be taken as most conclusively proved. The South could rest comfortably in the knowledge that there would be no actions from across the Atlantic to worry them. British rantings against slavery had about as much chance of proving effective as Southern condemnations of factory life had of altering the working system of Lancashire. The South and Lancashire were bound together by economic ties far too strong to be broken by moral qualms on either side. Change had to come from within the two societies.

In Britain, there were reformers anxious to push Parliament into a direct involvement in the affairs of the cotton industry. The chief Parliamentary exponent of shorter hours, especially for the factory children, was John Fielden. He was one of the leading manufacturers of the day, with a big steam mill in Todmorden, on the Lancashire–Yorkshire border. After the passing of the Reform Bill he was returned to Parliament as a radical MP for Oldham, having as his fellow MP the leading radical journalist of the day, William Cobbett. They made a formidable team. Cobbett spoke up for an older

174   *William Cobbett, passionate opponent of the new industrial society.*

Britain, deploring the changes that had reduced the independent yeoman to the role of wage slave; Fielden spoke for the new generation. He was the employer with a conscience. He favoured progress, the machine age and the new way of working that went with it, but he could not accept that it was necessary to buy prosperity at the expense of little children. Legislation was essential, Fielden argued, because without it, a well-meaning employer such as himself was forced to employ and overwork the little children or risk being ruined by less scrupulous competitors. His case was a good one, and he argued it forcibly and well. It was all the stronger just because he was no opposer of factories as such, but a factory owner himself. What he was opposing was not the use of factories, but their misuse.

Fielden received enthusiastic support from all the main textile areas, including Yorkshire where the woollen trade was belatedly following the cotton industry along the road to complete mechanisation. Now the other side of the British–American controversy was used as an argument. Again and again the point was made that those who were denouncing conditions in America were actively involved in creating worse conditions at home. The argument was stressed, with a fine flurry of italics, by a correspondent writing to the *Leeds Mercury:*

> The fact is true, thousands of our fellow-creatures and fellow-subjects, both male and female, the miserable inhabitants of a Yorkshire town, are this very moment existing in a state of slavery more horrid than are the victims of that hellish system, *colonial slavery.* These innocent creatures drawl out, unpitied, their short but miserable existence in a place famed for its professions of religious zeal, whose inhabitants are ever foremost in *professing* 'temperance' and 'reformation', and are stirring to outrun their neighbours in missionary exertions, and would fain send the Bible to the farthest corners of the globe; ay, in the very place where the anti-slavery fever rages most furiously, her apparent *charity* is not more admired on earth than her real *cruelty* is abhorred in heaven. The very streets which receive the droppings of an 'Anti-Slavery Society' are every morning wet by the tears of the innocent victims of avarice, who are *compelled*, not by the cart-whip of the negro slave-driver, but by the dread of the equally appalling thong or strap of the overseer, to hasten, half-dressed, but not *half-fed*, to those maga-zines of British infantile slavery – *the worsted mills in the town and neighbourhood of Bradford!*[8]

The result of the Parliamentary investigations could be read in the Blue Books, which brought out the worst of the conditions and displayed them to the public gaze. Legislation followed, aimed specifically at reducing the hours that children could work and the age at which they could start work. It was less effective than it might have been, as so few inspectors were appointed that the law could be, and was, evaded. Where employers did keep to the strict letter, the results were not always those envisaged by the law makers. Remnants of the family unit of domestic manufacture had survived into the factory age. Now, with the hours the children worked reduced, but the hours that the adults worked unaltered, the family unit was finally broken. The children worked shifts which no longer coincided with those of their parents, and the way was open to fresh abuses. And all the time, the pattern of employment was changing. More factories meant more and more operatives, but increasingly these were women and children, not adult males. As one contemporary put it, in a magnificent euphemism, there was a 'diminution in the more expensive class of operatives'.[9]

The legislature gradually brought in its rules, and throughout the nineteenth century there was a general easing of conditions in the textile mills. This was largely due to a feeling of greater ease and comfort among the employers and the country's rulers. When the Chartist movement was at its height, culminating in the great general strike of 1842, the revolutions that convulsed continental Europe were much in the rulers' minds. The mass of the people were lumped together as The Poor; fundamentally inferior, but potentially a dangerous mob. By the 1860s, the revolutionary threat seemed to have receded, and it became quite respectable at least to talk of giving these people a say in the government of their country. Similarly, in the textile industry the rush to capitalise on new inventions subsided. Employers found their profits established, and comfortably established at that, and were prepared to accept limitations to the hours that small children worked, such as those dictated by the Ten Hour Act of 1847, with few murmurings.

Among the workers too there were inevitable changes. By mid-century, there were few left who could remember any alternative way of life or the days of the old domestic system. The factory was firmly established, and memories of independence faded. But if memories of the past receded, memories of the ways in which change had been wrought proved to have bitten deeper into the collective consciousness. Disraeli spoke of Two Nations, rich and poor, but the divisions went deeper than that. Even if the economic gap narrowed, those on either side of the divide saw themselves as opponents. The process of industrialisation had been pushed through without regard for the individual worker, or even the great mass of workers. Trust was the first victim of the industrial revolution. Both sides of industry – the very language is that of division – developed their own attitudes. Employers saw workers as an input, a commodity to be got as cheaply as possible, just as the raw cotton was an input to be bargained over. Employees viewed wage increases as something that could never be obtained except by struggle, so that employers must look for any concessions they might want as being part of the same fight. Improvements in methods and machines might seem to an outsider to be very much to the advantage of everyone in the industry, but to the protagonists they were simply weapons to be used in the war over wages and conditions. Industrial relations were conducted with bitterness, even, on occasions, with violence. The concept of moving towards a common goal scarcely existed. Legislation had tempered the conditions, but had left the fundamental hostility untouched.

There was, however, a clearly-discernible improvement in conditions. The changes were dearly bought, but they were real. Society was on the move. Turning back across the Atlantic, the opposite appeared to be true. All was static. The slaves had no hopes of altering their own lives. They could only look for help from outside their ranks. There would be no assistance from the users of the cotton which was grown with their labour. However vehement the protestations against slavery might be, there was no appreciable movement to ban slave-grown cotton. There was not even any serious attempt to begin looking for alternative sources to develop for some future date. There was certainly no hope of finding a sudden change of heart among the planters. When change did come, it was to come through a bitter and bloody war.

In 1860, Abraham Lincoln was elected President of the United States. The South began to see her economic interests increasingly subordinated to those of the North. Two systems were in conflict, with slavery as only the most obvious mark of those differences. The slavery issue gave the conflict a moral element, but was never at the root of it. In December 1860, South Carolina announced its secession from the Union. In February 1861, Carolina was joined by six other states to form the Confederated States of America. Was America to be a loose confederation of states each maintaining its individual rights or an indissoluble union? The issue was to be decided on the battlefield.

The defence of Fort Sumpter where the American Civil War began.

Civil War

If ever the mutual dependence of the American South and Lancashire needed proving, that proof was supplied in the Civil War. As the South fought, Lancashire starved. It was the great turning point in the history of cotton.

As war began, the South immediately found itself faced with a blockade. Cotton shipments – apart from those on the few ships that managed to break through – virtually ended. The Confederacy had high hopes of British intervention on their side, as the effects were felt in Lancashire and other cotton districts. Southern propagandists set out their case to the British, largely through a pro-Confederate newspaper, *Index*. Their hopes soon collapsed. War can mean profits as well as losses. The effect on cotton may have been disastrous, but elsewhere British trade boomed. With American traders otherwise engaged, British maritime trade, which had been feeling the competition, prospered. Armament manufacturers and the metal trades as a whole had all the work they could handle. Even the textile manufacturers were able to salvage some profits by raising the prices on stocks they already had and on what they could produce with cotton from other sources. The unhappy operatives had no other resources: they felt the full weight of the disaster. Figures tell the story. Just consider these statistics for the cotton industry in Lancashire in the last week of November 1861 and the same week in 1862:

	1861	1862
Average weekly consumption of cotton (400-lb. bales)	49,000	18,000
Operatives working full-time	583,950	121,129
Operatives working short-time	–	165,600
Operatives out of work	–	247,230
Estimated loss of wages (weekly)	–	£169,744[1]

Here is a story of real hardship, but Britain was not about to go to war on behalf of unemployed cotton workers, even if there were a quarter of a million of them. There was, in any case, little sympathy for the Southern cause, except among the anti-democratic elements of society, but quite a lot for the North. The attitudes were neatly encapsulated in some of the popular ballads of the day. This ballad indignantly denounced the Unionists who had attacked a British merchantman attempting to run the Southern blockade:

> What did the valiant Yankee mean by manner so offensive
> To stop our craft upon the sea that had no force defensive?
> I tell you why: the quarrel for the everlasting Nigger
> Made Northern states 'gainst Southern states pull fratricidal trigger.
> The Southerners had hated long the Northern knavery
> Which spurn'd the name, but lov'd the gain, of woolly slavery.[2]

The bombardment of Fort Sumpter.

A rather different view was given in this ballad by 'A Factory Girl':

> ... hence it is that we
> Lack cotton to employ our industry;
> And cotton failing, causes work to fail,
> And labour is the poor man's capital.
> To be deprived of labour is to be
> Plunged in the depths of want and poverty:
> But can it be that free-born Britains have
> Depended on the labour of the slave?
> Yes! So supplies of cotton were assured,
> They cared but little how they were procured;
> So they had cotton, cared not tho' it were
> Stain'd with the blood of slaves, nor did they care,
> Tho', on the hands that pick'd it, there should be
> The galling chains of hateful slavery.[3]

If this was in any way typical of the attitudes among the unemployed of Lancashire then they were quite astonishing in their selflessness, for their suffering was great. A visitor from London toured the district, recording what he saw.[4] In Stockport, for example, he found a woman living in one of the mean, single-storeyed courtyard houses. Everything had been sold except the bed and its covering and her cooking pots. Her five children were with her but not her husband. He had obtained 9s and 11d worth of provisions on credit, and when he was unable to pay the debt he had been thrown into gaol. The visitor asked if she did not get any relief:

> 'Yes, Sir, I do, and very thankful I am for it; but I have only 3s 6d a week, and what is that? In good times my master used to make £1 to £1 5s a week, and then we thought we could only just live but now see what we have come to!'

Everywhere he went he found the most appalling poverty, yet the operatives he visited answered his questions, however impertinent, politely and cheerfully. At one house he was received kindly and only afterwards did he learn that the woman had just returned from burying her child. 'Do you think they are sustained in their trials by dependence upon Providence?' he asked in amazement. 'Or does their resignation result from sheer insensibility?' Luckily for him, he had left the district before he posed that question. He found the same story everywhere. Some families had sold everything and moved in to join friends in already overcrowded houses to save on rent. Many were helped by local traders, who allowed almost unlimited credit. Others, especially butchers, simply went out of business themselves and began sinking towards the poverty of their former customers.

There was much bitterness over the failure of the mill owners to help. In wealthy Preston, for example, less than £2000 was raised for the relief funds, and only forty-eight out of the seventy-one mills contributed anything at all. The greatest bitterness, however, was reserved for the Labour Test. The poor who applied for relief had to show their willingness to work. Men who were indoor workers, badly clothed and close to starvation, were sent out in mid-winter on jobs such as stone breaking. It was not merely cruel – in some cases it proved fatal.

Sermons were preached in the churches and chapels of Lancashire, though some offered little beyond pious platitudes. The preacher who began 'Everyone has heard of the terrible distress which God in His infinite wisdom has allowed to fall on our manufacturing population' can have done little to restore the faith of the unemployed in a benevolent providence. Others were more practical, demanding national relief for the sorrows of Lancashire:

The operatives suffer then in consequence of a national policy; therefore the relief of that suffering should also be national. Not, perhaps, if they had denounced that policy – if they had raised disturbances on account of it; if they had said, 'it is better to violate a principle of the international law of England than that we should starve.' But they have not said so: they have remained quiet; they have even fully concurred in that policy with an unanimity which is astonishing. The Government of the country owe a deep debt of gratitude to the quietude of Lancashire.[5]

That preacher looked at the fortitude of the unemployed, and did not see insensibility. He summed up his attitude in one, fine ringing phrase: 'To Lancashire we should give with pride, as to one who has honoured us, and who was noble in ruin.'

There was some relief offered by central government, but they still insisted that it was tied to the need to make work. Robert Rawlinson, the civil engineer, was given the job of seeing what could be done in the way of public works – paving streets, laying drains and creating public parks.[6] It was a cumbersome system. Rawlinson had to make his findings known to the local authorities, who then had to apply for a Government loan and then, if that was granted, the business of relieving poverty could begin. Even then it

182   *Public relief hand-outs for Lancashire cotton operatives.*

came a long way short of what was required. Because of the insistence of tying relief to work, of the estimated million and a half pounds available, more than a million had to be spent on materials – leaving only £400,000 for actual wages. But, as Rawlinson pointed out, the work generated employment among suppliers and subsidiary trades. And at least the work did have a useful end product – unlike most of the work handed out under the Poor Law. In a report of November 1864, he estimated that there were over six thousand directly employed and another two thousand finding subsidiary work. It was something, but set against the quarter of a million unemployed it was precious little. Private charity helped to pad out the meagre Government relief, but what was really needed was work, and work needed cotton. Lancashire was discovering the truth of what many had been saying for a long time – that it was dangerous to rely on one source. The Cotton Supply Association was set up and began to cast about for alternative sources.

There was only one obvious direction for Britain to turn: eastward back to the origins of the cotton trade – to India. One pamphlet, produced at the beginning of the war, managed with great economy to incorporate most of its argument into its title: *Be Just to India; Prevent Famine and Cherish Commerce.*[7] Old arguments were rehearsed and there was the now familiar condemnation of British policy which had allowed the supply of Indian cotton to fall to less than 10 per cent of the total used in Britain. Why did India not produce more? Everyone had an answer. Mr Mangles, a former Chairman of the East India Company, had his firm ideas on the subject: 'I have made the largest admissions with reference to the want of roads, which, I say, is the only real obstacle to the exportation of cotton in large quantities from India.'[8] There was certainly ample evidence of bad roads. An Indian civil servant described a journey of twelve miles which took seven hours of continuous, painful jolting: 'On his way, the *mamlutdar* amused us with several stories of accidents which had occurred on this road, one of which is related to the sad fate of a *banian*, or trader, who received such a jolt as to make him inadvertently bite the end of his tongue off.'[9]

Some improvements were made in roads, and new roads were designed and built specifically to serve the cotton regions; but the work went on slowly and fitfully and had little real impact on India's transport problems. The answer was widely felt to lie not with these roads but with railroads. The first great propagandist for railway construction was Lord Dalhousie, Governor General from 1848 to 1856. His dream was not primarily concerned with trade, but rather he planned a network of trunk routes to join the major cities of the coast with those of the interior. The plan was to be broad in concept and broad of gauge, for Dalhousie took evidence from Britain of the

The first train running on the Bombay to Thana line, India's first railway, in 1853.

relative merits of Stephenson's standard 4 ft 8½ in gauge and Brunel's 7 ft gauge and opted for compromise: a 5 ft 6 in gauge. The first companies, the East India Railway and the Indian Peninsular Railway, were formed in 1845, capital being raised on a curious guarantee system. The Government gave investors a guaranteed return of 3 per cent (which was soon raised to 5 per cent) on their investment, regardless of whether the railways made a profit or loss. Furthermore, the original investors had what amounted to a cash-back guarantee should they choose to sell up. As the Government could have borrowed the money from the banks at a lower rate of interest – and as none of the railways was to show a profit for some time – this was good value for shareholders but a pretty poor scheme for the Government. Nevertheless it was a start, and a certain amount of money came in from Lancashire investors, encouraged by a failure of the American cotton crop in 1846. Dalhousie himself was well aware where the Lancashire investors' interests lay. He wrote in April 1853:

> I know that the English sultocracy intend to endow India with railways with the exclusive view of extracting at diminished expense the cotton and other raw materials of their manufactures.[10]

Inevitably the Indian Mutiny brought railway construction to a temporary halt, and when work resumed without the inducement of the guaranteed return, the funds were notably less forthcoming. A Bombay merchant expressed his disgust in the *Daily News* in May 1861:

> It is a remarkable fact that though the Manchester interest has been constantly urging on government the duty of their developing the country, it has nevertheless entirely withheld its pecuniary support from the railway undertakings which were the first and most important step towards effecting this object.[11]

Yet the railways were built and the port of Bombay was connected to the cotton fields of the interior. This was an immense undertaking, for it involved pushing a line through the massive range of cliffs and ravines of the Western Ghats. Lord Elphinstone of the East India Company had prophesied that the passage of the Ghats would not be achieved without many casualties. 'Every possible means must be taken to lessen the risk – but it would be idle to expect that ... we should overcome the physical difficulties which we have to confront in making railroads in such a country as India without heavy sacrifice of human life.'[12] His words were to prove all too well founded. The men faced difficult terrain, attacks from wild animals and, in the rainy season, an atrocious climate. In the monsoons of 1859–60 all work was halted among the thirty thousand labourers, as cholera struck at some ten thousand of their number. But the work was completed by 1865. Further progress was to come with the realisation that railways would also help to provide a solution to the regular famines that afflicted India in the 1870s. The new lines were built as metre gauge – producing just that mixture of gauges Dalhousie had hoped to avoid.

Other critics of India's cotton production looked at the shortcomings of the East India Company, who collected rents from the land but who failed to use the money where it was most needed, in irrigation. In fact, they had actually made matters worse by failing to maintain the irrigation systems that were already there. In Poona, for example, in the years 1849–51, £185 was set aside out of a revenue of £80,500; in Belgum, £75 out of £125,000; and

The dockside in Bombay with cotton bales piled high, c. 1900.

Sholopoor was worst of all, spending nothing whatsoever. Yet in the Madras Presidency, £54,000 had been spent, bringing in £414,000 in revenue.[13]

The response by the Government was immediate, though actual development was slow. As the role of the East India Company in governing India finally ended in 1858, so a new irrigation programme was begun, including the construction of the Sirhind canal in the Punjab, which was to be the beginning of a canal network in the region that was to turn a semi-desert into a rich cotton-growing area. But such schemes take time to develop, and there were still the urgent problems to be solved – how to get more cotton from India to Europe, and cotton of the right quality.

Hand picking cotton in India.

Most commentators agreed that the root of the quality problem lay where it had always done, in the land tenure system. The cultivators, the *ryots*, were permanently in debt to the middlemen, the *usurers*, and both were preoccupied with a scramble to find ready cash to pay British taxes. So, the old difficulties remained. The cotton that was sent to Britain was poor quality, adulterated with poorer. The Cotton Fraud Act of 1863 imposed heavy penalties on anyone caught adulterating cotton or using unlicensed gins: but as the choice lay between possible prosecution under the act or certain punishment for non-payment of taxes, there was little practical difference. It was not this sort of legislation that was needed, but a whole change in attitude. What was needed was money for long-term investment.

There was no shortage of voices in favour of British investment:

The immense field that is open for the employment of European capital in India has never yet been conceived by capitalists at home. There are fortunes to be made in India with far greater facility than can be commanded in a country where every profession and every trade is overstocked. Without competing or attempting to compete with the native producer of the raw material, it would make the fortune of any man who, with a few thousand pounds of capital, would set up improved steam-worked machinery wherewith to clean cotton thoroughly up the country, and to screw it into bales for shipment to England at once.[14]

Nineteenth-century gins still in use at Karjan, Gujarat.

As Civil War in America became at first a threat and then a reality, so the clamour for investment in India became more insistent. The Manchester Cotton Company was formed with plans to raise a million pounds: by July 1862, they had just a little over £40,000. But they were able to collect enough cash to buy cleaning and pressing machinery which was duly despatched. Unfortunately, a promised new pier and new road in India were scarcely begun, and the expensive machines were left to rust on the beach. The scheme came to nothing – not one pound of cotton was ever brought to Lancashire by the Manchester company.

Yet there was a genuine surge of interest in extending and improving India's cotton supply, encouraged in large measure by the extraordinarily high prices that could be obtained throughout the Civil War years. *The Times of India* was crammed with advertisements for ginning machinery of which this, of 23 April 1862, is typical:

> All persons interested in machinery for separating cotton from the seed are invited to inspect the Patent Improved machinery for that purpose by Platt Brothers & Co., to be seen at the office of the undersigned, who is prepared to receive orders for the same.

The orders came in and venerable Platt gins are still to be seen at work in the cotton-growing districts of India.

The Indian growers began a period of unprecedented prosperity, and, in spite of all the shortcomings, they were able to do a great deal to plug the gap left by American cotton. Average imports of Indian cotton into Britain for the five years from 1855–60 ran at 192 million pounds per annum; in the next five years they more than doubled to 430 million pounds. But in spite of all the successes that could be shown, there was still a lack of faith in the long-term prospects for India. The men of Manchester were never convinced that this was more than a stop-gap measure. The war, they argued, could not last for ever and once it was over things would be as they were; old relationships would be re-established and everything would return to normal. In this they were proved to be entirely mistaken. Nothing was ever to be quite the same again.

Sampling cotton from bales stacked in the warehouse, c. 1872, by J. L. Kipling.

Aftermath

16

No one in the South ever doubted that defeat would mean changes that would encompass far more than the end of slavery. It had been a bloody and costly conflict and there was a price to be paid by a region already devastated by the passage of war. For the war itself had been fought entirely in the South: great cities such as Atlanta and Charleston had been laid waste; plantations had been destroyed; bales had been used to build barricades and cotton rotted in the fields. A cotton tax was imposed, and Government agents sent south to collect it. They were empowered to buy and sell cotton so as to pass on the tax, working on a commission basis. Many bought the cotton for themselves at artificially low prices, passed on the Government share and then resold at the true market value, pocketing the difference. Secretary Hugh McCulloch in Washington remarked that 'I am sure I sent *some* honest agents south; but it sometimes seems very doubtful whether any of them remained honest very long.'[1] The tax was estimated to have cost the planters some $68 million. The carpetbaggers who invaded the South in the years immediately following the war did little to help, and nor did those Northerners who bought up plantations in the belief that they then had only to sit on a verandah with a mint julep, counting the profits.

There were numerous tasks facing the Southerners who wished to rebuild the plantation system, and they often began from a very insecure financial base. Many planters had committed themselves to the war effort, and now all that they had left was worthless Confederate money and equally worthless Confederate bonds. Worst of all, in Southern eyes, the greatest capital asset that the plantations had possessed was removed from them overnight. The slaves were free. To the South, millions of dollars worth of property had been taken from them with no compensation whatsoever; to the North it was simply a case of the South being forced to acknowledge that man never could be counted as property to be bought and sold. To have paid compensation would have been to accept that a human being had a cash value in the first place. It was the one inevitable result of the war, but it was only now plain just how far the system had depended on the trading in human beings for its viability.

All these problems, great as they were, had recognisable dimensions. Debts could be paid and the land was still there. Given time, crops would grow again and prosperity could be rebuilt, however slowly. Other problems were less tractable. The South had built a mythology of 'the faithful slave'. The war revealed it for what it was. Slaves had 'deserted to the enemy', leaving the planters feeling both bewildered and betrayed:

> With us upon Savannah River, my favourite Board Hand, a Man who had rowed me to and from Savannah from my earliest recollections of Gowrie plantation ... a Negro we all of us esteemed highly. Singular to

191

say, this man 'Hector' was the very first to murmur, and would have hastened to the embrace of his Northern Brtheren, could he have forseen the least prospect of a successful escape.[2]

The planters who had prided themselves on their paternal attitudes towards the slaves now, in their rage, often turned them away penniless with nothing but the clothes on their backs. Other blacks took the decision for themselves. Not surprisingly, they headed off for the towns, eager to enjoy a taste of freedom. They were in no great rush to exchange total slavery for any new kind of subjection to their old masters. But, however reluctant the two sides were to renew acquaintance, some sort of relationship had to be cobbled together. Slave owner and slave tried to adapt to new roles as employer and employee.

The old plantation could not simply be converted into a new model. The most obvious system to move towards was that in which the field hands

192   *Charleston in ruins at the end of the Civil War.*

were paid in wages, but here the great difficulty to be overcome was shortage of cash. Money wages in the South as a whole plummeted from an average of nearly $140 a year in 1860 to $100 in 1868, and in many cases there was no money available at all until the crops were sold. Owners offered contracts to their labourers, specifying payments at the end of the season – but the blacks had no faith in their former masters' promises and no understanding of legal documents. Many plantations developed a system whereby gangs of workers under black overseers were given the means to live, occupied the former slave quarters and were offered a share in the crop. But that was too redolent of the old days and the old ways. Gangs broke up into family units and the families dismantled the old shacks and rebuilt them close to their own particular part of the plantation. The monumental structure of house and quarters with surrounding fields was broken down into what had become, in effect, a patchwork of smallholdings. From being a land of planters, the South was becoming a country of landowners and tenant farmers.

The tenants could be divided into three categories. At the top of the ladder were those who paid a regular cash rent for the land and then farmed it, providing all the necessities for farming out of their own funds and living on whatever profits were made. Slightly lower down the scale were those who, unable to raise the capital for a cash rent, paid their way by handing over a portion of the crop to the landlord. At the bottom were the former slaves who started with nothing – no home, no equipment, no seed and no money. Here the owners supplied the materials for farming and kept the families provided with the necessities of life until the harvest came round and the crops were sold. A share of the crops was handed over as rent and the year's accumulation of debts generally accounted for the remainder. In many cases when the entire crop was gone some part of the debt still remained. The tenant started the new year as he had begun the last, in debt, and the cycle began all over again. There was no escape from this ring of debt, and those who attempted to run away were hunted down and considered fortunate if they avoided a lynching. In effect, the landlord was hiring labourers and paying them in kind instead of cash, while binding them to their holdings as surely as slavery had ever done.

The black tenants were often given the best land, such as that of the Mississippi delta, yet, not surprisingly, they made little of it. With so little incentive, few prospered and crop yields were low. But it suited the owner well enough. He was getting his work done at rock bottom prices, and so he favoured the black tenants. No one else, as one planter noted, 'would be as cheerful, or so contented on four pounds of meat, and a peck of meal a week, in a little log-cabin 14 × 16 feet, with cracks in it large enough to afford free passage to a large sized cat.'[3]

A Share-cropper's cabin.

The 'cheerful' victims of this new system were the share-croppers who were to typify one aspect of the new South. Not all share-croppers were black, for there was still a large poor white population. But, as in slavery days, they could not be brought to work under the same system as the blacks. So they were left to farm the poorest lands, scratching what they could out of the thin soils of the hills, and only working in the richer lands of the plains when they could obtain some suitable rank, such as overseer on one of the few remaining large plantations. Poor white and poor black were still divided by the colour of their skins: it was to be a long time before some came to appreciate that they were also joined in poverty.

By 1880, cotton production was back to pre-war levels, even though the social life of the producers had undergone a major revolution. Changes were also felt within the manufacturing sphere. Many Northern mill owners had been prepared for the war, having bought heavily in the immediate pre-war years and having arranged for their cotton supplies to arrive by railroad through Ohio rather than through the Gulf ports. Nevertheless, there was cotton famine in New England just as there had been in Lancashire. The more prudent owners did what they could to keep their mills going. Some turned to spinning cotton waste to produce a coarse thread and found it a remarkably profitable trade. Others used their time to modernise the mills. Some simply closed up shop. In April 1861, the directors of the Merrimack Manufacturing Company of Lowell, Massachusetts, sold off their cotton stocks at, it must be said, a handsome profit, to other New England mills. Ten thousand Lowell operatives were simply turned out on to the streets. Charles Cowley, the historian of Lowell, writing shortly after the war, had no doubts about the implications of the decision:

> This crime, this worse than crime, this *blunder*, entailed its own punish-ment, – as all crimes do by the immutable law of God. When these companies resumed operations, their former skilled operatives were dispersed, and could no more be recalled than the Ten Lost Tribes of Israel. Their places were filled by the less skilled operatives whom the companies now had to employ. So serious was this blunder, that the smallest of the companies would have done wisely, had they sacrificed a hundred thousand dollars, rather than thus lose their accustomed help.[4]

For Lowell it marked the final stop to the story of the New England mill girls. When the mills reopened the immigrant population filled every vacancy.

At first it seemed that there would soon be a return to normality and the New England manufacturers began to expand as the flow of cotton was resumed. New mills were built and spinning capacity in the North went up 12 per cent between 1868 and 1870. But change was on the way as manufac-turers also began to look towards the South. There had been a small element in the South before the war (see Chapter 9), but it had always proved difficult to run a factory system within the context of a slave economy. Now that obstacle was removed, and new arguments appeared in favour of mill construction in the South. First, there was the social argument. There was a major problem over providing employment for the poor whites, who could not be prevailed upon to accept farm work on any basis that would equate them with the poor blacks. Mill building was also seen as part of the whole programme of Southern reconstruction, designed to integrate the Southern states into the main framework of American life. This view was forcibly expressed by Francis W. Dawson who wrote in 1880 that bringing the whites to mill work introduced them 'to elevating social influences, encourages them to seek education, and improves them in every conceivable respect.'[5] He also boasted of the economic gains to the community, quoting figures to show that South Carolina had 2296 operatives, upon whom 7913 persons were dependent for support, from a monthly wages bill of $38,034. As this represents a monthly wages bill of just over $16 per worker or, if you include all those dependents, less than a dollar per person per week, then it does not look over-generous. Dawson also reported that company profits were running at between 18 to 25½ per cent per annum. Whether philanthropy or profit ranked highest as a motive among those who invested in Southern mills must now be a matter for speculation. But some at least of those who moved south were quite honest in describing their motives. Lockwood Greene and Co. had this to say about their decision to move south:

An idealised view of the new Southern cotton industry of the post-war years.

As compared to New England and the Northeastern part of the country, the South has the advantage of longer hours of labor, lower wage scales, lower taxes, and legislation which gives a manufacturing plant a wider latitude than is usually possible in the North in the way of running over-time and at night. ..... the South is ... fortunate in having a supply of native American labor which is still satisfied to work at a low wage.[6]

The organisation of Southern mills very much followed the pattern established in the ante-bellum years, a pattern of paternalism. The company would provide – but in providing they came remarkably close to the old truck system that had obtained in some British mills in the early nineteenth century. Mill hands were tied to their jobs by bills run up at the mill commissary, just as share-croppers were tied to their holdings. The hand-outs of paternalism were given to counter-balance the effects of long hours and low wages. The programme succeeded only because it existed against a background of general poverty and deprivation. But succeed it did: families came down from the hills to camp out on the site of a new mill, waiting for

The reality: a little girl operative stands between rows of ring-spinning machines in a North Carolina mill.

197

jobs to be supplied and company houses to be built. In 1860 there had been some ten thousand employees in the Southern cotton mills, but by 1890 the figure had quadrupled. And the conditions for growth were improving.

America was entering a new period of expansion. The railways were thrusting their lines westward, and in 1869 the east and west coasts were joined. New floods of immigrants came in, reaching half a million a year by 1873, and all of them needing to be clothed – half a million new customers. And the opening up of the West also opened a route to the Far East, a new line of trade. It seemed to make less and less sense to view the American South as no more than a supplier of raw material for the mills of Lancashire. Increasingly it was seen as a supplier for the mills of the South. A new society was being built and though the process was to be long and often painful, there was to be no returning to the old ways.

Britain was slow to recognise the growing threat to her old dominance, just as manufacturers were slow to recognise the need to improve on the machinery developed in the first rush of inventive energy in the eighteenth century. Cotton spinning was still divided between the throstle, an adaptation of Arkwright's water frame to the use of steam power, and the mule. They had worked well, still did work well and had led to a century of profitable enterprise. So why should they not continue to work well? There was little excitement evident when John Thorp of Providence, Rhode Island, took out a patent for a new spinning machine, the ring frame. This used rollers to extend the yarn but twist was now delivered and the thread wound on by a 'traveller' moving round a ring set over the bobbin. It was a continuous process for stretching, twisting and winding on the yarn and far faster in operation than earlier machines. True, it was some time before it was perfected and the thread was somewhat inferior to that from the mules, but the British seemed to have lost their eagerness for exploring new inventions. This lack of enterprise was to be one of the factors which led towards the decline. The other main factor was the shift in old, traditional markets.

Once the Civil War was over, Britain dropped India as quickly as she had taken her up at the beginning of the cotton famine. Rather than seeing the war years as grim evidence of the effects of overdue reliance on one source of raw material under the control of a foreign power, they chose to see it as little more than an unfortunate interruption to the natural flow of events. India had served a purpose and now things could be allowed to return to normal. The strings of empire could again be manipulated to make India dance to the British tune. The puppet, however, was to prove to have a will of its own. It declined to perform.

It was by no means immediately apparent that any decisive shift had occurred. Indeed, first signs suggested quite the opposite. The price of cotton tumbled as American supplies were resumed and by 1872 exports to

Britain were down to a mere two-thirds of what they had been at the height of the war. Fortunes had been made in those years, the likes of which the Indian cotton trade had never seen before and, as is always the case, those who invested their quick gains foolishly crumbled into bankruptcy with the fall in prices, while those who had shown more prudence used their gains to advantage. The decline in sales to Lancashire did not mean that cotton could not be sold elsewhere. If India was no longer to be the major supplier of the raw material, then Britain no longer dominated the manufacturing world as she had done at the beginning of the century. The rest of Europe was beginning to take a leading role in the textile world and India's position was greatly improved with the opening of the Suez Canal in 1869, with its promise of faster and cheaper transport. Harry Rivett-Carnak, the Cotton Commissioner for the Central Provinces, noted the trend in his report for 1868–69:

> I have been very much struck with the direct trade in cotton between India and the Continent. Last year a French house in Bombay headed the list of shippers from that port. This year the number of foreign mercantile houses has largely increased. A French house has purchased land, and set up full presses in the Berars, and there appears to be a determination in France to deal direct with India for her cotton.[7]

Other European countries were also increasing their trade, and a new customer appeared in the East that was to take an ever-increasing share in the world of cotton, Japan.

Once the shock of the price collapse had died away, there was more or less a return to normality in the Indian cotton field, but with one important difference. The various works of improvement in transport and irrigation that had been begun in the war years were not allowed just to grind to a halt. They had shown their worth and had played their part in another war – the battle against famine. India might not be able to compete on equal terms with America, but matters were improving. There remained, however, the apparently insurmountable obstacle of the social system that kept the peasant farmers in permanent debt, unable to afford the necessary improvements to their holdings that would bring higher yields and better quality. Authority seemed to feel that it was none of their business, and would have presumably been content to ignore the problems of the peasants had the peasants not acted for themselves. In 1875 there was a widespread uprising against the money lenders: promissory notes and mortgages were simply taken away and destroyed. The revolt was soon quelled but at least authority was now forced to take an interest in the matter. New and better ways of financing the small farmer were clearly necessary, and one likely method was through the forming of co-operative societies of farmers which could raise funds to provide credit for the members. Deliberations were not speedy and it was 1904 before the first Co-operative Credit Societies Act was passed. It was a modest beginning, but it was to have a profound effect on the future.

One effect of the American Civil War had been to bring a great deal of money into India. In the first excitement of sudden wealth, many sank their funds into a variety of preposterous enterprises which collapsed as quickly as they rose. Among the rubble of fallen schemes a few were seen to be left standing, and among these were cotton mills. Such mills were not necessarily new. There had been early experiments – though not especially successful – in Pondicherry and Calcutta, but real progress began to be made when entre-preneurs started looking at opportunities on the West Coast. One of the earliest of these was an Indian merchant, Ranchhodal Chatalal. He had the money to invest but absolutely no knowledge of industry, as he candidly acknowledged when he wrote to England in 1848 on behalf of his consortium, asking for quotes for building and supervising a mill:

> These native gentlemen being totally unacquainted with machinery, either theoretically or practically, it becomes a matter of the greatest importance to them, when embarking in such an undertaking, that they should possess a guarantee that the machinery supplied will perform all that it is stated to be capable to do.[8]

That plan came to nothing, but at much the same time an Englishman, James Landon, had arrived in India to take over the running of the Cotton Experiments Centre which the East India Company had established in Broach. He went on to make a fortune and ran his own steam-powered gin. In 1851, he was approached by Ranchhodal, who proposed a partnership to establish a mill at Broach to spin cotton from the surrounding districts of Gujarat. They failed to agree terms and it was eventually Landon who went on to found the Broach Cotton Mill which began work in 1855. Ranchhodal went on to create the important Ahmedabad industry, whilst the Parsee merchant Cowarjee Davar established the even more important Bombay Mills.

The mill industry was well established, if only in a modest way, when investors began looking for new opportunities in the 1870s. Some money was available and, just as importantly, following the improvements in agriculture and the decline in the British market, cotton was available for spinning. The 1870s saw a mill boom centred on Bombay. At the beginning of the decade there were eighteen mills, by 1875 there were thirty-six and by the end of the seventies the number had risen to forty-two. By then, cotton

Power looms in a mill in Baroda, Gujarat.

textile manufacture was by far the biggest industry in India, employing over forty thousand mill workers.

From the start, India faced hostility from Manchester. British textiles came into India on very low tariffs – a source of constant complaint from the Indian authorities who suffered from a chronic shortage of revenue. Indian textiles, on the other hand, were heavily taxed when sent in the opposite direction. Attempts to obtain more favourable terms for India brought out one factor very clearly. India was being ruled for the benefit of Britain. Sometimes this fact was hidden, but some at least were honest enough to admit it with complete frankness. Sir John Strachey, the Minister of Finance, had this to say in his financial statement of 15 March 1877:

> We are often told that it is the duty of the Government of India to think of Indian interests alone, and that if the interests of Manchester suffer, it is no interest of ours. For my part, I utterly repudiate such doctrines. I have not ceased to be an Englishman because I have passed the greater part of my life in India and have been a member of the Indian Government ... though I have duties to India there is no higher duty in my opinion, than that which I owe to my country.

201

It was not an attitude likely to help Indian manufacturers – nor one likely to endear them to British rule.

Nevertheless, India continued to make headway, largely through an intensive programme of modernisation. In 1883, the first experiments were made with the use of ring frames – a development still largely ignored in Britain. The results were highly satisfactory and orders were sent to the famous Lancashire machine manufacturers, Platts. They refused to supply the Indian market, but Howard and Bullough of Accrington proved more accommodating. India was now able to compete in international markets, especially China.

This was inevitably viewed with extreme distaste in Lancashire, where the mill owners who had throughout the nineteenth century fought every attempt to improve the lot of the mill workers through legislation, now discovered a social conscience. They railed against the poor working conditions and low wages paid in Bombay, without mentioning the end product of low prices. It was an exercise in self-interest, yet the enquiry in Bombay did show up conditions little different from those that had prevailed during the darkest years of the industrial revolution in Britain. Here is James Cocker, a mill manager, from Bombay:

> Of course there is no lighting up in Bombay. There is no gas. The daylight there is very little different to what it is here, winter and summer taken together, but it is more equally divided. The consequence is that we start our mills in the height of summer, in the long days, about a quarter-past five in the morning, and close about ten minutes to seven at night. We allow half an hour out of this for the hands to have their food.
>
> *Do you stop the mill?*
> Yes. It is called half an hour, but in a great many cases it is reduced to twenty minutes, or even a quarter of an hour. The Factory Act is null and void there.
>
> *Is that for the day?*
> Yes. The hands there have no system of regular meals, as we have. They get their breakfast all hours, from seven to eleven, while dinner lasts from one till four o'clock. You will never go through the mill without finding some one, behind the mule gate, or in the carding room, eating. ... In winter time we commence at about twenty minutes past six in the morning, and we run until twenty to six at night. I am giving you the longest and the shortest time. The average working day is $12\frac{1}{4}$ hours, Sundays as well. We reckon to stop every other Sunday for cleaning purposes, but that is not a hard and fast rule – far from it. To explain myself fully: supposing, we will say, that the engine has something to

do with it any day in the week prior to the Stopping Sunday – say it breaks down on Thursday – and there would be a necessary stoppage of two hours to repair it, the consequence is that instead of stopping two hours only they would stop half the day and set the hands to clean – working all the next Sunday. We work about 80 hours per week.

What holidays have you besides those odd Sundays?

Nine full days in Bombay and two half days. I have made a kind of diary ... We should, as I said, have stopped every other Sunday, but, as showing the extent to which we actually do it, we only stopped eleven Sundays during 1887, and then three out of the eleven were stopped simply because we were forced to stop, because the engine broke down.[9]

It would seem on this evidence that India was to do no more than repeat the history of industrialisation in Britain. To some extent this was true, but in certain crucial areas the ways were sharply to divide. That, however, was not to happen until the twentieth century.

What then of Britain? What was happening in the world's first manufacturing society while these changes were convulsing societies to both east and west? The short answer must be – not a great deal. There was awareness that the rest of the world was stirring but there was a deal of complacency. Imperial preferences secured the markets of the empire for British goods, and there seemed little reason to believe that things would change. The great drive of inventiveness and expansion that had marked the years of the industrial revolution seemed spent. Where Britain had once relied on the lucrative export markets of Europe and America for the sale of her cotton piece goods, now she depended on the under-developed world and especially on India. In 1820 over 60 per cent of these goods went to Europe and America, while in 1880 the figure had dropped to less than 10 per cent, with the share to the under-developed world going up from 32 to 82 per cent in the same period.[10] Industry might appear healthy enough, expansionist even with decent profits, but in reality the rot was already nibbling into the fabric. Inefficiency was protected by empire and if empire were to go then nothing could stop the rot spreading. The American Civil War had brought more than local changes: the South would never again be a one-crop, purely agrarian society; and India was no longer content to accept a role determined by the interests of men in Manchester.

Immigrants, such as these girls from Lowell, worked for low wages in the Massachusetts mills, but still the industry moved south to even lower wages.

Full Circle

17

The cotton industry of the world is now a truly international business, no longer dominated as it was for so long by any one country or even any one region. Go into the most modern mill anywhere and you will find new machinery built and developed by different companies from different lands. Once the new ideas had been British: this ceased to be true in the nineteenth century when the Americans first introduced ring spinning. If we look at just two types of machine, one for spinning and one for weaving, we can see the new pattern. A British inventor, A. W. Metcalf, actually worked out a new spinning method which was patented in 1901 and is very similar to that used in the most modern machines of today – open-end spinning. This involves blowing the fibre along an airstream towards a very rapidly rotating cup. The fibres are layered in a groove of the rotor and as they are spun off, so they are twisted together. It is a highly-efficient machine, yet nothing was done with Metcalf's patent and it was not until 1960 that open-end spinning went into commercial use and then in Czechoslovakia. In weaving, it had long been recognised that a lot of time and effort went into pushing a heavy shuttle backwards and forwards across the loom and still more time was wasted in supplying the shuttle with weft. The modern automatic looms have a continuous supply of weft and the shuttle has disappeared completely to be replaced by one of two systems. In the first the thread is shot across the loom by a 'bullet' or 'gripper' which collects the yarn from the package and shoots it across the loom. The alternative uses 'rapiers' which shoot out from either side of the loom, one carrying the thread which is then collected by the second as they meet in the centre. Development and manufacture of these looms has been centred in Switzerland and America. Britain, the old innovating nation, has been left behind.

The British cotton industry, which was the mainspring of the world's first industrial revolution, has been winding down throughout the twentieth century. It might not have appeared that way at the beginning of the century when British mills still dominated the world scene, but now we see a rate of decline that has become a catastrophic collapse. Look at a photograph of any mill town in Lancashire at the turn of the century and you will see a forest of mill chimneys, each sending its portion to contribute to the pall of smoke that hung over the town. Visit that same town today and the chimneys have either gone or stand as little more than monuments to a dying industry. There is a cotton industry, but it is no more than a fraction of what it was.

The British cotton industry has always been an exporting industry. In the years before the First World War, the country was producing 8000 million yards of cloth of which 6900 million yards was exported, but everywhere the old, traditional markets were being assailed. The monopoly of the early years which had given Britain her leading role was ended, and

205

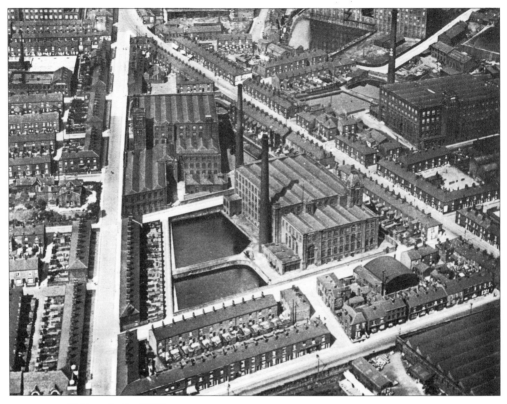

Oldham in the 1930s.

other countries were not merely supplying their own needs but were increasingly joining in the competition for overseas markets. They were doing so, what is more, using techniques and machinery that were often very efficient. The British industry in the early twentieth century was, to a remarkable degree, guilty of a smug complacency. It had always prospered, was prospering and, it was felt, would prosper. In the early 1920s, the years of high optimism that followed the end of the war, a great deal of money went into the cotton industry – not, as in other parts of the world, in development and improvement but in takeovers. There appears to be a curious pattern of alternation in economic thinking, between 'big is best' and 'small is beautiful'. These were the years of 'big'. Investors took over small textile companies in order to form 'more efficient units'. Unfortunately, the extra efficiency of the mergers seldom materialised. The investors, who often knew little if anything of textiles, failed to appreciate the fragmentary nature of the British industry. The small firms were often run by individuals in highly-individualistic fashion: they had found a way of working and their own corner of the market in which they could make a profit. Lumping a

Oldham today, with scarcely a mill in sight.

dozen such concerns together destroyed the old pattern and failed to put anything viable in its place. And all the time the opposition was getting stronger. Italy was taking an increased share of the Balkans market – helped by the take-up of the surplus supplies of raw material from India that had become available after the American Civil War. America itself, looking to its own factories and spread of industry in the South, was now changing from being an importer of cloth to being an exporter, able to attack the traditional British market in Canada. And in the Far East a new industrial power was rising far more rapidly than any – Japan. Even in India, one of the most important of all export markets for Britain, there was a drastic decline in imports for a number of reasons we shall look at shortly. And just to add to the problems facing the cotton trade there was a growing threat from a new competitor, the man-made fibre. The first fibres had been made in the 1890s and by 1904 Courtaulds, who had done much of the research and development work, took over the British rights to the manufacture of rayon.

All these factors demanded a vigorous response if Britain was to continue to hold a dominant position in the world. That response was not forthcoming, not necessarily through any fault of the manufacturers but for a whole variety of reasons in which Government economic policy was by no means the least important. In 1929, Britain was still a leader, but only just: as world demand for cotton goods rose, so Britain's share kept falling. Exports had declined through the 1920s. Before the First World War the country had held over two-thirds of the market – by 1925 it was down to almost exactly half.[1] It was down and falling – but then, as the twenties gave way to the thirties, things seemed to be falling apart everywhere. Depression had arrived.

Depression affected every industrial nation, and Britain was certainly not excluded from the general misery. All the traditional industries were heavily hit and if the actual unemployment figures in textiles look less bleak than those for, say, the shipbuilders of the North-East, then that is largely because they do not show the short-time working that was universal in the mills. With war putting an end to unemployment the depression years passed, but the post-war years have shown no halt in the steady decline of the trade. Where once Britain had sent cotton goods to the world, now the world sends them in to Britain – jeans from Hong Kong, shirts from Portugal and, back to where it all started more than three centuries ago, cotton goods from India. British cotton has been caught in an impossible situation. In the past, prosperity had been based on exports but now there was competition from countries which had machinery at least as efficient as that in Britain, and wage bills that were a good deal lower. Where some countries could fall

Manchester unemployed in the 1930s.

back on a vast home market to keep their industries alive, the British manufacturers faced precisely the same competition as they faced abroad. They were being undersold in all the markets of the world just as they had once themselves undersold the competition. The great age of British cotton is coming to an end, but even in the late nineteenth century there were some commentators who saw the gradual weakening of the British industry and saw the inevitable decline. They looked eastward to where a coffin was being built for the dying industry, but they refused to mourn:

> You know what will be buried in this coffin: all the outraged and murdered past; the little apprentice children, tortured as never Inquisition tortured ... Therein will be buried four generations of blighted and shortened lives, with unnumbered babes born blasted; therein will be buried all the manifold miseries of today, the accursed destroying drudgery of men, women and children; therein will be buried all the pale, sickly faces, the crooked legs and bent backs, the thin frames, the puny, wailing infants, generated and born on the cheap. [2]

The days of greatness of the world's first industrial nation are over. The pioneering work is done, and the pioneers are being elbowed aside by the next generation. And what has the result been for Britain, the place where the world changed? The industrial revolution had shown that industrialisation could bring prosperity, but had never answered the question – prosperity for whom? The revolution had bred an industrial world of conflict which at times erupted into open warfare. The legacy of those years of conflict is with the country still. If this is true of Britain, what can one say about those who came after?

The new industry that was born in the American South certainly prospered, and much as the first mill workers in Britain had welcomed the opportunity to break out of the circle of poverty that had enclosed the rural populations, so now the poor whites welcomed the opportunities to take on mill work. In the North, however, early enthusiasm was now far in the past and discontent with pay and conditions led to several attempts to introduce trade unions to the American mills. The spread of unionism in the North was greeted with as much enthusiasm by the mill owners as their counterparts had shown in Britain. One result of the process was that Northern mill owners simply moved their operation down to the more tractable South. Here they were frequently able to turn complaints against the mill into other channels, by exploiting the racial issue. Nevertheless, the poor working conditions, long hours and low pay – and on all these counts the Southern workforce fared worse than their Northern counterparts – eventually bred sufficient discontent for the unions to begin recruitment in the South.

The South has always been a conservative region, which makes it the more surprising to find the more political, communist-led unions making progress. The National Textile Workers Union was able to recruit members in spite of its politics – which is perhaps as strong evidence as there can be that conditions were often intolerable. They were not especially successful with their strikes, but they followed a pattern which was to be typical of much of the union-management struggle of the twenties. A strike at the Loray mill in North Carolina in April 1929 was quickly broken. Strikers were

A modern mechanical cotton picker in America, clearing two rows of cotton at a time.

evicted from their company houses and they set up camp on the edge of town. On 7 June, the police moved in to clear the camp, shots were exchanged and the police chief was killed. Sixteen union leaders were arrested which did little to calm the situation. There were more violent clashes and a union worker, twenty-nine-year-old Ella May Wiggins, was killed. In the end it all came to nothing. The union leader Fred E. Beal jumped bail and escaped to the Soviet Union. He soon became disillusioned with the realities of Russian communism and returned to the States in 1938, where he was arrested and jailed.

Moderate unions fared no better, and were met with equal violence. In June 1929, workers at the Baldwin Manufacturing Company in Marion, North Carolina, joined the United Textile Workers and a public meeting was called to discuss grievances. As a result, twenty-two trade unionists were sacked and the union promptly demanded reinstatement, a reduction of the working day from twelve to ten hours and the establishment of a grievances committee. The terms were refused and a strike called. It was an ill-organised affair, but an agreement of sorts was reached which very much favoured the employers, though it was agreed that the sacked twenty-two would be reinstated. Work began again, at which point the company president R. W. Baldwin refused to honour his part of the bargain. There was no reinstatement and on 2 October the night shift left the mill and formed pickets to keep the day shift out. Baldwin called in the sheriff. An eye witness described what happened next:

> The Sheriff ordered the people to stand back ... twice he asked them to stand back. 'I am not going to ask you to stand back any more' the Sheriff threatened as he called to workers who wanted to come through the gates 'Come on in, those of you who want to go to work'.
>
> Only one man passed. The Sheriff then jerked out his tear-gas pistol and fired it at Slick Mills, one of the strikers. Mills was blinded and staggered out of the crowd. Deputy Sheriffs Broad Robbins, Charles Tate and James Owen then began firing their revolvers.
>
> The crowd scattered, running in all directions. None of our people had guns and none of us tried to resist the officers.[3]

Six workers were killed and twenty-five seriously wounded. Baldwin was among the first to applaud the Sheriff's action and all murder charges were dropped. Such cases were by no means uncommon, though few strikes ended as bloodily as that at Marion. Trade unionism never did gain a strong footing in the Southern mills, though time was to lead to a steady improvement in both wages and conditions. It was a pattern not dissimilar to that which was followed in Britain in the nineteenth century. Americans in passing through their version of the industrial revolution found the going no easier than their counterparts in Britain had done. But, unlike Britain, America was also a supplier of the raw materials of industry. Cotton was grown in the South, not merely spun, woven and sold.

The share-cropping system prevalent throughout the South did little to encourage an intelligent use of the land. Cotton crop followed cotton crop on to land that became ever more impoverished. At the same time, the cotton fields were attacked by a previously unknown scourge, *Anthonomus grandis*, the boll weevil. The adult insect chews into the cotton boll to lay its eggs and the damage done by the adult is multiplied by the hungry grubs when they hatch. It came to the South from Mexico in 1894 and began moving north at a rate varying between 40 and 160 miles a year. The pest has never been eradicated and even today pest control and losses from the uncontrolled insect cost in the region of $200 million a year. Between them, soil erosion and the boll weevil laid waste great tracts of the cotton country. In retrospect not everyone saw this as a disaster. Many, forced to abandon cotton cultivation, turned to more profitable crops. Georgia, for example, now has no cotton, the land having been turned over to crops such as peanuts and forestry. The citizens of Enterprise, Alabama, were so impressed by the improvement that they erected a statue to the boll weevil in the town square.

There may have been benefits in the long term, but they were by no means apparent in the short term. The ravages of the boll weevil, and the impoverishment of the soil combined to bring the share-croppers to the point of desperation. Then, as those problems were partially overcome and crops improved, the depression sent prices plummeting to an all-time low. The New Deal was designed to solve the problem through the Agricultural Adjustment Agency (AAA). In 1933, the AAA diagnosed the problem as over production – there was too much cotton so prices were low, but if less was produced then prices would rise. They began a policy of ploughing under the cotton crops; over ten million acres were taken out of production and the farmers given relief payment. This was fine for the landlords, but precious little of the relief funds found their way down to the croppers. A survey of some three thousand croppers in Alabama disclosed that 80 per cent were in debt and had been for at least a year. They were found to be living under conditions that had not improved since the end of the Civil War.

Just as the mill workers had done, the croppers began to band together and the Southern Tenant Farmers Association was formed in Arkansas. It was unique among Southern institutions of the time in having both black and white members. Blacks were given positions of authority, and introduced by name as 'mister'. It enraged many Southerners and if methods employed against mill unions were violent, they were as nothing compared to the response to the croppers' association. A white organiser was told in no uncertain terms that 'We don't need no Gawd-damn Yankee Bastard to tell us what to do with our niggers.' Black leaders fared even worse in what was to become a reign of terror in Arkansas. A. B. Brookins, the union chaplain, described what happened to him, and many other blacks could tell a similar story. 'They shot up my house with machine-guns, and they made me run away from where I lived at, but they couldn't make me run away from my Union.'[4] Croppers were evicted from their homes, but as soon as the authorities had gone, their neighbours took the furniture back in again and defended the property. It was during this period that the now famous protest song 'We shall not be moved' was first sung.

It was neither union activity nor New Deal legislation that was ultimately to change the life of the share-cropper. There was a certain amount of movement in the early twentieth century as the growth of other industries, notably the automobile industry, created new opportunities for workers. But that was a matter of choice for the workers. The biggest change came when the croppers and other workers on the land had the chance of employment taken away from them. Just as mechanisation had changed the pattern of life for industrial workers, so too it now changed the pattern of life on the farm. The mule was replaced by the tractor, new and improved machines took over the work of ploughing, sowing and hoeing. But the most important change of all occurred when the machines also took over the job of picking the cotton.

In the 1930s two brothers, John D. and Mack Rust, produced the first spindle cotton picker in which rotating vertical spindles, studded with spikes, pulled the cotton boll off the plant. Their first effort in 1931 was a machine that could pick one bale a day – by 1933 it was picking five bales. Plantation records for the last century suggest that at the height of the season when the plants were covered in bolls, the slaves were averaging slightly over 150 pounds a day but that this fell to around 120 as the season drew near a close.[5] So the machine was thirteen times as efficient or, to put it another way, one man and a machine could do the work of thirteen. The Rust brothers were genuinely concerned about the effects of their invention. They saw the obvious advantages of taking cotton picking away from human hands, relieving men and women of back-breaking work in the heat of the fields, but they also saw the evils of mass unemployment. They tried at first to limit the use of the machine and then proposed putting profit into a foundation that would fund the displaced farmers. These schemes did little to help and in the forties they abandoned manufacture. Others took over. In 1946, there were just over a hundred spindle pickers at work – by 1953 there were over fifteen thousand.

Today, hand picking has gone and the croppers have gone too. The big plantations have returned, owned by individuals or corporations. There are, however, great differences between the old and the new. The modern plantation is as much an industrial unit as a farm. An interesting example is the Delta and Pine Land Company plantation in Mississippi. It was formed out of a number of small plantations in 1911 specifically to serve British manufacturers, Fine Spinning of Lancashire, and was later taken over by Courtaulds. A company town was formed and the plantation became a self-contained unit where at the height of its prosperity there were thirty-four thousand acres under cotton. It was the first plantation to use arsenic to control the boll weevil and the first to use aircraft for crop-spraying – the latter activity proving so profitable to the sprayers that they were able to go on and develop their business into what is today Delta Airlines. Delta Pine began breeding better cotton and developed a successful seed business. Courtaulds left in 1978 and now the plantation has changed in character. Like many others in the South, it has diversified – largely moving into soya beans and a little rice and wheat. It has a thriving cotton-seed business using the most modern equipment. It is interesting to note, however, that though the gins are vast in comparison to those of Whitney's day, they still work on the same principle. Mechanisation can be seen on every hand. Yet in terms of yield per acre, plantations such as this in the rich Mississippi delta, the heartland of the old South, must yield in productivity to the new plantations of the South-West, in California and Arizona. There in the arid lands, the crops can be irrigated in totally controlled conditions, but at a price. Water is a scarce and valuable commodity and there is far from universal approval of the methods used.

The patterns of the old South have been broken but not destroyed. Growing has steadily shifted towards the west and the new efficient methods have ensured very high yields. The mill industry of the South has grown and where in the nineteenth century American cotton was grown mainly for the export market, today half of it goes to American mills. But the old problems of over production that had plagued the South in the thirties are still there. The 1982–83 crop was estimated at 12 million bales: 5.4 million would go to the domestic market and 5 million to export, leaving 1.6 million to add to stocks that already stood at 6.6 million bales.[6] The answer has been the same as before, to cut production. The Government has introduced a Payment in Kind (PIK) programme in which farmers are paid in effect for not growing cotton – and not using the land. For every acre of cotton field that is left bare, the Government passes on an equivalent amount of cotton to that which would have been grown on the land. So production is reduced, the farmer receives compensation and the Government can let someone else worry about disposing of the surplus cotton. In other ways too the pattern has been changed. Slavery is dead and thanks to the heroic efforts of the Civil Rights movement segregation has been removed from the statute books. The black population of the plantations has largely moved on, heading for the cities and towns, but racial peace and equality still seem at best to be distant dreams.

Looking at the American South today, one can see how the present differs from the past – yet how much of the past is still at work in modern life. The same could be said of India, where, if anything, change has been more dramatic and more revolutionary than in either Britain or America. Everything that has happened to Indian cotton in the twentieth century has been dominated by the long fight for freedom from British rule and the social policies pursued since independence.

Mahatma Gandhi spinning in his cabin on his way to the London Conference on India in 1931.

Farmers still use bullock carts to bring their cotton to the Karjan Co-operative Gin.

Indians long ago recognised that, to the British, India existed as a supplier of raw materials and as a market for manufacture. It was, in other words, part of an economic empire and the British were susceptible to attack on the economic front line. This was the origin of the Swadeshi movement which began in 1905 and encouraged the boycott of British goods and the purchase of Indian goods. It provided an enormous stimulus to Indian mills and an even greater stimulus came when the movement was extended through the boycott led by Mahatma Gandhi. But Gandhi was not content with the notion that English manufacture should be replaced by Indian manufacture. He wanted to spread the movement so that the effects of the demand for Swadeshi should be felt not just by the minority who lived in towns and worked in factories but by the multitudes of village India. From Swadeshi there came the Khadi movement – the production of cloth in the villages by traditional means, by spinning on the *charkha* and weaving on the hand loom. Gandhi's views have sometimes been represented as vaguely William Morrisy – a yearning for an older, simpler life – and Gandhi's own use of spinning as an almost mystic activity seems to support that view. But, in fact, he saw Khadi quite clearly as an economic necessity in a country with such appalling problems of rural poverty. He wrote 'Khadi is the only true economic proposition in terms of the millions of villagers until such time, if ever, when a better system of supplying work and adequate wages for every able-bodied person is found in every one of the villages of India.'[7] He saw

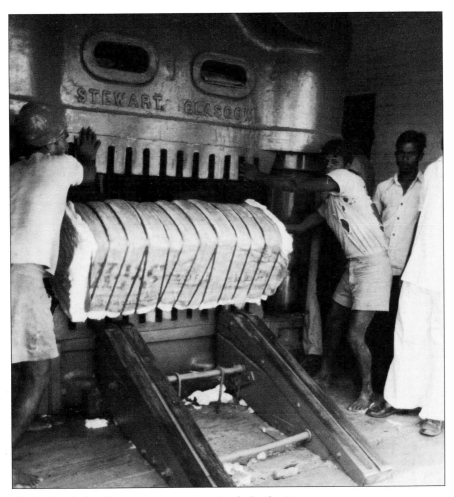

The Karjan hydraulic press turns out another bale of cotton.

Khadi as being a movement by the poor for the poor. 'The hand looms have suffered because of their having to sell their output to the same middle class which buys its clothing from foreign and Indian mills … the problem of rural uplift is to be viewed as one of setting up within each locality numerous lines of production which tends to be locally consumed.'[8] In the 1940s there was much concern among many Indians that whatever might be the future of Khadi and the cottage industry movement, the process of industrialisation should not follow the path of the West. The National Planning Committee put it in plain terms: 'social injustice, economic discontent, class conflict, – these are unhappy brood of individualist Industrialism.' In fact, the Indian cotton industry was to follow a very different route from that established in Europe, and still finds unique solutions to the problems of industrialisation.

217

From the first, the Indian mills had to come to terms with the complexities of Indian social life, including the special problems of caste. Where a British mill simply recruited labour and the new mills of the American South established their company towns, Indian mills worked by employing gangs of workers hired by jobbers. The Bombay jobber stood in relation to his gang much as the head man stood in relation to the village community. He was, in fact, the link between village and town, field and factory. He hired the workforce, took responsibility for their welfare, arranging credit and finding lodgings – and received *dasturi*, which might be described as bribes, from those who wished to join the gang. He administered a complex system and was the link between the English or Gujarati-speaking owners and overseers and the mainly Maharastra-speaking workforce. There were further complications caused by the fact that the workers still regarded themselves as villagers first and mill hands second. They not only sent money back to the villages, but at harvest times or when family occasions demanded, returned there themselves. So every gang consisted of the 'permanent' hands and 'badlis' or reserves who could be called in to replace the absentees as required. It seemed to European eyes to be a chaotic system but, like so many Indian institutions, it fitted the particular circumstances of Indian life very well. It was a halfway stage, a bridge between the life of the village and the life of the industrial town.

218   *The unchanging scene: women wind on bobbins for the hand-loom weavers of Panipat.*

As the industry grew, so the jobbing system declined and disappeared and it seemed that India would move closer to the familiar Western model of confrontation between management on one hand and trade unions on the other. To some extent this happened, notably in Bombay: elsewhere the Indian system threw up some uniquely Indian solutions. The most remarkable example is the story of the Ahmedabad strike of 1918.

It was a complex dispute that began over payments made to workers who stayed on in the mills while the town was afflicted by plague. The extra payments were later withdrawn and complaints on this subject became entangled with discussions over pay and conditions. When the strike began there were three principal figures involved – Ambalal and Anasuya Sarabhai, brother and sister, and Gandhi. The Sarabhai family were leading mill owners, but Anasuya had spent some time in Britain where she became involved with the suffragette movement and when she returned to India she went to see Gandhi to offer her help. Gandhi pointed out that as she had been brought up in the Ahmedabad textile industry, she could best help by organising the workers. So, at the start of the strike, brother and sister stood in opposite camps – Ambalal as leader of the owners, Anasuya heading the workers with Gandhi lending her his full support. It was more than a strike for wages, it was an argument over principle, as Ambalal was clearly aware when he criticised Gandhi's philosophy:

> He assumes that mills are run out of love for humanity and as a matter of philanthropy, that their aim is to raise the condition of the workers to the same level as that of the employers. We beg to say that his approach in this respect is wrong ... employment of labour and conditions of employment are determined purely on the basis of supply and demand.[9]

The workers had few resources to sustain them through the strike and Gandhi, to demonstrate his total support, decreed that he too would not eat while the strike lasted. It was the first of the Gandhi fasts and it had an immediate effect. Ambalal at once proposed that the issue be settled by arbitration while gently suggesting to Gandhi that the fast was a form of blackmail when used against a friend. Gandhi agreed at once and the strike was over. As Gandhi told the mill workers: 'I have never come across the like of it. I have had experience of many such conflicts or heard of them but have not known any in which there was so little ill will or bitterness as in this.'[10]

The end result was the formation of the Ahmedabad Textile Labour Association under the leadership of Anasuya Sarabhai, dedicated to settlement by arbitration rather than strike. It has been remarkably successful, with Ahmedabad enjoying an industrial peace unknown in other parts of India, or indeed anywhere else. It is generally regarded as a satisfactory

Pride of the co-operative movement: a modern spinning mill at Ichalkaranji.

system though one that is not without its problems for the owners. As an Ahmedabad mill owner told the author, the union now has one of the best staff of experts on industrial relations in India and it is rare indeed that their lawyers lose a case – so rare that most owners settle without incurring the high costs of legal procedures.

The most profound changes of all came with independence. First the agonies of partition resulted in the cutting-off of many of the principal growing areas from the manufacturing centres, the latter staying in India, the former in newly-formed Pakistan. Indian growers have had to work hard, experimenting with new hybrid plants and new techniques in order to achieve their objective of making India entirely self-sufficient in cotton and even, in time, a net exporter. The problem still lies mainly with a method of cultivation which depends on the village smallholding. This is true even of Gujarat, which produces over a quarter of the country's cotton though it has far less than a quarter of the total cotton acreage.[11] Much of the improvement is due to the work of the co-operative movement, working with Government backing. A typical co-operative, such as the Karjan Co-operative Ginning and Pressing Society, runs the local gin and press and copes with the majority of the marketing for the local farmers. The farmer brings in his cotton and is immediately paid 75 per cent of the estimated price it will fetch and receives the rest when the crop is sold, some deduction being made for expenses. The farmer makes an average 10 per cent more than he would if he sold the crop at auction. But the co-operative is more than just a ginning and marketing body, it is also a channel for funds and for new ideas. Under it are eighty-nine village co-operatives, representing over four thousand share-holders within a twenty-mile radius from the gin. Improvements in crop types, in pest control and cultivation methods are fed down to the level of the smallest village. Slowly, desperately slowly, but surely the levels of productivity and income are rising. And the gains are being spread to every corner of the community. No one viewing the co-operative gin with its hundred-year-old machines or the villages that surround it could fail to see that much remains to be done. India as a whole has 19.4 million acres under cotton as compared to 12.8 million in the USA, yet produces only 7.8 million bales as against the American production of 15.7 million – in other words American yields are three times those of India.[12] Yet, equally, no one can fail to be impressed by what has been achieved, nor with the will that exists to keep moving forwards.

The most remarkable feature of all appears when one turns to the production of cotton cloth. At the time of independence, the cotton world of India was already showing a bewildering complexity. There was a large-scale mill industry, Khadi was already established as a major force in the villages and there was also a multiplicity of small units, using both hand looms and power looms. It would have been expected that the small units would have disappeared as the mills grew in number, size and efficiency. The mills did indeed grow, from 378 in 1951 to 723 in 1982.[13] More and more yarn was produced by the Indian mills until a point was reached when the country had returned to the position that had prevailed before the European traders arrived – growing and spinning all the cotton the country needed. The figures show that the number of spindles turning in these mills rose in the same period from 11 million to 21.8 million: just what one would expect to find. But turn to the figures for looms in the mill and there is a complete change – throughout the period the number of looms remained constant at approximately two hundred thousand. There was, it is true, a move towards replacing ordinary looms by automatic looms, but the total figure scarcely changes. This was not because the mill owners had no wish to add extra looms, but because they were prevented from installing them. Government has decreed that wholesale use of labour-saving machinery makes little or no sense if the sole end product is profit for a few and unemployment for thousands. So it has been decreed that the cloth woven in India will be equally divided between three sections – mills, power looms and hand looms. No one pretends that the hand loom can match the power loom for efficiency, nor that the power loom can match the mill loom – this is a decision taken entirely on the basis of human need. It has been made possible because India is a vast country of huge population which can be self-sufficient in all its clothing needs. And it is argued that every rupee earned by a village worker that lifts that worker above the subsistence level is a rupee that he can spend as a customer. To a Western visitor, brought up on the notion that the hand loom is an antique machine of interest only to a few in the arts and crafts movement, it is a revelation to visit a small Indian town and find forty thousand of them at work. It is almost as startling as finding the idea that success can only be measured in terms of productivity challenged on every hand.

Is India showing a wisdom lacking in the West, or simply trying to ward off the inevitable progress of that industrial revolution that first began to change the world two centuries ago? Are the methods of directing industry to serve the needs of the poorest members of the community going to work in the long term and are they applicable to other countries? It is too soon to judge, but certain things are already clear. The visitor to Britain's textile industries will see closure and decay, with just a few bright spots of development and success. The overall mood is one of gloom and pessimism. In America there is a feeling that a static position has been reached – that most technical problems have been solved but there are still social problems that seem intractable. Neither country faces problems which even approach the magnitude of those that affect India, yet it is in India for all the horror of its poverty that one finds optimism. Such impressions are necessarily subjective and this one, final example is little more than one visitor's impression of just one part of the Indian textile world.

In Ichalkaranji, in Kolhapur, I visited three spinning mills run by co-operatives formed by the local power-loom weavers: and the co-operation of these local people produced a modern, efficient and growing industry. There was pride in the mills, pride shown in their competitiveness – to produce the finest prize roses from the flower beds that surround the mills. Here, at least, the old pattern of rural poverty is beginning to crumble. Not so very long ago, this was an area like many another in India, where a Maharajah's palace sat in the middle of cotton fields. There the peasant farmers strove to live on the crops that would be sent across the seas to distant Britain. Now that same cotton goes to the local mill and the yarn from the mill goes to the power looms, and all have a share in the gains. And here one can find a potent symbol of the new India. The old palace still stands, ornate and beautiful. But it is no longer home to a Maharajah – it has been bought by the co-operative as a training centre for young textile students. King Cotton has had a long and often tyrannical reign. Here at least, in the heart of India, that reign has ended. His kingdom has been given back to the people.

Appendix

Life in the mill and on the plantation was governed by carefully formulated rules. The rules for the plantation overseer are typical of many such sets of regulations, whereas the plantation manual is more detailed than most and has been included to show the extent to which the owner could attempt to regulate all aspects of slave life. Mill rules vary in detail, but all appear to have one thing in common: the rule maker stretches his imagination as far as possible in attempting to foresee the misdemeanours into which his employees might be drawn.

1   Rules for the Overseer or Manager, Willis P. Bocock Plantation. Marengo County, Alabama.

1   He must not indulge in swearing, drinking, or any immorality on the place. The morals of the negroes must be strictly attended to, and unless the overseer conducts himself like a gentleman no improvement can be expected of the negroes.

2   He should not enter into conversations with the negroes except on business. Familiarity breeds contempt.

3   Occasionally and at odd times he should patrol the negro quarters to see that nothing amiss is going on.

4   He must not injure the negroes, never strike one in a passion, or with any thing that might do mischief. If they do wrong & need correcting let it be done without cruelty! and avoid taunting them with their misconduct afterwards. Avoid torture of mind or body.

5   A brisk lively motion both for Mules and negroes should generally be required, but no rushing. It is desirable for everything to last as long as possible, which cannot be the case if overworked.

6   Breeding & suckling women should be worked near the house if possible, & carefully.

7   Mules & horses should be well rubbed & attended to every day, & negroes should be alllowed a specified time for that purpose, say one hour at 12 o'clock in winter, and the time lengthened as the days grow long & hot. In hot weather hands & mules must have 2 hours rest at 12 o'clock.

8   At night let the negroes employ themselves as they please till the bell rings, without any interference unless they are violating some rules of the plantation.

9   The women must be allowed time every week for washing and mending, & the largest girls must help their mothers. If a rainy day comes in the week let them have it then. If not, allow them two or three hours by Sun on Saturday evening.

10   About once a month, say on the 1st Saturday, after the weather begins to get warm, have a cleaning up about the houses, yards, and under the houses, and haul off the litter. Cleanliness is necessary to health.

11   Negroes are allowed to come up to see Mistress and Master on Sunday mornings and late Sunday afternoons. At all other times they must ask leave of the overseer before they come. The house hands do not go to the quarters without permission.

12   Men are allowed a rooster and 3 hens, two hens additional for their wives, and one for each child that works in the field. These they have to start with at the first of the year. The chickens & eggs they raise are for their own use, not to be sold off the place.

13   As we try to raise Meat and all supplies for the place, the overseer must pay as much attention to the stock of all kinds as to the crops. Have them counted frequently, & count himself & list at least once a month.

14   Notice houses fences & gates, put and keep them in as good condition as practicable. Attend to the gear of all kinds, and all plantation tools wagons, plows &c; let all be kept in good order & good repair, and when not in use put in their right places, not left exposed to hot sun & wet weather.

15   The great rule of managing is – Keep every thing in good condition & repair; Waste nothing; take care of everything,

16   Especially when likely to be scarce. And the rule for cropping is, first make an abundance to live and feed on, including plenty of vegetables for the negroes; then as much market crop as convenient.

17   The overseer raises nothing for sale, except for his employer, and sells nothing off the place except by authority of his employer, then for cash only which he at once hands over.

18   The overseers' time is paid for by his employer, and belongs to his employer. It is not right for the overseer to use that or anything else that belongs to his employer, in going about, in visiting, or in entertaining, or in any way but for his employer.

19   He keeps a book, prepared & furnished him at the beginning of each year, in which the rules are written down. & he sets down every thing in the course of the year according to the heads.

20   And when his employer is absent he writes to his employer at the end of every week an account of matters on the place. Sending at the end of every month a report of his stock &c.

Marengo County Alabama, July 15th 1860

This agreement witnesseth that Lewis A. Collins has agreed to live for Willis P. Bocock at Waldwick as his overseer or manager from the above date till the end of this year. He agrees to give his whole time & attention, his best skill, industry, & judgment, to carrying on the business and carefully managing every thing under his charge; to attend to and observe the wishes & directions of his employer when made known; to be careful of the good conduct health & cleanliness of the negroes; to take care of the sick; & to see that they comply in a reasonable manner with the rules laid down for them, also to conduct himself with prudence & sobriety, and a faithful regard to his employers' interest.

Said Bocock on his part agrees in consideration of said Collins' services so rendered, to furnish him an animal to ride about said business, he furnishing his own Saddle & bridle; to allow for his family that stay with him on the place a reasonable finding of such things as are raised on the plantation to be used without waste, also a woman of the place to cook & wash for them, and to pay him wages at the end of his time at the rate of five hundred dollars for twelve months, said Collins accounting for all time lost from his employer's business.

As evidence that said Collins intends to be faithful it is further agreed that whenever said Bocock becomes dissatisfied he may put an end to this agreement by paying s^d Collins up to that time; and further, at the Said Collins' own request, that if he drinks any spirits in the time he is not to receive any wages.

July 16, 1860   Lewis O. Collins

                           W. P. Bocock

2   Plantation Manual, origin unknown.

Allowances.

Allowances are given weekly. No distinction is made among work-hands, whether full hands, or less than full hands in the field, or adjuncts about the yard, stables, etc. A peck of meal apiece is given every Sunday morning. The peck measure is filled and piled up as long as will remain on it, but not packed or shaken. Meat and syrup are given out on Monday night. When meat alone is given, 3 pounds of pickled pork, or bacon, apiece is the allowance. Fresh meat, salted over night, may be given at any time at rates of $3\frac{1}{2}$ pounds of beef or pork. In summer but one-half of the allowance may be of fresh meat. As soon as cold weather sets in fresh pork allowance begins. Of hog offal 4 pounds. With one quart of syrup, the meat allowance is reduced to 1 3/4 pounds of pickel pork, or $2\frac{1}{2}$ of hog offal. No deductions are made for light sickness of a day or so, or for pregnancy. A ditcher who does each task without occasioning annoyance for a week receives on Wednesday night an extra pound of meat. The driver is allowed a small extra of meat and molasses whenever he may apply for it, which is but rarely done. Each ditcher receives every night, when ditching (fall & winter) a dram (jigger), consisting of 1/5 water and 4/5 whiskey, with as much asofoetida

225

as it will absorb, and a long string of peppers in the barrell. The dram is a good sized wine glass full. In cotton picking time, when sickness is prevalent, every hand gets a dram before leaving for the field. After a soaking rain all exposed to it also get a dram before changing their clothes. Drams are never given as rewards and only as medicinal. From second hoeing, or early in May an occasional allowance of tobacco is given to those that use it, about 1/8 of a pound, usually after some general operation as a hoeing, ploughing, etc. This is continued until the crops are gathered when each negro can provide for himself. Each man gets in the fall 1 cotton shirt and 1 pair woolen pants and 1 woolen jacket. In the spring they get 1 shirt and 1 pair of cotton pants. Each woman gets 6 yards of woolen cloth and 3 yards of cotton shirting in the fall, with a needle, skein of thread and $\frac{1}{2}$ dozen buttons. In the spring they get 6 yards of cotton drillings, 3 yards of shirting with needle thread and buttons. A. stout pair of shoes is given to each in the fall and blanket every third year.

Children

There is a separate apartment under the charge of a trusty nurse where the children are kept during the day. Weaned children are brought to it at the last horn blown in the morning, about good day light. The unweaned are brought in at sun rise, after sucking, and left in cradles in charge of the nurse. Allowance is given out daily to the children. 4 quarts of meal, 3 quarts of hominy and 2 pounds of bacon are found sufficient for about 20 children. They have also 1 pint of skimmed milk each day. Their breakfast consists of hominy and milk. At mid-day their meat is made into soup-pot liquor generally, with vegetables boiled in it if any are to be had and dumplings or bread. In the afternoon, an hour or so before sun-set they have hominy and milk again. They are never allowed fresh meat except the bony parts of beef to make soup. $1\frac{1}{4}$ pints of molasses are given among the same number every Wednesday morning. Each child gets a shirt and the girls a frock also; the boys a pair pantaloons reaching the neck and with sleeves every fall and spring, of the same goods as the work hands. A child's blanket is given to each of them every third year. Children born can have a blanket at the time of birth or the fall following according to the necessities of the Mother. All children are required to appear in entirely clean clothes twice a week. It is the duty of their mothers to attend to it and of the nurse to see that it is done or immediately to report it. The nurse must also see that no child changes its clothes from thicker to thinner clothes or the reverse at improper times or has on any wet garment at any time.

Plantation Hours.

The first morning horn is blown one hour before daybreak. Work hands are expected to rise and prepare the cooking. etc. for the day. The second horn is blown at good daylight, when it is the duty of the driver to visit every house and *see that all have left for the field. The plough hands leave their houses for the stables at the summons of the plough driver 15 minutes earlier than the gang, the overseer opening the stables. At $11\frac{1}{2}$ A.M. the plough hands stop to feed. At 12.00 A.M. the gang stop to eat dinner. At 1 P.M. through the greater part of the year all hands return to work. In summer the intermission increases with the heat to the extent of $2\frac{1}{2}$ hours. At 15 minutes before sunset the plows stop for the day and at sun set the rest of the hands. No nightwork is ever exacted. At night the negroes are allowed to visit among themselves until horn-blow – at $8\frac{1}{2}$ o'clock in winter and 9 o'clock in summer, after which no negro must be seen out of his house and it is the duty of the driver to go around and see that he is in it.*

Sucklers are not required to leave their houses until sun-rise when they leave their infants at the children's house before going to the field. The period of suckling is one year. For six months they return three times a day to suckle their infants – in the middle of the morning, at mid-day and in the middle of the afternoon. Their work lies always within half a mile of the quarter. They are required to cool before commencing to suckle, to wait fifteen minutes at least in summer after reaching the children's house before nursing. It is the duty of the nurse to see that none of them are heated when nursing as well as of the overseer and his wife occasionally to do so. They are allowed 15 minutes at each nursing to be with their children. After 7 months they return to nurse but twice a day missing at mid-day. At ten months they return at mid-day only. Each woman on weaning her child is required to put it in charge of some woman without a child for two weeks and not to nurse it at all during that time. A. suckler does about 3/5 of a full hands work, a little increased toward the last.

Such hands as cannot follow with the prime gang from age or deformity are put with the sucklers. Pregnant women at 5 months are put with the sucklers gang.

The regular plantation midwife shall attend all women in confinement. Some other woman learning the art usually assists her. The confined woman lies up one month, the midwife remaining with her the first 7 days.

There is a hospital adjoining the children's house where all the sick are confined. Every reasonable complaint is promptly attended to and with any marked or general symptom of sickness a negro may lie up a day or so at least. Homeopathy is exclusively used. As no physician is allowed to practice on the place, there being no homeopathist convenient, each case has to be examined carefully by the master or overseer to ascertain the disease. The remedies next are to be chosen with the utmost discrimination. The vehicles for preparing and administering with are to be thoroughly cleansed. The directions for treatment, diet, etc. most implicitly followed; The effects and changes cautiously observed, and finally the medicines securely laid away from accidents and contaminating influences. In case where there is uncertainty the books must be taken to the bedside and a thorough and careful examination of the case and comparison of medicines made before administering them. The head driver is the most important negro on the plantation. He is to be treated with more respect than any other negro by both master and overseer. He is on no occasion to be treated with any indignation calculated to lose the respect of the other negroes without breaking him. He is required to maintain proper descipline at all times. To see that no negro idles or does bad work in the field, and to punish it with discretion on the spot. The driver is not to be flogged except by the master but in emergencies that will not admit of delay. He is permitted to visit the master at any time without being required to get a card though in general he must inform the overseer when he leaves the place and presents himself on returning. He is expected to communicate freely whatever attracts his attention or he thinks information to the owner.

Marriage is to be encouraged as it adds to the comfort, happiness and health of those entering upon it, besides insuring a greater increase. No negro can have a wife, nor woman a husband, not belonging to the master. Where sufficient cause can be shown on either side a marriage may be broken but the offending party must be punished. Offenders can not marry again after such divorces for three years. As an encouragement to marriage the first time any two get married a bounty of $5.00 to be invested in household goods or an equivalent of articles shall be given. If either has ever been married before the bounty shall be $2.50 or equivalent. A third marriage shall not be allowed but in extreme cases and in such cases or where both have been married before no bounty shall be given. No marriage shall take place without the master's expressed consent to it.

Negroes living at one quarter having wives at the other, are privileged to visit them only between Saturday night and Monday morning and must get a pass for each visit. The pass card must be delivered immediately on reaching the destination and a return card given ready to return. All are subject to the regulation of the place they are at any time upon and it is as much the duty of the overseer and driver to observe them as the others under their ordinary charge. Each male work-hand shall be allowed to go to town once a year, on a Sunday between crop-gathering and Christmas. Not more than ten can go the same day. Adjoining each negro house is a piece of ground convenient for a garden. They have also patches in various parts of the plantation to cultivate little crops of their own. There is also a small field planted and worked, generally in pindars, the same as the rest of the crop the produce of which is divided among them. At Christmas three or four days holyday are given on one of which is a barbacue of beef or mutton and pork, bread and coffee are provided. Also a holyday and cue in August.

Horses and Mules.

Every horse and mule when in use is curried in the morning before taken from the stable and at 12 o'clock; also at night whenever they appear unusually sweaty and fatigued. They are fed twice a day; at night as much corn as they can eat, generally nearly a peck and about 8 hs. of fodder, hay or shucks apiece: and at 12 o'clock 6 ears of corn and about 2½ hs. of fodder each. When idle they require one third less and are curried but once a week, on Sundays. Watering is done 3 times a day when idle and 4 times when at work: always morning and night and before and after 12 o'clock feeding when at work but only before when idle. One gill of salt of best quality is given every other day unless soaked corn is used. When soaked corn is fed it is put in a barrel in the morning and 2/3 of a gill of salt to each mule sprinkled over it and water enough added to cover it. This fed only at night. A. gill of dry salt besides is given to each horse twice a week. Horses are haltered in separate stalls. Mules are left lose in another stable. Fresh straw is added daily so as to keep a dry bed always at night.

Hogs in pasture are fed every other day. They are not to be fed constantly at one spot. The amount given at a feeding is about 1 bushel of inferior corn to every 50 little and big. The overseer attends to this in person assisted by such negroes as may be required. A. counting of them must be made and entered on the plantation book at least once every month and marking, cutting and speying at least once in every three months. No hogs must be left at large except a few shoats about the lot.

3   Rules for Water-Foot Mill, Haslingden, September 1851

1   All the Overlookers shall be on the premises first and last.

2   Any Person coming too late shall be fined as follows:– for 5 minutes 2d, 10 minutes 4d, and 15 minutes 6d, &c.

3   For any Bobbins found on the floor 1d for each Bobbin.

4   For single Drawing, Slubbing, or Roving 2d for each single end.

5   For Waste on the floor 2d.

6   For any Oil wasted or spilled on the floor 2d each offence, besides paying for the value of the Oil.

7   For any broken Bobbins, they shall be paid for according to their value, and if there is any difficulty in ascertaining the guilty party, the same shall be paid for by the whole using such Bobbins.

8   Any person neglecting to Oil at the proper times shall be fined 2d.

9   Any person leaving their Work and found Talking with any of the other workpeople shall be fined 2d for each offence.

10   For every Oath or insolent language, 3d for the first offence, and if repeated they shall be dismissed.

11   The Machinery shall be swept and cleaned down every meal time.

12   All persons in our employ shall serve *Four Weeks' Notice before leaving their employ*; but *L. Whitaker & Sons, shall and will turn any person off without notice being given.*

13   *If two persons are known to be in one Necessary together they shall be fined 3d each; and if any Man or Boy go into the Women's Necessary he shall be instantly dismissed.*

14   *Any person wilfully or negligently breaking the Machinery, damaging the Brushes, making too much Waste, &c., they shall pay for the same to its full value.*

15   *Any person hanging anything on the Gas Pendants will be fined 2d.*

16   *The Masters would recommend that all their Workpeople Wash themselves every morning, but they shall wash themselves at least twice every week, Monday Morning and Thursday morning; and any found not washed will be fined 3d for each offence.*

17   *The Grinders, Drawers, Slubbers and Rovers shall sweep at least eight times in the day as follows, in the Morning at $7\frac{1}{2}$, $9\frac{1}{2}$, 11 and 12; and in the Afternoon at $1\frac{1}{2}$, $2\frac{1}{2}$, $3\frac{1}{2}$, $4\frac{1}{2}$ and $5\frac{1}{2}$ o'clock; and to notice the Board hung up, when the black side is turned that it is the time to sweep, and only quarter of an hour will be allowed for sweeping. The Spinners shall sweep as follows, in the Morning at $7\frac{1}{2}$, 10 and 12; in the afternoon at 3 and $5\frac{1}{2}$ o'clock. Any neglecting to sweep at the time will be fined 2d for each offence.*

18   *Any person found Smoking on the premises will be instantly dismissed.*

19   *Any person found away from their usual place of work, except for necessary purposes, or Talking with any out of their own Alley will be fined 2d for each offence.*

20   *Any person bringing dirty Bobbins will be fined 1d for each Bobbin.*

21   *Any person wilfully damaging this Notice will be dismissed.*

The Overlookers are strictly enjoined to attend to these Rules, and they will be responsible to the Masters for the Workpeople observing them.

References

Chapter 1

1   Celia Fiennes, *Through England on a Side Saddle*, 1695.
2   John Dyer, *The Fleece*, 1757.
3   Daniel Defoe, *A Tour through the whole Island of Great Britain*, 1724–6.
4   Quoted in John Irwin and Katharine B. Brett, *Origins of Chintz*, 1970.
5   Samuel Pepys, *Diary*, 27 February 1664.
6   Quoted in Thomas Ellison, *The Cotton Trade of Great Britain*, 1886.
7   Defoe, *The Trade to India*, 1720.
8   Defoe, *A Brief State of the Question between the Printed and Painted Callicoes and the Woollen and Silk Manufacture*, 1719.
9   Defoe, *A Plan of the English Commerce*, 1728.
10   See, for example, John Asgill, *A Brief Answer to a Brief State of the Question*, 1719.
11   Quoted in G. P. Baker, *Calico Painting and Printing in the East Indies in the XVII and XVIIIth Centuries*, 1921.
12   Defoe, *A Plan of the English Commerce*.
13   *Ibid.*

Chapter 2

1   Details of Kay's life are from John Lord, *Memoir of John Kay of Bury*, 1903.
2   John Dyer, *The Fleece*, 1757.
3   Letter to Sir Leicester Holt, quoted in Edward Baines, *History of the Cotton Manufacture in Great Britain*, 1835.
4   Dyer, *op cit.*

Chapter 3

1   Andrew Ure, *The Philosophy of Manufacture*, 1835.
2   Quoted in W. English, *The Textile Industry*, 1969.
3   For the most detailed account of Arkwright's career see R. S. Fitton and A. P. Wadsworth, *The Strutts and the Arkwrights 1758–1830*, 1958.
4   Erasmus Darwin, *The Botanic Garden*, 1791.
5   Stanley D. Chapman, 'Fixed Capital Formation in the British Cotton Industry 1770–1815', *Economic History Review*, 1970.
6   *Derby Mercury*, 13 December 1771.
7   Quoted in Fitton and Wadsworth, *op cit.*
8   Frances Collier, *The Family Economy of the Working Classes*, 1965.
9   Obituary in *The Gentleman's Magazine*, 1792.
10   John Byng, Viscount Torrington, *The Torrington Diaries*, 1936.
11   Frederick Strutt, 'Jebediah Strutt' in Charles Cox, *Memorials of Old Derbyshire*, 1907.
12   Fitton and Wadsworth, *op cit.*

13 Collier, *op cit*.
14 Sir Frederick Eden, *The State of the Poor*, 1797.
15 Byng, *op cit*.
16 Josiah Wedgwood to Thomas Bentley, 9 October 1779.
17 *Manchester Mercury*, 12 October 1779.
18 Robert Owen, *A New View of Society*, 1813.
19 *The Trial of a Cause*, 1785.

Chapter 4

1   Richard Burn, *Statistics of the Cotton Trade*, 1847.
2   See, for example, Burn, *op cit*. and Edward Baines, *History of the Cotton Manufacture in Great Britain*, 1835.
3   The Shaftesbury Papers, *Collection of the South Carolina Historical Society*, Vol. 5, 1897.
4   *Ibid*.
5   Thomas Ellison, *The Cotton Trade of Great Britain*, 1886.
6   Letter from the Chairman and Deputy Chairman of the East India Company to the President of the India Board, 16 March 1842.
7   Reports and Documents connected with the proceedings of the East India Company in regard to the Culture and Manufacture of Cotton-wool, Raw Silk and Indigo in India, 1836.
8   *Ibid*., letter to London, 30 May 1812.
9   Thomas Ellison, *A Handbook of the Cotton Trade*, 1858.
10 Note to Bombay, 1810, quoted in J. Forbes Royle, *On the Culture and Commerce of Cotton in India*, 1851.
11 Reports and Documents, 1836.
12 Royle, *op cit*.

Chapter 5

1   From a paper 'The Negro and Jamaica' read to the Anthropological Society of London, 1 February 1866.
2   J. D. B. De Bow, *The Industrial Resources of the Southern and Western States*, 1852.
3   Genesis, Ch. 9, v. 25.
4   Revelation, Ch. 1, v. 14.
5   Quoted in Leslie Howard Owens, *This Species of Property*, 1976.
6   Francis E. Hyde, Bradbury B. Parkinson and Sheila Marriner, 'The Nature and Profitability of the Liverpool Slave Trade', *Economic History Review*, 1953.
7   Advert from South Carolina State Gazette, 6 September 1784, quoted in Ulrich B. Phillips, *Plantation and Frontier Documents 1649–1863*, 1909.
8   G. W. Featherstonhaugh, *Excursions through the Slave States*, 1844.

9   Templeman and Goodwin Account Book, Southern Historical Collection (SHC) North Carolina.

10 For details of Whitney's life and later career, see Constance Mclaughlin Green, *Eli Whitney and the Birth of American Technology*, 1956.

Chapter 6

1   The details of Crompton's life are taken from Gilbert J. French, *Life and Times of Samuel Crompton*, 1859.

2   Arthur Young, *A Six Months Tour Through the North of England*, 1769.

3   John Byng, Viscount Torrington, *Diaries*, 1792 (published 1936).

4   J. H. Plumb, *England in the Eighteenth Century*, 1950.

5   Quoted in E. P. Thompson, *The Making of the English Working Class*, 1963.

6   Eden, *op cit*.

7   Valerie Morgan 'Agricultural Wage Rates in late Eighteenth Century Scotland', *Economic History Review*, 1971.

Chapter 7

1   Unless otherwise stated, all the information on Styal comes from the Greg MSS, Manchester Reference Library.

2   Andrew Ure, *The Philosophy of Manufacture*, 1835.

3   John Brown, *A Memoir of Robert Blincoe*, 1832 (reprinted 1977).

4   Report of the Select Committee on the State of Children in the Manufactories of the United Kingdom, 1816.

5   Robert Owen, *A New View of Society*, 1813.

6   *Ibid*.

7   Quoted in John Butt, *Industrial Archaeology of Scotland*, 1967.

8   Robert Southey, *Journal of a Tour in Scotland in 1819*, 1929.

9   W. Hutchinson, *An Excursion to the Lakes*, 1776.

10 William Howitt, *The Rural Life of England*, 1838, quoted in Pamela Horn, *Labouring Life in the Victorian Countryside*, 1976.

11 First Report of the Commissioners enquiring into the Employment of Children in Factories, 1833.

Chapter 8

1   Quoted in John Foster, *Class Struggle and the Industrial Revolution*, 1974.

2   Rev. Richard Warner, *A Tour through the Northern Countries of England*, 1802.

3   *The Manchester Directory*, 1772.

4   *The Business Directory of Manchester*, 1868–9.

5   A pamphlet addressed to the Committee for the Regulation of the Police, in the towns of Manchester and Salford, 4 January 1792 by John Ferriar.

6   John Ferriar, *Proceedings of the Board of Health in Manchester*, 1805.

7   John Fielden, *The Curse of the Factory System*, 1836.

8   The English text is that prepared by the Institute of Marxism-Leninism, 1969.

9   Details of Cartwright's life from M. Strickland, *A Memoir of Edmund Cartwright D.D.*, 1843.

10   Letter to Samuel Oldknow, Oldknow Papers, John Rylands Library, Manchester.

11   Quoted in W. English, *The Textile Industry*, 1969.

12   Edward Baines, *History of the Cotton Manufacture of Great Britain*, 1835.

13   Statistics are drawn from: J. D. B. De Bow, *The Industrial Resources of the Southern and Western States*, 1852; Thomas Ellison, *The Cotton Trade of Great Britain*, 1886; and Richard Burn, *Statistics of the Cotton Trade*, 1847.

14   De Bow, *op cit*.

Chapter 9

1   Nathan Appleton, *Introduction of the Power Loom, and Origin of Lowell*, 1858.

2   Quoted in Arthur L. Eno Jr (ed.), *Cotton was King*, 1976.

3   *Ibid*.

4   Regulations for the Boarding Houses of the Middlesex Company, 1846, Lowell Historical Society.

5   Eno, *op cit*.

6   Harvey T. Cook, *The Life and Legacy of David Rogerson Williams*, 1916.

7   Ernest McPherson Lander Jr. *The Textile Industry in Antebellum South Carolina*, 1969.

8   J. D. B. De Bow, *The Industrial Resources of the Southern and Western States*, 1852.

Chapter 10

1   J. F. H. Claiborne, *Life and Correspondence of John A. Quitman*, 1860.

2   Diary of Everard Green Baker, Mississippi, 1848–58.

3   Diary of Mary E. Bateman, Mississippi, 1856.

4   Letter dated 3 March 1839, Thompson Papers, SHC.

5   Frances Anne Kemble, *Journal of a Residence in a Georgian Plantation, 1838–9*, 1863.

6   Quoted in Leslie Howard Owens, *This Species of Property*, 1976.

7   Baker diary.

8   John Nevitt's Journal, 1826–30. Clermont Estate, Mississippi, SHC.

9 Nevitt, 3 May 1827.
10 Baker diary, 28 September 1854.
11 Edwin Adams Davies, *Plantation Life in the Florida Parishes of Louisiana 1836–46*, 1943.
12 Susan Dabney Medes, *A Southern Planter*, 1889.
13 Baker Diary, 30 June 1954.
14 Kemble, *op cit*.
15 Quoted in Eugene D. Genovese, *Roll Jordan, Roll*, 1975.
16 Burnley papers, SHC.
17 John Harland, *Ballads and Songs of Lancashire*, 1865.

Chapter 11
1 There is a full discussion in Thomas P. Goven, 'Was Plantation Slavery Profitable', *Journal of Southern History*, 1942.
2 Plantation Manual, origin unknown, SHC.
3 Rules of Highland Plantation from Edwin Adam Davies, *Plantation Life in the Florida Parishes of Louisiana, 1836–86*, 1943.
4 Papers of David Crenshaw Barrow of Georgia, SHC.
5 *Ibid*.
6 Letter from George A. Bratton, 31 May 1893, quoted in Katharine M. Jones, *The Plantation South*, 1957.
7 Letter from Archibald Arrington to his wife from his Alabama plantation, 28 June 1856.
8 Barrow papers.
9 *Ibid*.
10 Letter from Barclay Salkeld of Liverpool, 18 May 1819.
11 Minor papers.
12 Overseer's rules from Willis P. Bocock Papers, SHC (See Appendix 1).
13 Green River Plantation Rules, SHC.
14 George A. Bratton, overseer of Mississippi plantation in Jones, *op cit*.
15 Arrington papers. Letter to his wife, 25 June 1857.
16 Bocock rules.
17 Hugenin Plantation Book, 6 May 1836.
18 Hugenin book, first entry, 1838.
19 Entry for 3 August 1840 in Bennet H. Barrow's diary, quoted in Davies, *op cit*.
20 Kemble, *op cit*.
21 Francis Frederic, *Slave Life in Virginia and Kentucky*, 1863.
22 Barrow papers.
23 Hannah Hinman Day to John P. Broun, Alabama, 3 April 1842, Broun papers, SHC.

Chapter 12

1 John Wade, *Extraordinary Black Book*, 1831.
2 Evidence of William Hallam, 25 February 1778.
3 John Blackner, *History of Nottingham*, 1815.
4 The ballad John O'Grinfield is one of several on a similar theme. This version is from John Hartland, *Ballads and Songs of Lancashire*, 1865. See also Roy Palmer, *A Touch on the Times*, 1974 and Roy Palmer, *Poverty Knock*, 1974.
5 Hartland, *op cit*.
6 Reproduced in W. Bennett, *The History of Burnley*, Vol 3., 1948.
7 From 'The Trades' Newspaper', Place Collection, British Museum.
8 Quotations are drawn from newspaper cuttings in the Place Collection, British Museum, mainly from the *Bolton Chronicle* and *Manchester Mercury* for April 1826.
9 *Bolton Chronicle*, 29 April 1826.
10 Second Report from the Select Committee on Emigration from the United Kingdom, 1827.
11 Reports on Petitions of Cotton Weavers, 1809, 1811.
12 Place Collection.
13 Francis Place to John Doherty, 7 April 1829.
14 A Report of the Proceedings of the Meeting of Cotton-spinners at Ramsey, 1829.
15 Constables of Manchester to Sir Robert Peel, 26 May 1830, HO papers.
16 *Annual Register*, 1838.
17 G. Hardwick, *History of the Borough of Preston*, 1857.
18 Henry Ashworth, *The Preston Strike*, 1854.
19 *Ibid*.
20 From Roy Palmer, *A Touch on the Times*, 1974.
21 Ashworth, *op cit*.
22 Hardwick, *op cit*.

Chapter 13

1 Quoted in full in Herbert Aptheker, *A Documentary History of the Negro People in the United States*, 1951.
2 Susan Dabney Medes, *A Southern Planter*, 1889.
3 Aptheker, *op cit*.
4 Slave autobiography, Library of Congress.
5 Frederick Law Olmsted, *A Journey in the Seaboard Slave States*, 1856.
6 Solomon Northrup, *Twelve Years a Slave*, 1970.
7 John Nevitt's Journal 1826–30, Clermont Estate, Mississippi.
8 Undated letter, Peter Jaillet to Major J. Crawford, Farrish Carter Papers, SHC.

9   Lewis Plantation Book 1858– 61, Green County, Alabama SHC.

10   J. F. H. Claiborne, *Life and Correspondence of John A. Quitman*, 1860.

11   Everard Green Baker, Diary and Plantation notes, Mississippi, 25– 28 December 1852.

12   *Ibid.*, 20 September 1857.

Chapter 14

1   Andrew Ure, *The Philosophy of Manufacture*, 1835.

2   Robert Rawlinson, *Public Works in Lancashire*, 1898.

3   J. H. Ha, *Two Letters on Slavery in the United States* (undated).

4   E. N. Elliott, *Cotton is King and Pro-Slavery Arguments*, 1860 (3rd edition).

5   *Ibid.*

6   Letter from Samuel Watt 27 March 1843, Correspondence of the British and Foreign Anti-Slavery Society, 1839– 68.

7   Deputation to Lord Palmerston, 9 November 1839.

8   *Leeds Mercury*, 29 September 1830.

9   Thomas Ellison, *The Cotton Trade of Great Britain*, 1886.

Chapter 15

1   Figures given to the Central Relief Committee, quoted in Thomas Ellison, *The Cotton Trade of Great Britain*, 1886.

2   George Martin Braune, *The Marine Council of Trent*, 1862.

3   'A Factory Girl', *The Cotton Famine*, 1862.

4   Anon. *A Visit to the Cotton Districts*, 1862.

5   Sermon preached in 1862, published in a group entitled *Distress in Lancashire*.

6   Robert Rawlinson, *Public Works in Lancashire*, 1898.

7   Henry Ashworth, *Be Just to India; Prevent Famine and Cherish Commerce*, 1861.

8   *Ibid.*

9   Quoted in Thomas Ellison, *A Hand-book of the Cotton Trade*, 1858.

10   Quoted in Amba Prasad, *Indian Railways*, 1960.

11   Quoted in Peter Harnett, *Imperialism and Free Trade: Lancashire and India in the Mid-Nineteenth Century*, 1972.

12   Quoted in Ministry of Railways, *Indian Railways One Hundred Years*, 1953.

13   Lt. Col. A. Cotton, *Public Works in India*, 1854.

14   'An Indian Civil Servant', *Usurers and Ryots*, 1856.

Chapter 16

1   Quoted in E. Merton Coulter, *The South During Reconstruction, 1865– 1877*, 1947.

2   Diary of Louis Manigault, May 1862.

3   C. Van Woodward, *Origins of the New South, 1877–1913*, 1951.

4   Arthur L. Eno Jr (ed.), *Cotton was King*, 1976.

5   Woodward, *op cit.*

6   Broadus Mitchell and George Sinclair Mitchell, *The Industrial Revolution in the South*, 1930.

7   Quoted in M. L. Dantwala, *A Hundred Years of Indian Cotton*, 1947.

8   S. D. Mehta, *The Cotton Mills of India, 1854 to 1954*, 1954.

9   Manchester Chamber of Commerce, *Bombay and Lancashire Spinning Inquiry*, 1888.

10   E. J. Hobsbawm, *Industry and Empire*, 1968.

Chapter 17

1   Statistics from Charles Loch Mowat, *Britain Between The Wars 1918–1940*, 1955.

2   Bonani, *The Doom of the Cotton Trade*, 1895.

3   *New York Times*, 3 October 1929.

4   David Eugene Conrad, *The Forgotten Farmers*, 1965.

5   Lewis Plantation Book, Green County, Alabama 1858–61.

6   National Cotton Council of America, *The Economic Outlook for U.S. Cotton*, 1983.

7   Ratilal Mehta, *The Story of Khadi*, 1974.

8   Evidence to the Cottage Industries Sub-Committee of the National Planning Committee, 30 July 1940.

9   Eric H. Erikson, *Gandhi's Truth*, 1970.

10   *Ibid.*

11   Office of the Textile Commissioner, *Cottons of India*, 1980.

12   The Indian Cotton Mills Federation, *Handbook of Statistics on Cotton Textile Industry*, 1982.

13   *Ibid.*

Index